STUDIES IN MAIMONIDES
AND
HIS INTERPRETERS

STUDIES IN MAIMONIDES
AND
HIS INTERPRETERS

Marc B. Shapiro

University of Scranton Press
Scranton and London

Library of Congress Cataloging-in-Publication Data

Shapiro, Marc B.
  Studies in Maimonides and his interpreters / Marc B. Shapiro.
    p. cm.
  English and Hebrew.
  Includes bibliographical references.
  The English section consists of essays by Marc Shapiro; the
Hebrew section consists of letters and selections on Maimonides
by various authors.
  ISBN 978-1-58966-165-3 (pbk.)
  1. Maimonides, Moses, 1135-1204. I. Title.
  BM546.S53 2007
  296.1'81--dc22

                                                  2007043969

Distribution:

University of Scranton Press
Chicago Distribution Center
11030 S. Langley
Chicago, IL 60628

PRINTED IN THE UNITED STATES OF AMERICA

In Honor of My Parents

CONTENTS

CONTENTS: HEBREW SECTION

PREFACE

In 2004, as one of the participants in an international conference commemorating the eight-hundredth anniversary of the death of Maimonides, I was asked to prepare my paper for publication in *Maimonidean Studies*. Unexpectedly, it came to some seventy-five pages. Therefore, I was not surprised when I was told that it was too long to be published. Professor Arthur Hyman, the editor of *Maimonidean Studies* and one of the organizers of the conference, suggested that I submit a much shorter essay to him,[1] and publish the full version as a separate monograph. The volume you are now holding is the result of his advice. When the opportunity to publish a volume on Maimonides presented itself, I decided to also include a revised and expanded version of my article "Maimonidean Halakhah and Superstition," which also appeared in *Maimonidean Studies*.[2]

While each of these chapters stands alone as an independent piece of research, they are also connected in that they both focus on important aspects of Maimonides' legacy and how these have been understood through the centuries. Throughout the book, I attempt to utilize the best insights of both the traditional and academic interpreters. It was my late teacher, Professor Isadore Twersky, who always insisted that no proper examination of Maimonides can be undertaken without careful examination of what the traditional commentators have written. One advantage of this method is that I am able to illustrate how some of the approaches identified with academic studies actually have precursors in the traditional world. In addition, the traditional interpreters succeeded in identifying many problems that the academic researcher, on his own, might well have overlooked. While I certainly don't pretend that I am the one best qualified to write the history of interpretation of Maimonides, and in particular the history of *Mishneh Torah* interpretation, I hope that the essays included in this

---

1. Published in *Maimonidean Studies* 5 (2008), pp. 27–53.

2. Vol. 4 (2000), pp. 61–108. I thank Prof. Hyman for granting me permission to republish material from my essays that appeared in the last two volumes of *Maimonidean Studies*.

book have succeeded in identifying at least some of the issues that will be part of any such investigation.

The "Note on Maimonides and Muhammad" found at the end of the English section requires a bit of explanation, as it speaks to the times in which we live and the sometimes precarious state of scholarship when it comes up against larger political forces. In 1993, I published an article in *Judaism* entitled "Islam and the Halakhah."[3] In the version of the article submitted to the journal, I mentioned that Maimonides referred to Muhammad as a "madman," and in a few lines I also explained the origin of the term. When the article appeared in print, I was surprised to find that this had been removed without my knowledge. Naively, I thought that this was an innocent mistake, and I inquired as to what had happened. Imagine my shock when I was told that my article had been censored because the journal did not want to publish anything that could be seen as offensive to Muslims. While some may see this as understandable in the wake of the 1988 Salman Rushdie episode, it was nevertheless a betrayal of scholarship, which cannot be guided by political correctness. I would hope that any Muslims who see the "Note on Maimonides and Muhammad" will understand that its intent is not to insult their prophet, but rather to clarify a historical issue.

Since this book is directed towards specialists (and this explains the numerous Hebrew citations throughout), I have also included a Hebrew section that I think students of Maimonides will find interesting. The first document, a lengthy letter from Nahman Isaac Fischmann (1809–1878) to Samuel David Luzzatto, reflects the great nineteenth-century battles over the legacy of Maimonides. Luzzatto, for reasons of his own, resurrected the anti-Maimonidean tradition and began polemicizing against Maimonides and his philosophical teachings.[4] Such a disrespectful attitude towards Maimonides did not go over well in Haskalah circles, and led to great literary debates in the

---

3. *Judaism* 42 (Summer, 1993), pp. 332–343.

4. For Luzzatto's views on Maimonides, and a host of other issues, see Monford Harris, "The Theologico-Historical Thinking of Samuel David Luzzatto," *JQR* 52 (1962), pp. 216–244, 309–334.

periodicals of the day, with Luzzatto's main opponent being R. Solomon Judah Rapoport (Shir) of Prague.[5]

Among those who attacked Luzzatto was Fischmann. He was a conservative maskil from Lemberg who, together with three other like-minded fellows, published two volumes of *Ha-Roeh* (1837, 1839). These were devoted to sharp critiques of the writings of such leading figures as Luzzatto, Rapoport, Leopold Zunz, and Isaac Samuel Reggio.[6] Isaac Barzilay, who studied the writings of these men (known as *Ha-Roim*), concluded that while "they claim to be defending both truth and religion," in fact, "they seem motivated rather by personal ambition, jealousy and hate, emotions they hope to satisfy best by debunking the great authorities of Jewish scholarship of their time, notably Shir."[7] In the letter to Luzzatto published here, there is certainly strong opposition to the latter's style and content, and even some personal criticism, but I leave it for readers to judge for themselves whether it also crosses the line into "jealousy and hate."

Fischmann's letter appears courtesy of the Library of the Jewish Theological Seminary (MS 10584). Although most of the letter, in a later and slightly different form, was actually published by Fischmann in *Ha-Roeh* 2 (1839), pp. 32–56, enough new material is found in Fischmann's original letter to Luzzatto to make its publication here worthwhile. (The first few pages, the conclusion, and many of his very sharp comments were omitted from the printed version.) His missive,

---

5. See Isaac Barzilay, *Shlomo Yehudah Rapoport (1790–1867) and His Contemporaries: Some Aspects of Jewish Scholarship of the Nineteenth Century* (Israel, 1969), pp. 101ff. See also Meir Hershkovitz, *Maharatz Chajes: Toldot Rabbi Zvi Hirsch Chajes u-Mishnato* (Jerusalem, 2007), ch. 12.

6. J. L. Landau writes about Fischmann, who was also a great poet: "[His] name is hardly remembered, and his poetical productions are relegated to the literary lumber-room. It is very strange indeed that while poems of very doubtful merits which had been lying buried in private collections for centuries are being revived, beautifully printed and edited with introductions and annotations, although their loss would hardly be felt, the works of a man, whose creative power as an original poet cannot be disputed, are altogether forgotten." *Short Lectures on Modern Hebrew Literature: From M. H. Luzzatto to N. I. Fischmann* (London, 1938), p. 262. See also Naomi Zohar, *Be-Or Hadash* (Ramat Gan 2001), ch. 6.

7. *Shlomo Yehudah Rapoport,* p. 85. See also Simon Bernfeld, *Toledot Shir* (Berlin, 1899), pp. 98ff.

focusing as it does on varying interpretations of Maimonides, ties in very nicely with one of the themes of this book. In transcribing it, I corrected certain obvious mistakes (e.g., misspelled words), as well as various errors of quotation (especially when he is quoting Luzzatto). I have also inserted some paragraph breaks.

Rabbi Joseph Kafih was one of the premier twentieth-century interpreters of Maimonides, and while he should be viewed as a traditional interpreter, he was also very much aware of the academic approach. Anything from his pen with regard to Maimonides is precious,[8] and I have therefore included three letters of his in the Hebrew section. I thank Menachem Kellner and Karmiel Cohen, each of whom provided one of these letters; the other one was sent to me. (To make the letters to Cohen and myself understandable, I have also included our letters to Kafih.) Rabbi Jehiel Jacob Weinberg, the subject of my first book who remains one of my main scholarly interests, gave a great deal of thought to a number of the issues discussed in the present book. I therefore thought it worthwhile to provide a selection of relevant material from his writings. I am grateful to Aharon Batt for providing the letter from Weinberg to Rabbi Yehoshua Hutner, and to Gabriel Cohn for providing the two letters that Weinberg sent to him.

I would like to thank the following people for their scholarly assistance: the late Isadore Twersky, David Berger, Raphael Jospe, and Yair Shiffman. A special thank you goes to Chaim Rapoport, who read the volume and provided many helpful sources. I have indicated his contribution by citing his initials (CR) after the sources to which he called my attention. As in the past, I am indebted to Leah Levy for her expert assistance in the fine points of the English language. I also thank Zalman Alpert of Yeshiva University's Gottesman Library for his assistance on many occasions.

---

8. It is only in recent years that scholars have begun to take advantage of Kafih's enormous contribution to the study of the *Mishneh Torah*. See R. Aviad Ashual, *Mishnat ha-Shemitah* (Kiryat Ono, 2000), *id., Birkat Moshe* (Kiryat Ono, 2007); R. Aharon Kafih, *Yeriot Aharon* (Jerusalem, 2003), *id., Minhat Aharon* (Jerusalem, 2007); and various essays in the four volumes of Yosef Farhi, ed., *Mesorah le-Yosef* (Netanya, 2005, 2007).

My wife, Lauren, and my in-laws, Alex and Bobbi Sobel, have been greatly supportive throughout the writing of this book, even if they didn't always understand what I found so appealing about the time I spent in my basement office. My children, Aliza, Yael, Danielle, Joshua, and Jacob, no doubt felt the same way; but they never let this deter them from barging in and demanding that I return to the real world. For this, I thank them.

Finally, I must thank my parents, Edward and Daryl Shapiro, to whom this book is dedicated. My mother deserves special credit for always instilling optimism in my brothers and me. My father has been particularly involved with my scholarly growth, and I will never be able to thank him enough for this. Together, they gave me the best possible home in which to grow up.

ABBREVIATIONS

EJ	*Encyclopedia Judaica* (1972 edition)
HUCA	*Hebrew Union College Annual*
JJS	*Journal of Jewish Studies*
JQR	*Jewish Quarterly Review*
MGWJ	*Monatsschrift für Geschichte und Wissenschaft des Judentums*
PAAJR	*Proceedings of the American Academy of Jewish Research*
TUMJ	*Torah u-Madda Journal*

PRINCIPLES OF INTERPRETATION IN MAIMONIDEAN HALAKHAH: TRADITIONAL AND ACADEMIC PERSPECTIVES

When considering the methodology of great figures, one assumes that there is a system behind their works, and that they are comprised of more than simply a hodge podge of thoughts. Any contrary assumption will usually be regarded as an insult to the figure under consideration.[1] Maimonides' *Mishneh Torah* is so carefully crafted[2] as to make it obvious that he, too, must have been guided by systematic principles of interpretation that spanned the work as a whole, rather than reaching his conclusions on an *ad hoc* basis.[3]

It is perhaps surprising that the Introduction to the *Mishneh Torah* does not provide sufficient details of his methodology, especially considering that Maimonides was very clear about his method of classification in the Introduction to his previous work, the *Sefer ha-Mitzvot*. What he does say is the following:

> This text will be a compilation of the entire Oral Law, including also the ordinances, customs, and decrees that were enacted from the time of Moses our teacher until the completion of the Talmud, as they were explained by the geonim in the texts they composed after the Talmud.

---

1. See, e.g., R. Jehiel Jacob Weinberg's comments in this regard vis-à-vis Hanokh Albeck's assumption that the Mishnah was not edited in any real way by R. Judah the Prince, but is simply a collection of earlier sources arranged according to content. *Kitvei ha-Gaon Rabbi Yehiel Yaakov Weinberg* (Scranton, 1998, 2003), vol. 1, no. 91, vol. 2, p. 430.

2. There are exactly one thousand chapters in the *Mishneh Torah*, certainly no coincidence. Surprisingly, this fact seems to have gone unnoticed until it was pointed out by Simon A. Neuhausen, *Torah Or le-ha-Rambam* (Baltimore, 1941), p. vii. See also J. Avida, "Mispar ha-Perakim ba-Mishneh Torah le-ha-Rambam Z"L," *Sura* 2 (1955), pp. 267–276, who was unaware of Neuhausen. I was surprised to see that Herbert A. Davidson, in his outstanding *Moses Maimonides: The Man and His Works* (Oxford, 2005), p. 215, mistakenly gives the number as 982, an error which appears in early editions of the *Mishneh Torah*.

3. One scholar who does not share this assumption is Jacob Levinger, who argues that there are times when Maimonides does, in fact, decide matters on an *ad hoc* basis. See *Darkhei ha-Mahashavah ha-Hilkhatit shel ha-Rambam* (Jerusalem, 1965), pp. 170ff., where he uses this approach to explain how Maimonides could record halakhot, some of which imply that cruelty to animals is a biblical prohibition, and others that it is only a rabbinic prohibition.

However, Maimonides does not provide us with the principles he used in arriving at his decisions. For example, in this same Introduction, in describing the value of his new codification in simplifying the halakhah, he says that there is confusion "with regard to the Talmud itself, both the Jerusalem and the Babylonian Talmuds." Yet he does not tell us what the Jerusalem Talmud's exact role is in his halakhic codification.[4] The same can be said for the halakhic midrashim and the Tosefta, which are also mentioned in the Introduction. Similarly, in his letter to R. Pinhas of Alexandria, Maimonides writes that everything in the *Mishneh Torah* that appears without an indication that it is his original deduction is taken from the "Babylonian or Jerusalem Talmuds, or from *Sifra* or *Sifrei*, or an explicit Mishnah or Tosefta."[5] The fact that Maimonides chooses to mention the Jerusalem Talmud, halakhic midrashim, and Tosefta shows that they indeed play a role, although it is not clear what this role may be. Presumably, they are to be used when the Babylonian Talmud is silent or unclear on an issue, but then, of course, we have another problem; namely, why does Maimonides resort to these sources in some cases, but not in others?

While it is possible that these sorts of questions can be answered on an *ad hoc* basis, scholars have understandably attempted to identify

---

4 The most recent study of this issue is Yerahmiel (Robert) Brody, "Li-Fesikat ha-Rambam al pi ha-Talmud ha-Yerushalmi be-Nigud la-Talmud ha-Bavli," *Maimonidean Studies* 4 (2000), p. 1–11 (Hebrew section). For one case study, see Israel Francus, "Ha-Yerushalmi ki-Mekor li-Fesikat ha-Rambam," *Sinai* 102 (1988), pp. 32–44. For some relevant quotes from the Vilna Gaon, see R. Zvi Yehudak Kook's note in R. Abraham Isaac Kook, *Mitzvat Re'iyah* (Jerusalem, 1985), p. 206.

5. *Iggerot ha-Rambam*, ed. Sheilat (Jerusalem, 1988), vol. 2, p. 443. Sheilat, *ibid.*, suggests that the reason Maimonides doesn't mention *Mekhilta de-Rabbi Yishmael* together with *Sifra* and *Sifrei* is because it is mostly an aggadic work. For alternative approaches, see Louis Finkelstein, "Maimonides and the Tannaitic Midrashim," *JQR* 25 (1935), pp. 473–474; David Metzger, introduction to *Kovetz Meforshei ha-Mekhilta* (Jerusalem, 1999). In the Introduction to the *Mishneh Torah*, Maimonides mentions *Mekhilta de-Rabbi Yishmael* and the *Mekhilta* of Rabbi Akiva, which, according to R. Menahem M. Kasher, is simply another way of saying the *Mekhilta* of Rabbi Simeon Bar Yohai, a book Maimonides made good use of. See Kasher, *Ha-Rambam ve-ha-Mekhilta de-Rashbi* (Jerusalem, 1980), p. 12 n. 5. Metzger (mentioned previously in this note) offers a different approach. See also Y. N. Epstein, "Mekhilta ve-Sifrei be-Sifrei ha-Rambam," *Tarbiz* 6 (1935), pp. 99–138.

principles of Maimonidean halakhah that provide a more holistic approach. Many of these principles are scattered throughout later rabbinic literature, as well as in works such as R. Malakhi ha-Kohen's *Yad Malakhi*[6] and R. Hayyim Hezekiah Medini's *Sedei Hemed*,[7] which belong to what is known as the *kelalim* literature. It is interesting that a work of this nature, entitled *Seder Olam* and focused on the Talmud, was actually attributed to Maimonides. R. Nissim Gerondi mentions this work,[8] and a few passages from it survive in the writings of R. Betzalel Ashkenazi[9] and R. Hayyim Joseph David Azulai.[10] Even absent a passage stating that Rav lived for three hundred years, there would be no reason to regard it as authentic.

As generation upon generation put their minds to the *Mishneh Torah*, conflicts arose about the principles of Maimonidean halakhah, and new approaches were suggested whose tenability must surely be questioned. The rise of modern Maimonidean scholarship has raised many of the same issues, but the assumptions of academic study often lead to differing conclusions. What is significant, however, is that one can find precursors in traditional rabbinic works for even the most nontraditional academic interpretations.

Let me begin with a principle, indeed a *leitmotif*, which runs through traditional studies of the *Mishneh Torah* in recent centuries.[11] This principle states that there is an answer for every perplexity. The possibility that Maimonides made a simple error, or that he overlooked a rabbinic passage—which entails bringing Maimonides down

---

6. (Bnei Brak, n.d.), pp. 182–187.

7. (New York, 1967), vol. 9, pp. 135–139.

8. See *Hiddushei ha-Ran*, ed. Frank and Werner (Jerusalem, 1966), *Moed Katan* 10a.

9. See *Shitah Mekubetzet, Ketubot* 88b; Alexander Marx, "Die Kelalei ha-Talmud des R. Bezallel Aschkenasi," *Festschrift zum siebzigsten Geburtstage David Hoffmann's* (Berlin, 1914), p. 375.

10. *Ayin Zokher* (Jerusalem, 1962), *ma'arekhet alef* no. 44, *ma'rekhet heh* nos. 51, 60.

11. I am not referring to the philosophical sections of the *Mishneh Torah*. Concerning these sections, scholars who were otherwise most deferential to Maimonides had no difficulty in asserting that he erred. R. Jacob Kamenetsky goes so far as to say that the first four chapters of *Yesodei ha-Torah*, which Maimonides viewed as basic to Judaism, are not to be regarded as Torah but as פילוסופיא בעלמא. See *Emet le-Yaakov* (New York, 1998), pp. 15–16.

to the level of a mere mortal—is not an operating principle.[12] For the traditional commentator, exegesis of Maimonides would be impossible if this approach was adopted. Even if he acknowledged that, in theory, Maimonides could have erred, he would also insist that these errors are not of the sort that his successors, who did not measure up to him, would be able to identify. Rather, the traditionalist commentator must struggle to find an answer, either by providing a new source or a new conceptualization of the halakhah in question. If, at the end of the day, the traditionalist commentator is unable to solve the problem, he acknowledges the difficulty but asserts that "if our rabbi [Maimonides] was before us, he would properly explain matters."[13]

While many approach all of Maimonides' works in this way, the *Mishneh Torah* carries special weight in this regard. It has been placed on a much higher pedestal than any of Maimonides' other works—or, for that matter, the works of other scholars. Thus, while contradictions in the *Mishneh Torah* have exercised the minds of our best and brightest for almost a millennium, one does not find the same level of concern over the numerous contradictions found in the *Shulḥan Arukh*.[14] The attention to detail lavished on the *Mishneh Torah* by traditional commentators is simply not duplicated for any other works. This fact is reflected in the principle recorded by R. Malakhi ha-Kohen in his classic *Yad Malakhi*: "All of Maimonides' words are exact (בתכלית הדיוק) and you should scrutinize and apply casuistry to them

---

12. See, e.g., R. Jacob Emden, *Leḥem Shamayim* (Jerusalem, 1958), *Shekalim* 8:8: אמנם על כרחנו צריך שנפרש שנפרש דברי הרמב"ם ז"ל בענין שיסכימו להלכה ואל האמת, כי אי אפשר להמאור הגדול שיטעה בדבר ברור . . . ואף אנו יודעין כמה קושי יש בהבנה זו. ומה נעשה ועצר גדול היה לנו להחליט הטעות ח"ו בדברי הרמב"ם ז"ל. על כן לא נמנענו מללמוד עליו זכות מה, שכך היא חובתינו וכך יפה לנו.

13. R. Joseph Kolon, *She'elot u-Teshuvot Maharik* (Jerusalem, 1988), no. 126 (end). I have actually paraphrased, as the original reads: אלו הוה רבינו קמן היה פותח לנו פתח רוחב יותר מפתחו של אולם. The same language is found in R. Levi ben Habib, *She'elot u-Teshuvot Ralbaḥ* (Lemberg, 1865), no. 12 (beginning).

14. Concerning the *Shulḥan Arukh*, R. Samuel Aboab went so far as to claim that the work was edited by R. Joseph Karo's students, and this is what led to the contradictions; see *Devar Shmuel* (Venice, 1702), no. 255. While there is absolutely no evidence for this, it struck Aboab as the most plausible explanation for the contradictions, just as Bible critics point to different authors to explain the contradictions in the Torah.

just as you are able to do with the Talmud."[15] In fact, similar formulations are already found in R. Shem Tov Ibn Gaon's *Migdal Oz*.[16]

While such a hagiographic approach is not likely to resonate in academic circles, it is significant that even in traditional commentaries we find examples where Maimonides' perfection is challenged. To be sure, it is no surprise that in medieval times scholars asserted that Maimonides indeed made simple errors, forgot things, and was not exact in his language.[17] Unlike traditional scholars of later centuries, it is to be expected that many medievals would refuse to regard Maimonides' formulations with the same reverence given to the Mishnah and Talmud.[18] They would also have been skeptical of Maimonides' reported comment that in his youth, he did not suffer from forgetfulness.[19] After all, these men were Maimonides' contemporaries and near contemporaries, and one can hardly be more strident in pointing to Maimonides' supposed errors than R. Abraham ben David of Posquières (Rabad). Even the author of the *Sefer ha-*

---

15. (Livorno, 1767), *kelalei ha-Rambam*, no. 3. Because of its citation in this standard reference work, this principle has become more famous than the source in whose name it is quoted: R. Samuel Kalai, *Mishpetei Shmuel* (Venice, 1599), no. 120 (p. 152b). This passage is also cited at the beginning of chapter 1 of Jacob Levinger's *Darkhei ha-Mahashavah*, as an illustration of the traditional approach with which he disagrees. (R. David Pardo is adamant that the *Mishneh Torah* is not *more* exact in its language than the Mishnah. See *Mikhtam le-David* [Salonika, 1772], *Yoreh Deah* no. 43, *Hoshen Mishpat* no. 12 [p. 195a]: ולמימר דהרמב"ם ז'ל דייק בלישניה טפי מהתנא וזה לא יתכן [CR]).

16. See his commentary to *Shehitah* 6:8: ודברי הרמב"ם ז"ל מקובלים מפי רבותיו נ"ע מפי הגאונים ז"ל וכפי לשון התלמוד לא פחות ולא יותר ותדקדק על לשונו כמו שתדקדק על לשון הגמרא; *Ma'akhalot Asurot* 12:9: והרוצה לדקדק בגמ' יוכל לדקדק בר"ם ז"ל כמו שידקדק בגמ'.

17. Yet when Nahmanides, in his criticism of *Sefer ha-Mitzvot* (Additions to Positive and Negative Commandments), speaks of *mitzvot* that Maimonides "forgot" to include, I don't think this is to be taken literally (contrary to R. Hayyim Hirschenson, *Malki ba-Kodesh* [St. Louis, 1919], vol. 1, p. 103 [CR]). Similarly, when Abarbanel writes that Maimonides' words in the *Mishneh Torah* אינם כפי העיון מדוקדק (Commentary to *Guide* 2:35), this only means that in his halakhic writings Maimonides saw no need to offer detailed philosophical explanations, and thus his inexact formulations are intentional.

18. See, e.g., R. Solomon ben Adret, *She'elot u-Teshuvot ha-Rashba* (Jerusalem, 1998), vol. 4, no. 118: ויצא לך דקדוק זה . . . . ודקדקת . . . . באת לדקדק בלשונו כאלו דקדקת מלשון המשניות ואף זה אינו ממה שכתב הרמב"ם. This source was noted by R. Yaakov Hayyim Sofer, *Berit Yaakov* (Jerusalem, 1985), p. 236.

19. See Eugen Mittwoch, "Ein Geniza-Fragment," *Zeitschrift des Deutschen Morgenländischen Gesellschaft* 57 (1903), p. 63.

Hinnukh, who was greatly influenced by Maimonides, does not deny that the latter erred. Rather, he regards as a sign of Maimonides' greatness the fact that he made so few errors.[20]

Yet it is significant that also in subsequent centuries we continue to find assertions that Maimonides made mistakes in his works, including the *Mishneh Torah*.[21] For example, R. Simeon ben Zemah Duran feels comfortable in stating that "there is no doubt" that Maimonides forgot to record a certain halakhah. In this same responsum, after noting an apparent internal contradiction in the *Mishneh Torah*, Duran states: "Perhaps Maimonides forgot what he originally wrote." According to Duran, this explains why the two contradictory texts were not brought into line.[22] R. Joseph Karo, referring to one passage in the *Mishneh Torah*, flatly states that Maimonides erred.[23] Elsewhere, he notes that in a responsum to the sages of Lunel, Maimonides overlooked a text in the Jerusalem Talmud.[24] R. Elijah of Vilna (the Vilna Gaon), who claims that Maimonides forgot something when writing a responsum,[25] also explains a certain contradiction in the *Mishneh Torah* by suggesting that Maimonides changed his mind and neglected to correct one of his texts.[26] This same approach,

---

20. *Sefer ha-Hinnukh*, no. 573.

21. One interesting example is R. Isaac bar Sheshet, *She'elot u-Teshuvot Rivash* (Jerusalem, 1975), no. 285, who, based on a faulty text of the *Mishneh Torah*, declares that Maimonides erred (CR).

22. *She'elot u-Teshuvot ha-Tashbetz* (Lemberg, 1891), vol. 3, no. 274. More recent authorities have offered various answers to explain the contradiction to which Duran refers. Yet it is noteworthy that R. Joseph Kafih, Commentary to *Sefer Torah* 7:16, is not convinced. He follows Duran in suggesting that this halakhah is one that Maimonides corrected later in life, but neglected to follow through with a correction to the other relevant text. For another pertinent comment by Duran, see *She'elot u-Teshuvot ha-Tashbetz*, ed. Catane (Jerusalem, 1998), vol. 1, no. 147, where, in referring to Maimonides, he writes: ומתוך שבא לכלל כעס בא לכלל טעות (CR).

23. See *Kesef Mishneh*, *Na'arah Betulah* 3:2: וזה שלא בדקדוק.

24. See *Kesef Mishneh*, *Nedarim* 12:1: ומ"ש שלא נזכר בשני התלמודים נכתב שלא בהשגחה. This exact comment is also found in *Beit Yosef* (*Bedek ha-Bayit*), *Yoreh Deah* 234:57–58 (p. 536 in the Makhon Yerushalayim edition. All citations of the *Tur* and its commentaries will be to the Makhon Yerushalayim edition, which divides each section into subsections).

25. *Beur ha-Gra, Orah Hayyim* 301:42. This comment of the Vilna Gaon is referred to by R. Naphtali Zvi Judah Berlin, *Ha-Amek She'elah* (Jerusalem, 1999), vol. 1, p. 348. See also R. David Solomon Shapiro's note in *Ha-Darom* 3 (1957), p. 73.

26. *Beur ha-Gra, Orah Hayyim* 68:1.

concerning another example, is also suggested by R. David Ibn Zimra.[27]

Maimonides' great-great-grandson, R. Joshua ha-Nagid, when confronted with a contradiction in the *Mishneh Torah*, noted that one should pay no regard to what Maimonides wrote when the halakhah in question is incidental to the topic under discussion.[28] This is another way of saying that when Maimonides wrote this passage, he did not give it the same attention as he did when this halakhah was the focus of his concern, thus testifying to a certain negligence on Maimonides' part.[29] Without mentioning R. Joshua, R. David Ibn Zimra also says that, when confronted with a contradiction that cannot be explained, one should rely on the text that is the main place the halakhah is discussed, and ignore anything else.[30]

Yet as the centuries passed and Maimonides' unique status in the rabbinic pantheon was solidified, these types of approaches came to be viewed by most as lacking in basic respect, as they speak to a certain carelessness in Maimonides' editing. In addition, they were thought to undermine the proper study of Torah. These ideas were best put by R. Hayyim Joseph David Azulai in reply to a scholar[31] who thought it proper, in order to answer a certain perplexity, to claim that Maimonides' formulation was less than exacting:

---

27. *She'elot u-Teshuvot ha-Radbaz* (New York, n.d.) vol. 2, no. 755. For a strong assertion that Maimonides erred by a relatively unknown figure, see R. Abraham Hayyim Viterbo in Eliezer Ashkenazi, ed., *Ta'am Zekenim* (Frankfurt, 1855), p. 45b. This text is cited by David Henshke, "'Le-Nokhri Tashikh': Le-Toledot Shitat ha-Rambam," in Binyamin Ish Shalom, ed., *Be-Darkhei Shalom: Iyunim be-Hagut Yehudit Mugashim le-Shalom Rosenberg* (Jerusalem, 2007), p. 566.

28. Quoted in *Kesef Mishneh, Sefer Torah* 7:16. See *Teshuvot R. Yehoshua ha-Nagid*, ed. Ratsaby (Jerusalem, 1989), no. 15. See also R. Eleazer Fleckeles, *Teshuvah me-Ahavah* (New York, 1945), vol. 1, no. 67.

29. The passage could also mean that when a particular halakhah was incidental to his main focus, Maimonides *saw no need* to record it exactly. Yet this begs the question: Why would he intentionally adopt such a confusing approach?

30. *She'elot u-Teshuvot ha-Radbaz*, vol. 5, no. 1382: ואפילו את"ל דקשיא מדידיה אדידיה אפסקא דהלכות מאכלות אסורות סמכינן שהוא עיקר והתם אגב גררא ולא דק בה . . . ולא כתבתי זה אלא אם תמצא כיוצא בו ולא תדע לתרץ שתדע על אי זה משני הלשונות תסמוך להלכה.

31. The scholar is R. Mordechai Carmi, author of the halakhic work *Ma'amar Mordekhai* (Livorno, 1884–1886). In his responsum printed in Azulai, *Hayyim Sha'al* (Lemberg, 1886), vol. 1, no. 14, Carmi writes: ונראה דהרמב"ם בה' א"ב [איסורי ביאה] לא נחית

If such approaches are adopted every insignificant student will be able to offer them, and what value is there in writing such things? Furthermore, Maimonides' greatness is renowned. A number of Maimonides' words are difficult to understand, yet the later authorities found a proper explanation, for all of his words are carefully formulated. Therefore, if due to the weakness of our intellect we cannot resolve his words, assume that the fault lies with us, and if it is empty, it is because of us.[32] This is something that doesn't need to be said and is obvious, and so have I received from my teachers that in our day far be it to offer such explanations. . . . The great authorities of years past were masters of the Torah and they could say whatever appealed to them, but not us.[33]

To put it another way, the intensive Torah study that revolves around analysis of Maimonides' rulings is subverted if there is always an easy way out; one may assert that the matter is abstruse, not because of its profundity, but because of the master's carelessness.

Even when we are not dealing with a suggestion of carelessness, but a simple assertion that certain information was unavailable to Maimonides, we encounter resistance. For example, when R. Joseph Karo points out, in explanation of a certain formulation in the *Mishneh Torah*, that perhaps Maimonides was unaware of a *takkanah* of the geonim,[34] Azulai again jumps to the master's defense. Repeating an earlier assertion by R. David Ibn Zimra[35] (although without mentioning him by name), Azulai states that Maimonides was aware of *all* the decisions of the geonim.[36] While this is obviously an exaggeration, and one wonders how Azulai himself could have been sure of the accuracy of his statement, it is another good illustration of the resistance to positing gaps in Maimonides' knowledge in order to arrive at a solution. In fact, Azulai's hagiographic portrayal of Maimonides is even more extreme, as we see from the following. There are a number

---

לדקדק כ"כ בדין זה שהרי דין זה לענין טומאה וטהרה הוא ואין כאן מקומו וסמך עמ"ש בה' מו"מ [משכב ומושב] כי זה מקומו.

32. See Jerusalem Talmud, *Peah* 1:1, commenting on Deut. 32:47.

33. *Hayyim Sha'al*, vol. 1, no. 15.

34. *Kesef Mishneh, Shevuot* 11:13.

35. *She'elot u-Teshuvot ha-Radbaz*, vol. 1, no. 281, vol. 6, no. 2265.

36. *Birkei Yosef* (Vienna, 1859), *Yoreh Deah* 16:3.

of talmudic disputes concerning which Maimonides does not offer a halakhic ruling, and these omissions have exercised commentators over the centuries. R. Ezekiel Landau, in discussing one such example, states that Maimonides' omission was caused by a simple inability to come to a decision.[37] Azulai's response is again quite strong, defending the honor of Maimonides and asserting that the master was able to rule on *all* halakhot.[38] To offer one more example, R. Moses Zacuto explained that when Maimonides wrote the *Mishneh Torah*, he changed an earlier ruling of his that had appeared in the *Commentary on the Mishnah* because he subsequently found a relevant text in the Jerusalem Talmud.[39] Once again, Azulai is insistent that one must assume that Maimonides was aware of all classic rabbinic texts.[40]

Returning to our main point, the readiness to posit that Maimonides erred was never totally submerged. Thus, R. Menahem Azariah de Fano deals with a difficulty in the *Commentary on the Mishnah* by asserting that it was written in Maimonides' youth. As such, one does not assume that all of its perplexities can be explained.[41] In other

---

37. *Noda bi-Yehudah* (Jerusalem, 1994), first series, *Orah Hayyim*, no. 39 s.v. *u-va-zeh*: שהרמב"ם מסתפקא ליה בהך פיסקא . . . ולכן השמיט הרמב"ם כל פלוגתא זו שלא הי' לו בזה הכרעה. *Maggid Mishneh*, *Nizkei Mamon* 3:2, writes: ותימה איך עירב רבינו את המחלוקת, ואפשר שנסתפק לו פסק ההלכה כמי וכתב שתי הדעות. See also R. Zvi Hirsch Chajes, Commentary to *Sukkah* 41a, and R. Yaakov Hayyim Sofer, *Zera Hayyim* (Jerusalem, 1988), pp. 20–21 (who cites the sources just mentioned). See also R. Abraham ben Mordechai ha-Levi, *Ginat Veradim* (Jerusalem, 1970), *Even ha-Ezer* 4:19: ול"נ שהרמב"ם ז"ל ספוקי מספקא ליה ובסם פיקא לא מעיל נפשיה ולכן לא בירר דין זה (CR). Regarding Maimonides not offering a final decision, see Dror Fixler, "Ha-Mahlokot ha-Movaot ba-'Mishneh Torah' le-ha-Rambam," *Me'aliyot* 13 (1993), pp. 189–194. See also Chaim Tchernowitz, *Toledot ha-Poskim* (New York, 1946), vol. 1, p. 239; Levinger, *Darkhei ha-Mahashavah*, p. 148; Eliav Schochetman, "Ve-ha-Davar Tzarikh Hekhre'a: Le-Verur Da'at ha-Rambam bi-She'elat Hiddush ha-Semikhah," *Shenaton ha-Mishpat ha-Ivri* 14–15 (1988–1989), pp. 231ff.

38. *Yosef Ometz* (Jerusalem, 1987), no. 28: ועמו הסליחה שזה זה לא ניתן ליאמר על הרמב"ם ז"ל דכל רז לא אניס ליה ומ"קראות [!]שאין להם הכרע מכריע הוא את כולם.

39. *Kol Ramaz* (Amsterdam, 1719), *Sanhedrin* 2:2.

40. *Hayyim Sha'al*, vol. 1, no. 89 (p. 39a): דזה לא ניתן להאמר על הרמב"ם דבפירושו לא ידע בריתא במקומה בירושלמי ואח"כ ידעה דכל רז לא אנס ליה אש"ר ישב לחוף ימים ים הבבלי וירושלמי ובריתא במקומה המלך לא ידעה.

41. *She'elot u-Teshuvot ha-Rama mi-Pano* (Jerusalem, n.d.), no. 117: דברים הרבה ממה שכתב בפי' המשניות וזו אחת מהן דקטנותא נינהו ולא מקשינן ליה מנייהו (The expression דקטנותא נינהו is based on a passage in *Gittin* 29b [CR]). See, similarly, R. Judah Rosanes, *Mishneh la-Melekh*, *Yom Tov* 7:1 (end), and the sources cited by Neriah Guttel, "Derekh ha-Melekh ba-Mishnah," in Yosef Eliyahu Movshovitz, ed., *Kovetz ha-Rambam* (Jerusalem,

words, instead of offering solutions to difficulties in this work, one can adopt the straightforward approach of assuming that Maimonides erred. Similarly, R. Joseph Corcos writes, also with reference to the *Commentary*, that Maimonides was not as exacting as he could have been.[42] R. Vidal of Tolosa advances the possibility that even in the *Mishneh Torah* Maimonides made a careless error.[43] R. Jacob Emden is more certain, pointing to what he regards as a definite mistake in this work.[44] R. Naphtali Zvi Judah Berlin is quoted by his nephew as commenting that in writing the *Mishneh Torah*, Maimonides indeed erred, and also overlooked certain halakhot that should have been included. He noted that these mistakes could have been reduced had Maimonides not engaged in solitary study.[45] While not dealing with actual errors, R. Vidal of Tolosa,[46] R. David Ibn Zimra,[47] R. Joseph Karo,[48]

2005), p. 112 n. 35. Many negative comments about the *Commentary on the Mishnah* were due to scholars not having access to a good translation of the text. They were also unaware that Maimonides continued to revise this work throughout his life. Thus, many of the supposed difficulties and contradictions between it and the *Mishneh Torah* disappear when one examines Kafih's edition. Of course, difficulties and contradictions remain, and although in his notes to the *Commentary* Kafih refers to many of them, others are not noted. To give one example, in his *Commentary* to *Sanhedrin* 7:4, Maimonides states that there is no court-administered punishment, neither biblical nor rabbinic, for lesbianism. Yet in *Issurei Biah* 21:8, he writes: וראוי להכותן מכת מרדות. While not an actual contradiction, the formulation is certainly different than that of the *Commentary*.

42. Commentary to *Terumot* 11:11 (found in the Frankel edition of the *Mishneh Torah*): כי לא דקדק במשנה כל הצורך.

43. *Maggid Mishneh, Shevitat Yom Tov* 7:18: הוא טעות . . . מה שנמצא בספרי רבינו סופרים או אגב שטפא.

44. See *Mitpahat Sefarim* (Jerusalem, 1995), p. 29: לכן שיבוש גמור הוא זה לר"ם ז"ל. (See above, p. 4 n. 12, where Emden offers a different perspective.) It is actually Emden who errs; see the commentaries of Kafih and Rabinovitch to *Tzitzit*, 2:2; R. Yaakov Hayyim Sofer, *Hadar Yaakov* (Jerusalem, 2005), vol. 4, pp. 134–137.

45. See R. Barukh Halevi Epstein, *Mekor Barukh* (Vilna, 1928), pp. 1772–1773. Maimonides is compared negatively in this regard to R. Solomon ben Adret. I must note, however, that I am skeptical of the authenticity of this story.

46. *Maggid Mishneh, Shehitah* 1:26. This is perhaps not a good example, as Maimonides is quoting the Talmud which, according to R. Vidal, is also not exacting in its language (CR).

47. Commentary to *Terumot* 7:23.

48. *Kesef Mishneh, Gerushin* 2:3: ומה שהזכיר פה סופר אשגרת לישן הוא ולאו דוקא. See also *Kesef Mishneh, Ishut* 14:13 (quoting R. Isaac bar Sheshet, *She'elot u-Teshuvot ha-Rivash*, no. 364 [CR]); *Arakhim ve-Haramim* 8:5, *Nedarim* 12:8, *Beit ha-Behirah* 1:17, *Ma'aseh ha-Korbanot* 12:23, *She'ar Avot ha-Tum'ah* 12:3, *Malveh ve-Loveh* 27:1 (quoting R. Isaac bar Sheshet, *She'elot u-Teshuvot ha-Rivash*, no. 142).

R. Judah Rosanes,[49] R. Abraham di Boton,[50] R. Shabbetai ha-Kohen,[51] and R. Isser Zalman Meltzer[52] all speak of inexact formulations in the *Mishneh Torah*.

TO ERR IS HUMAN

Let us begin by looking at examples where we seem to confront mistakes, carelessness, and forgetfulness by Maimonides. Although no apologies are needed for such an investigation in an academic work, we would be remiss in not calling attention to the fact that Maimonides, by mentioning his own human frailties, virtually invites us to use such an approach, at least when dealing with difficulties in his later writings. For example, in a famous letter to the sages of Lunel, Maimonides acknowledges that in his old age he indeed suffers from forgetfulness.[53] In another letter, Maimonides mentions that he once temporarily forgot the source of a halakhah.[54] Elsewhere, with reference to something he wrote in the *Commentary on the Mishnah*, Maimonides states that it is an error that is due to him not having examined the matter properly.[55] In the Introduction to the *Commentary*, Maimonides states that he is unsure if he has included all the laws in a certain category,[56] and in the conclusion to the *Commentary*, he acknowledges the possibility of errors, due to the difficult circumstances under which he wrote this work.[57]

Even R. Abraham Maimonides feels compelled, in one case, to suggest that perhaps his father forgot about a talmudic passage.[58] The

---

49. *Mishneh la-Melekh, Tum'at Tzara'at* 16:3, s.v. *ve-od.*

50. *Lehem Mishneh, Shevuot* 5:18: ורבינו ז"ל לא דקדק שם בלשונו. See also *Lehem Mishneh, Shevuot* 3:5 (CR), *Zekhiyah u-Matanah* 3:7, *Shekhenim* 7:5, *Shegagot* 15:4, *Melakhim* 7:1. Despite these comments, see his criticism of Karo in *Lehem Mishneh, Arakhim ve-Haramim* 8:5: ובמחילה מכבוד תורתו . . . איך אפשר לומר על כל כמה פעמים שהזכיר רבינו ז"ל תוספת פרוטה באה שלא בדקדוק אלא אורחא דמילתא.

51. *Shakh, Hoshen Mishpat* 115:5 (CR).

52. Unlike the others mentioned, Meltzer only offers this as a possibility. See *Even ha-Azel* (Jerusalem, n.d.), *Keriat Shema* 1:1 (p. 9a): רק דאפשר דלא דייק כ"כ (CR).

53. *Iggerot ha-Rambam*, vol. 2, p. 503.

54. *Iggerot ha-Rambam*, vol. 2, pp. 444–445.

55. *Teshuvot ha-Rambam*, no. 217.

56. Vol. 1, p. 10 (CR).

57. Vol. 6, pp. 455–456.

58. *Birkat Avraham* (Lyck, 1859), no. 13. See also *ibid.*, no. 5, that after Maimonides corrected one halakhah, he should have also corrected a later halakhah.

problem he confronted is that in the *Mishneh Torah*, *Shegagot* 7:6, Maimonides writes "it appears to me," and yet—as the commentators are quick to point out—this view, offered as his own insight, is found explicitly in *Bava Kamma* 2a. While I am unaware of any later commentators who offer this approach to explain the problem at hand, instead suggesting all sorts of solutions, R. Abraham saw simple forgetfulness as a possible scenario.[59] Among academic scholars, this approach was used in particular by Jacob Levinger in seeking to explain Maimonidean omissions in the *Mishneh Torah*.[60] Yet there remain many omissions concerning which such an answer will simply not work, and we must continue the search for reasonable explanations. To give just one example, which as far as I know has never been adequately explained: Why did Maimonides not codify the famous and uncontested halakhah that a father is obligated to teach his son a craft (*Kiddushin* 29a)?[61]

There are a few types of error that can easily be explained by the possibility of forgetfulness. The first area to consider is that of biblical verses. Rabbinic literature of all genres is full of examples in which scholars cite biblical verses incorrectly. In fact, there is a much discussed Tosafot[62] which claims that the amoraim themselves did not

---

59. Unlike other commentators, R. Joseph Corcos, *ad loc.* (printed in the Frankel edition of the *Mishneh Torah* and quoted in *Kesef Mishneh*) suggests a textual approach, namely, that Maimonides' version of *Bava Kamma* was missing the words in question. Had this been so, R. Abraham Maimonides would have noted it, and there is no manuscript evidence confirming the absence of these words (see *Bava Kamma*, ed. Frankel [Jerusalem, 1996]). R. Betzalel Ashkenazi, *She'elot u-Teshuvot Rabbi Betzalel Ashkenazi* (Jerusalem, 1968), no. 38, objects to Corcos' approach, arguing that it is not a valid principle of interpretation: ואין דרכנו לתרץ לשון הרב ז"ל בחילוף גירסא אי לא אשכחן לה בשום ספר כתיבת יד והכא לא אשכחן שינוי בזה בספרים.

60. See *Darkhei ha-Mahashavah*, pp. 120, 128. On p. 120 Levinger writes: הנחה כזאת מן הסתם לא תניח את דעתם של הרבה קוראים, ואעפ"כ לגבי דינים רבים, שהרבו להתפלפל בהם מדוע אינם באים במ"ת, היא נראית כמסתברת ביותר. עכ"פ החוקר שאינו רוצה לגשת למ"ת מתוך דעה קדומה על אישיותו העל-טבעית של הרמב"ם חייב להתחשב באפשרות כזאת.

61. Maimonides does record it as halakhah in his *Commentary on the Mishnah, Kiddushin* 1:7. For discussions of Maimonides' omission, see R. Jacob Ettlinger, *Binyan Tziyon* (Jerusalem, 1989), no. 125; R. Hayyim Eleazar Shapira, *Divrei Torah* (Jerusalem, 1998), vol. 8, no. 18; Eliav Schochetman, "Al Hovat ha-Av le-Lamed Beno Umanut," *Dine Israel* 20–21 (2000–2001), pp. 397–417.

62. *Bava Batra* 113a s.v. *tarvayhu*. See also *Teshuvot Geonim Kadmonim* (Berlin, 1848), no. 78.

always properly remember biblical verses.[63] Related to this, it is worth noting that Nahmanides declares that the famous Torah scroll of R. Meir, which read "Behold, death was good" (טוב מות), was actually carelessly written this way by R. Meir himself (although Nahmanides does not attribute the error to forgetfulness).[64]

Since the invention of printing and universal acceptance of a standard biblical text, it is easy to determine when we are dealing with an error. Leaving aside typographic mistakes, these are due to the scholar erring because he was citing from memory. When dealing with texts from earlier centuries matters are less clear, since in addition to forgetfulness, we have to consider the possibility that the "mistaken" quotation actually preserves a variant text. When dealing with Maimonides matters are simpler, at least with regard to the text of the Pentateuch, since after coming to Egypt he was able to make use of the Ben Asher codex in writing his own Torah scroll.[65] Although only a very small section from the Pentateuch survives in this codex, we know that the letters of the Ben Asher Pentateuch were identical to the current Yemenite text (which differs slightly from Ashkenazic and Sephardic Torah scrolls).[66] It is, of course, also vital that we have good texts of Maimonides' works, which is no longer a problem due to the

---

63. The same opinion is offered by R. Asher ben Jehiel and quoted in *Shitah Mekubetzet, Bava Batra* 113a. For detailed discussions of this issue, see R. Hayyim Hezekiah Medini, *Sedei Hemed* (Brooklyn, 1949), *ma'arekhet alef*, no. 299, *Peat ha-Sadeh, ma'arekhet alef*, no. 21, *Shiyurei ha-Peah, ma'arekhet alef*, no. 41; R. Aharon Magid, *Beit Aharon* (New York, 1978), vol. 11, pp. 520–525. A typical reaction to the Tosafist comment is expressed by R. Hayyim Joseph David Azulai, *Petah Einayim* (Jerusalem, 1962), *Bava Kamma* 54b: דאין לתלות בוקי סריקי באמוראים דלא ידעי מקרא שכתוב ח"ו.

64. *Kitvei Ramban*, ed. Chavel (Jerusalem, 1963), vol. 1, p. 184: ר' מאיר היה לבלר, וכשכתב ספר תורה אחד היה מחשב בלבו כי והנה טוב מאד ירמוז אפילו למות ולאפיסות כולם, והלך ידו אחר לבו.

65. *Sefer Torah* 8:4. I see no reason to assume that Maimonides carefully examined this codex for its text of the Prophets and Hagiographa. See e.g., *Iggerot ha-Rambam*, vol. 1, p. 229, where Maimonides, following Is. 33:1, writes: ואתה בוגד ולא בגדו בך. Yet as R. Meir Mazuz, *Arim Nisi* (Bnei Brak, 2008), p. 77, has pointed out, the Ben Asher codex reads: בוגד ולא בגדו בַ.

66. In five places Ben Asher and the Yemenite text differ with regard to the proper separation of words; see Jordan S. Penkower, *Nusah ha-Torah be-Kheter Aram Tzovah: Edut Hadashah* (Ramat Gan, 1993), pp. 67ff. For the differences between the Yemenite text and the Ashkenazic-Sephardic text, see my *The Limits of Orthodox Theology: Maimonides' Thirteen Principles Reappraised* (Oxford, 2004), p. 97 n. 41. See also Maimonides, *Commentary on the Mishnah*, vol. 3, p. 24 n. 5.

efforts of R. Chaim Heller, R. Joseph Kafih, R. Nachum Eliezer Rabinovitch, R. Yitzhak Sheilat, and the scholars who have produced the Frankel edition of the *Mishnah Torah*.[67]

Following the next paragraph I point to examples of Maimonides' forgetfulness and carelessness when citing biblical verses, and some of the latter are no more than slips of the pen.[68] While most of these examples are misquotations, in some of the cases Maimonides quoted the verse correctly but was mistaken about the

---

67. Neuhausen, *Torah Or le-ha-Rambam*, the only comprehensive study of biblical passages in the *Mishneh Torah*, is severely flawed because it relies on faulty texts of Maimonidean works and also omits a number of examples. In addition, Neuhausen operates under the mistaken assumption that the *Mishneh Torah* preserves variant biblical readings. Nevertheless, I have made good use of this work. R. Joseph Kafih's index of biblical verses in Maimonidean works, *Ha-Mikra ba-Rambam* (Jerusalem, 1972), was invaluable for this chapter.

68. It must be noted that even the Oxford ms. of the *Mishneh Torah*, which carries Maimonides' attestation, contains scribal errors, and no one assumes that Maimonides actually went through it carefully. See Shlomo Zalman Havlin, ed., *Mishneh Torah le-ha-Rambam, Mada ve-Ahavah: Ha-Sefer ha-Mugah* (Jerusalem, 1997), p. 18. This manuscript was corrected in numerous places, on many occasions apparently by the original copyist. Some errors certainly went undetected, especially those that only concern one letter. For example, in *Berakhot* 6:19 the Oxford ms. reads: רצווי הרבה צוו חכמים. Clearly, the first word was originally written in the plural and the final *nun* or *mem* (and presumably also an additional *yud*) were mistakenly omitted. See also *Teshuvah* 4:2, where the Oxford ms. has the word יתזכה. It is possible that this is a copyist's error for יזכה, and this is what appears in Kafih's version (which is based on Yemenite mss.). There are many other examples where other mss. appear to have a better reading than the Oxford ms. This is sometimes also the case with regard to biblical verses. For example, in the Introduction to the *Mishneh Torah*, the Oxford ms. cites Deut. 31:26 as לקוח את ספר התורה הזאת. Yet all other mss. used by Frankel have הזה, which is what appears in the verse. In the List of Commandments at the beginning of the *Mishneh Torah*, neg. com. 178, the Oxford ms. misquotes the verse. The better reading is certainly that which is found in most other mss., especially since this reading agrees with what Maimonides writes elsewhere (*Sefer ha-Mitzvot*, neg. com. 178, *Ma'akhalot Asurot* 2:14). In the List of Commandments at the beginning of the *Mishneh Torah*, neg. com. 270, we have an interesting example where the Oxford ms. originally cited the verse properly, and the "correction" created a nonexistent verse. The Oxford ms. has been published in Rabinovitch's edition, but it is necessary to compare his transcription with the original; I have found errors as well as single letters which were later added to the ms., yet they are not enclosed in brackets. For example, in *Tefillah* 12:5 Maimonides records the prayer חיי עולם נטע בתוכנו. In the ms. a *heh* is suspended above the last letter of נטע, signifying that the word should be נטעה. Yet Rabinovitch neglected to place the *heh* in brackets. This is a particularly unfortunate omission, because there is a medieval dispute about precisely this *heh*. See Kafih, *Yeriot Aharon*, p. 72; David Flusser, "Hayei Olam Neta'ah be-Tokhenu," *Tarbiz* 58 (1999), pp. 147–153. The unsuspecting reader assumes

subject to which it referred. Although I have attempted to provide a complete list, I have undoubtedly overlooked some examples. I have only recorded those cases where, in my opinion, the manuscript evidence is conclusive; for if there is contradictory manuscript evidence, it is often impossible to determine which manuscript has been corrupted or corrected. Where there is strong evidence, but in my opinion not conclusive, I have put the example in the notes. I have not listed cases where a *vav* is omitted from the beginning of a word at the start of a quotation, because it is impossible to know if these are errors or if the *vav* was omitted for stylistic reasons. In addition, it is hard to rely on the accuracy of manuscripts in cases such as these. I have, however, listed the examples where Maimonides mistakenly adds a *vav* at the beginning of words, as these appear to be errors rather than stylistic changes (although whenever the issue is a single letter, there is always the possibility that we are confronted with scribal error).[69] I have not listed those cases where Maimonides himself later corrected his error. I have also not cited examples where it is clear, to me at least, that Maimonides has not misquoted a verse, but simply abridged it for simplicity's sake (even if he doesn't add וכו' between the two sections of the verse).[70] In order to avoid confusion, as the Hebrew in this book is without vocalization, when quoting

---

that the version given by Rabinovitch is actually the Oxford ms., when in reality, both here and elsewhere, Rabinovitch has also incorporated the additions to the ms. Rabinovitch appears to be careful to place all added *words* in brackets, and one can only wonder why he did not see the necessity of doing so with individual letters as well. For another error regarding the corrections to the Oxford ms., see *Yesodei ha-Torah* 6:7, where the correction cites Deut. 12:3 as תשרופון, yet Rabinovitch's edition mistakenly has תשרפון, which is how the word actually appears in the Bible (with a *sheva* under the *resh*). For a list of all corrections to the Oxford ms., see Havlin, ed., *Mishneh Torah*, pp. 71–79.

69. I have not cited *Mattenot Aniyim* 1:14, where Maimonides, in citing Deut. 24:19, writes: וכי תקצר קצירך בשדך. Although the initial *vav* is lacking in the original, in this case the *vav* simply signifies Maimonides' citation of a second relevant verse; see Kafih's commentary, *ad loc.* A number of times, Maimonides cited a verse inaccurately, but corrected the error himself. See *Commentary on the Mishnah*, vol. 1, p. 13 n. 12, vol. 4, p. 102 n. 13, vol. 5, pp. 46 n. 42, 90 n. 34, vol. 6, pp. 25 n. 9, 293 n. 2. See *Commentary on the Mishnah*, *Orlah* 1:2 (and Kafih's note, *ad loc.*) where Maimonides first misquoted a biblical verse, and although he later recognized the error and attempted to correct it, he did not do so completely.

70. See, e.g., *Sefer ha-Mitzvot*, neg. com. 110 (also found in many Yemenite mss. of the List of Commandments at the beginning of the *Mishneh Torah*, neg. com. 110).

from the Bible I have sometimes cited words as plene (with an extra *vav* or *yud*), even though they appear in the Bible as defective.

There is no question that this extensive list shows that, when writing his various works, Maimonides did not hesitate to cite biblical texts from memory. In fact, Kalman Kahana pointed to the forgetfulness we shall see in order to cast doubt on the accepted view [71] that the famous manuscript of the first five books of the *Commentary on the Mishnah* [72] was written in Maimonides' own hand. [73] Here is not the place to show in any detail why Kahana is mistaken; suffice it to say that we shall also see many examples of forgetfulness in the *Mishneh Torah*. In addition, it is noteworthy that in a number of cases Maimonides made the same mistake in more than one place, showing that the error was ingrained in his memory (although more often he does cite the verse correctly elsewhere [74]). It is also clear from this list that Maimonides sometimes recorded halakhot from memory, without checking the underlying talmudic text; for had this text been in front of him he would not have misquoted the biblical verse, or cited a mistaken verse. This assumption—that Maimonides would record halakhot from memory (and we know that his memory was not perfect)—has implications for all sorts of Maimonidean difficulties. [75]

---

71. See Simon Hopkins, ed., *Maimonides's Commentary on Tractate Shabbat* (Jerusalem, 2001), p. xvii.

72. The facsimile edition was published by Solomon D. Sassoon (Copenhagen, 1956–1966). Kafih based his edition upon this manuscript. Because of a strange error on Kafih's part, he assumed that the ms. did not contain Maimonides' *Commentary* on *Avot*, *Avodah Zarah*, and *Horayot*. See Yitzhak Sheilat, *Hakdamot ha-Rambam* (Jerusalem, 1992), pp. 14–15. New editions of Maimonides' *Commentary* to these tractates have recently appeared. See below, p. 20 n. 81. It should also be noted that in the facsimile edition the end of *Hagigah* was mistakenly omitted and was thus never translated by Kafih (or anyone else). See Catriel D. Kaplin's introduction to Solomon D. Sassoon, *Natan Hokhmah li-Shelomoh* (Jerusalem, 1989), p. 14.

73. "Perush ha-Mishnah shel ha-Rambam bi-Khetav Yado?" *Ha-Ma'ayan* 26 (Tevet 5746), pp. 58ff.

74. As the footnotes have grown too large as it is, I have not generally provided these references. They can be easily located using the Bar Ilan Responsa CD-Rom.

75. When an error appears in the *Mishneh Torah* as well as in other sources, I have placed it in the *Mishneh Torah* list. At this point, I should note R. S. H. Kanievsky's view, *Kiryat Melekh* (Jerusalem, 1983), p. 250, that Maimonides purposely altered and shortened

Commentary on the Mishnah, Introduction to *Zeraim*, p. 17: Maimonides cites Deut. 12:17 as לא תוכל לאכל בשעריך מעשר דגנך תירושך ויצהרך. Yet the verse reads ותירושך. A similar verse in Deut. 14:23 reads תירושך, and no doubt this led to the confusion.

Commentary on the Mishnah, *Peah* 6:2, *Nedarim* 7:4, *Eduyot* 4:4, *Kelim* 2:4: Maimonides cites Neh. 7:3 as ויגיפו הדלתות. Yet the verse reads יגיפו, without the *vav*.

Commentary on the Mishnah, *Kilayim* 2:5: Maimonides cites Is. 37:30 as אכול השנה ספיח והשנה השנית שחיס. Yet the verse reads ובשנה השנית.[76]

Commentary on the Mishnah, *Shevi'it* 1:1: Maimonides cites Lev. 25:11, לא תזרעו ולא תקצרו את ספיחיה, as referring to the Sabbatical year. Yet the verse speaks of the Jubilee year.

Commentary on the Mishnah, *Ma'aser Sheni* 1:2: Maimonides cites Lev. 27:10, לא יחליפנו ולא ימיר, as referring to tithes of cattle. Yet the verse speaks of animals given as offerings to the Lord.

Commentary on the Mishnah, *Ma'aser Sheni* 3:2: Maimonides cites Lev. 7:18 as ואם האכל יאכל מבשר זבח השלמים וכו' פיגול הוא לא ירצה. Yet the verse reads: ואם האכל יאכל מבשר זבח שלמיו . . . פגול יהיה. Citing from memory, Maimonides was confused by Lev. 19:7: ואם האכל יאכל ביום השלישי פגול הוא לא ירצה.

Commentary on the Mishnah, *Ma'aser Sheni* 3:2: Maimonides cites a verse[77] as והנותר ממנו באש תשרפו. Yet there is no such biblical verse. He either intended Ex. 12:10, והנותר ממנו עד בקר באש תשרפו, Lev. 7:17, והנותר בבשר, or Lev. 8:32, והנותר מבשר הזבח ביום השלישי באש ישרף, ובלחם באש תשרפו.

---

biblical verses. He provides no evidence for this assertion, and it is presumably based upon his hagiographic view of Maimonides. As I was completing this chapter, I came across Dror Fixler, "Sefarad, Eretz Yisrael, u-Mitzrayim be-Ferush ha-Mishnah la-Rambam," *Netuim* 8 (2002), pp. 58–61, who also provides a list of mistakes by Maimonides in the *Commentary on the Mishnah*. He alerted me to some examples I overlooked. Yet his list is also not complete. For example, together with Kafih, he neglects to note that Maimonides misquotes a verse in *Zavim* 2:4.

76. The verse has been corrected in the ms. used by Kafih, written by Maimonides. However, the correction is not in Maimonides' handwriting and there is no reason to assume that he was responsible for it.

77. Throughout this chapter, the term "verse" is used as a form of shorthand; it does not mean that the words quoted are necessarily a complete verse.

Commentary on the Mishnah, Orlah 1:2: Maimonides cites Lev. 19:23 as ונטעתם לכם כל עץ. Yet the word לכם does not appear in the verse.

Commentary on the Mishnah, Bikkurim 1:4: Maimonides cites Deut. 26:3 as אשר נשבעת לאבותינו. Yet the verse reads: אשר נשבע ה' לאבותינו.

Commentary on the Mishnah, Eruvin 1:7: Maimonides cites Num. 19:16 as כל הנוגע בחלל חרב. Yet the verse reads: וכל אשר יגע על פני השדה בחלל חרב.

Commentary on the Mishnah, Beitzah 1:1: Maimonides cites Ex. 12:19 as שבעת ימים שאור לא ימצא בבתיכם כי כל אוכל חמץ. Yet the verse reads: כי כל אוכל מחמצת.

Commentary on the Mishnah, Yoma 5:2: Maimonides cites Lev. 16:19, מן הדם באצבעו שבע פעמים, as a proof text; yet this verse is not relevant. The correct verse is Lev. 16:14: שבע פעמים מן הדם באצבעו. Because the verses are so similar, it is easy to see how, citing from memory, Maimonides confused the two.

Commentary on the Mishnah, Yoma 8:1: In listing the five verses in which the Torah states that one must afflict oneself on Yom Kippur, Maimonides cites Lev. 16:34: והיתה זאת לכם וכו'. However, this verse is not relevant, and Maimonides should have cited Lev. 16:29, which mentions self-affliction and is cited by the Talmud, *Yoma* 76a, as one of the five verses. Its opening words, והיתה לכם, are very similar to the verse Maimonides cites, and this led to the confusion.

Commentary on the Mishnah, Yevamot 7:6: Maimonides cites Lev. 22:13 as ובן אין לה. Yet the verse reads: וזרע אין לה.

Commentary on the Mishnah, Yevamot 11:5: Maimonides cites Lev. 6:23, לא תאכל באש תשרף, as a proof text. Yet the correct verse is Lev. 6:16: כליל תהיה לא תאכל.

Commentary on the Mishnah, Nazir 6:5, *Sefer ha-Mitzvot*, neg. com. 207: With reference to the prohibition of a Nazirite rendering himself unclean for the dead, Maimonides cites Lev. 21:11: לאביו ולאמו לא יטמא. Yet this verse is stated with regard to the High Priest. The correct verse is Num. 6:7: לאביו ולאמו לאחיו ולאחותו לא יטמא.[78]

Commentary on the Mishnah, Nazir 6:5: Maimonides cites Lev. 14:9 as יגלח את כל ראשו ואת זקנו ואת גבות עיניו. Yet the verse reads: וגלח את שערו את ראשו ואת זקנו ואת גבות עיניו.

---

78. He actually cites the correct verse shortly following this. See *Commentary on the Mishnah, Nazir* 7:1.

Commentary on the Mishnah, *Sotah* 3:5: Maimonides cites Lev. 6:22 as כל זכר בכהנים יאכלנה. Yet the verse reads: כל זכר בכהנים יאכל אותה.

Commentary on the Mishnah, *Sotah* 3:6: Maimonides cites a verse as וסקלתם אותו. Yet there is no such biblical verse. He no doubt intended Lev. 24:14, ורגמו אותו, which is the relevant proof text cited in *Sotah* 23b and *Sanhedrin* 45a.

Commentary on the Mishnah, *Kiddushin* 1:8: Maimonides cites the word והגיש as appearing in the Bible. Yet there is no such word. Perhaps he had in mind Lev. 2:8, והגישה.[79]

Commentary on the Mishnah, *Kiddushin* 2:9: Maimonides cites a verse as קודש היא. Yet there is no such biblical verse. He intended Lev. 25:12: יובל היא קודש תהיה.

Commentary on the Mishnah, *Bava Metzia* 2:10, *Sefer ha-Mitzvot*, neg. com. 208: Referring to the prohibition against a Nazirite's entrance into a house with a dead body, Maimonides cites Lev. 21:11: על כל נפשות מת לא יבוא. Yet this verse refers to the High Priest. He should have cited Num. 6:6: על נפש מת לא יבוא.

Commentary on the Mishnah, *Sanhedrin* 1:5: Maimonides cites Deut. 18:20 as והנביא אשר יזיד. Yet the verse reads: אך הנביא אשר יזיד.

Commentary on the Mishnah, *Sanhedrin* 11:6: Maimonides cites Lev. 21:9 as ובת כהן כי תחל לזנות.[80] Yet the verse reads: ובת איש כהן.

Commentary on the Mishnah, *Makkot* 3:1: Maimonides cites Lev. 25:14 as לא תונו. Yet the verse reads: אל תונו.

Commentary on the Mishnah, *Shevuot* 1:2: Maimonides cites Lev. 5:7, 11 as ואם לא תשיג ידו וכו' ואם לא תגיע ידו. Yet the verses should be reversed: ואם לא תגיע ידו וכו' ואם לא תשיג ידו.

Commentary on the Mishnah, *Shevuot* 5:1: Maimonides cites Lev. 5:25 as ואת אשמו יביא לה' והביא את אשמו לה' איל תמים. Yet the verse reads: איל תמים.

Commentary on the Mishnah, *Eduyot* 5:1: Maimonides cites Lev. 15:2 as דבר אל בני ישראל. Yet the verse reads דברו. It is possible that

---

79. See below, s.v. *Commentary on the Mishnah, Menahot* 5:5.

80. Kafih's version mistakenly cites the verse correctly. To see what Maimonides actually wrote, one must consult the facsimile edition of the autograph copy of Maimonides' *Commentary*; see above, p. 16 n. 72.

Maimonides' version of *Shabbat* 83a and *Niddah* 34a were the same as ours; these, too, contain the error, and perhaps Maimonides simply copied from one of these texts without realizing the mistake.

Commentary on the Mishnah, Eduyot 6:3: Maimonides cites Lev. 11:39 as והנוגע בנבלתם. Yet the verse reads: הנוגע בנבלתה.

Commentary on the Mishnah, Eduyot 7:1: Maimonides cites a verse: ופטר חמור וכו' וכל בכור אדם בבניך תפדה. Yet there is no such biblical verse. He intended either Ex. 34:20, ופטר חמור תפדה בשה ואם לא תפדה וכל פטר חמור תפדה בשה ואם לא, or Ex. 13:13, וערפתו כל בכור בניך תפדה תפדה וערפתו וכל בכור אדם בבניך תפדה.

Commentary on the Mishnah, Eduyot 8:4: Maimonides cites Lev. 11:38 as וכי יפול מים על זרע. Yet the verse reads: וכי יתן מים על זרע. Maimonides conflated this verse with the one immediately preceding it (11:37): וכי יפול מנבלתם על כל זרע.

Commentary on the Mishnah, Avodah Zarah 3:8: Maimonides cites Num. 25:3 as ויצמד ישראל לבעל פעור ויאכלו זבחי מתים. Yet the last three words do not appear in the verse and actually come from Ps. 106:28: ויצמדו לבעל פעור ויאכלו זבחי מתים.[81]

Commentary on the Mishnah, Avot 2:13: Maimonides cites Prov. 2:19 as כל באיה לא ישובון ולא יסיגו. Yet the verse reads ישיגו.

Commentary on the Mishnah, Avot 4:5: As an example of a verse dealing with forgiveness for an unwitting sin, Maimonides cites Lev. 19:22: ונסלח לו מחטאתו אשר חטא. However, this verse does not deal with such a case. He should have cited either Lev. 4:35, על חטאתו אשר מחטאתו אשר חטא ונסלח לו, or Lev. 5:10, חטא ונסלח לו.

Commentary on the Mishnah, Avot 4:18: Maimonides cites Eccl. 5:15 as כל עמת שבא כך הלך. Yet the verse reads ילך.

Commentary on the Mishnah, Horayot, Introduction: Maimonides cites Lev. 4:32 as יביא קרבנו נקבה תמימה. Yet the verse reads: יביא קרבנו לחטאת נקבה תמימה.

---

81. For Maimonides' *Commentary* on *Avodah Zarah*, it is essential to use Dror Fixler's edition (Jerusalem, 2002); for *Avot*, Yitzhak Sheilat's edition (Jerusalem, 1994); for *Horayot*, Yitzhak Sheilat's *Tikkun Mishnah* (Jerusalem, 2002), since for these tractates, Kafih's edition is not based on Maimonides' own manuscript. See also *Me'aliyot* 20 (1999), pp. 21–87, for R. Haim Sabato's supercommentary to Maimonides' *Commentary* on *Horayot*.

Commentary on the Mishnah, Horayot 2:1: Maimonides cites Lev. 4:3 as והקריב על חטאתו אשר חטא פר בן בקר לחטאת. Yet the verse reads: פר בן בקר תמים לה' לחטאת.

Commentary on the Mishnah, Horayot 2:5: Maimonides cites Lev. 5:17 as ואם נפש אחת תחטא. Yet the verse reads: ואם נפש כי תחטא.

Commentary on the Mishnah, Horayot 3:1: Maimonides cites Lev. 4:23 as על חטאתו אשר חטא. This expression is found six times in Leviticus, and three times in chapter 4. Yet the word על does not appear in 4:23.

Commentary on the Mishnah, Zevahim 2:1: In the corrected version of his *Commentary*, Maimonides cites Lev. 6:3 as על בשרו ולבשם. Maimonides' correction actually made matters worse, for in the first version of the *Commentary* he had ילבשם על בשרו. This citation contains only a small error, in that the first word should read ילבש.[82]

Commentary on the Mishnah, Zevahim 2:1: Maimonides cites Ex. 40:31 as ורחצו אהרן ובניו ממנו את ידיהם ואת רגליהם. Yet the verse reads: ורחצו ממנו משה ואהרן ובניו את ידיהם ואת רגליהם.

Commentary on the Mishnah, Zevahim 2:1: Maimonides cites Ex. 40:32 as בבאם אל אהל מועד ובקרבתם אל המזבח ירחצו חקת עולם לו ולזרעו. Yet the verse reads: בבאם אל אהל מועד ובקרבתם אל המזבח ירחצו כאשר צוה ה' את משה. In the concluding words of his citation, Maimonides was confused by Ex. 30:20-21: והיתה . . . בבאם אל אהל מועד ירחצו מים להם חק עולם לו ולזרעו לדרתם.

Commentary on the Mishnah, Zevahim 2:2: Maimonides cites Lev. 7:18 as פגול הוא לא ירצה המקריב אותו לא יחשב לו פגול יהיה ואכליו עונו ישא. Yet the verse reads: לא ירצה המקריב אותו לא יחשב לו פגול יהיה והנפש האוכלת ממנו עונה תשא. The phrase ואכליו עונו ישא, used by Maimonides, appears in Lev. 19:8.

Commentary on the Mishnah, Zevahim 2:3, *Menahot* 3:1: Maimonides cites Lev. 7:18 as מבשר זבח השלמים. Yet the verse reads שלמיו.

Commentary on the Mishnah, Zevahim 4:3: Maimonides cites a verse as וקמץ ממנו בקמצו. Yet there is no such biblical verse. He intended either Lev. 2:2, והרים ממנו בקמצו, or Lev. 6:8, וקמץ משם מלא קמצו.

Commentary on the Mishnah, Zevahim 5:6: With reference to the sin offering, Maimonides cites Lev. 10:13: ואכלתם אותה במקום קדוש. Yet

---

82. See below, p. 38, s.v. *Kelei ha-Mikdash* 10:6.

this verse refers to the *minhah* offering. He should have cited Lev. 6:19:
במקום קדוש תאכל.

Commentary on the Mishnah, Zevahim 8:12: Maimonides cites Lev.
22:3 as וטמאתו עליו ונכרת. Yet the verse reads ונכרתה.

Commentary on the Mishnah, Zevahim 12:1: Maimonides cites a verse
as הכהן המקריב אותה יאכלנה. Yet there is no such biblical verse. No
doubt he intended Lev. 7:9: לכהן המקריב אותה לו תהיה.

Commentary on the Mishnah, Zevahim 14:1: With reference to the
Red Heifer, Maimonides cites a verse as חטאת היא. Yet there is no such
biblical verse. He presumably intended Num. 19:17, שרפת החטאת.

Commentary on the Mishnah, Zevahim 14:2: In explanation of a mishnaic halakhah, Maimonides cites Ex. 22:29: שבעת ימים יהיה עם אמו
וביום השמיני תתנו לי. Citing from memory, Maimonides confused this
verse, which has no relevance to the Mishnah, with Lev 22:27: והיה
שבעת ימים תחת אמו ומיום השמיני והלאה ירצה לקרבן אשה לה'.

Commentary on the Mishnah, Zevahim 14:9: Maimonides cites Deut.
12:11 as תביאו עולותיכם וכו'. Yet the verse reads: תביאו את כל אשר אנכי
מצוה אתכם עולותיכם . . .

Commentary on the Mishnah, Menahot, Introduction (p. 66):
Maimonides cites Num. 15:12 as כמספר אשר תעשה ככה תעשה לאחד
כמספרם. Yet the verse reads תעשו (twice).

Commentary on the Mishnah, Menahot 5:3: Maimonides cites the following verse as applying to both the "*minhah* for sin" and the "*minhah*
for jealousy": לא יתן עליו שמן ולא ישים עליו לבונה. Yet there is no such
biblical verse. Lev. 5:11, referring to the *minhah* for sin, reads: לא ישים
עליה שמן ולא יתן עליה לבונה. Num. 5:15, referring to the *minhah* for jealousy, reads: לא יצק עליו שמן ולא יתן עליו לבונה.

Commentary on the Mishnah, Menahot 5:5: Maimonides cites the
word והגיש as appearing in the Bible. Yet there is no such word.[83]

Commentary on the Mishnah, Menahot 7:6: Maimonides cites Num.
15:4 as והקריב המקריב לה' את קרבנו. Yet the verse reads קרבנו לה'.

Commentary on the Mishnah, Menahot 13:3: Maimonides cites a verse
as וערך עליה העצים. Yet there is no such biblical verse. Maimonides

---

83. Maimonides couldn't have intended והגישה, because he also cites this word in his
Commentary here. Cf. above, p. 19, s.v. *Commentary on the Mishnah, Kiddushin* 1:8.

combined Lev. 1:12, ‏וערך הכהן אותם על העצים‎, and Lev. 6:5, ‏ובער עליה‎ ‏הכהן עצים‎.

Commentary on the Mishnah, Hullin 1:5, *Kelim* 1:1, 2:1 (twice): Maimonides cites Lev. 11:33 as ‏וכלי חרש‎. Yet the verse reads: ‏וכל כלי‎ ‏חרש‎.

Commentary on the Mishnah, Hullin 9:3: Maimonides cites the *Sifra* to Lev. 11:39: ‏תלמוד לומר טמא‎. He thus mistakenly reproduces the error in the *Sifra*, as the verse reads ‏יטמא‎.

Commentary on the Mishnah, Bekhorot 4:1: Maimonides cites Num. 3:15, ‏מבן חדש ומעלה תפקדם‎, as referring to firstborn males. Yet the verse refers to the census of the Levites. He should have cited Num. 18:16, ‏ופדויו מבן חדש תפדה‎.

Commentary on the Mishnah, Bekhorot 4:1: Maimonides cites a verse as ‏כל הקהל‎. Yet there is no such biblical verse.

Commentary on the Mishnah, Bekhorot 5:2: Maimonides cites Num. 18:18 as ‏וכשוק התרומה‎. Yet the verse reads: ‏וכשוק הימין‎.

Commentary on the Mishnah, Bekhorot 8:1: Maimonides cites Ex. 13:2 as ‏פטר רחם בישראל‎. Yet the verse reads: ‏פטר כל רחם בבני ישראל‎. This verse is also cited incorrectly in the standard text of *Bekhorot* 46a and 47a.[84] If this was Maimonides' text as well, it no doubt contributed to his confusion.

Commentary on the Mishnah, Arakhin 3:2: Maimonides cites Lev. 27:22 as ‏יקדיש איש לה'‎. Yet the verse reads: ‏יקדיש לה'‎.

Commentary on the Mishnah, Arakhin 3:2: Maimonides cites Num. 31:28 as ‏והרמתם מכס‎. Yet the verse reads: ‏והרמת מכס‎.

Commentary on the Mishnah, Temurah 3:2: Maimonides cites Lev. 7:12 as ‏לחם התודה‎. Yet the verse reads: ‏זבח התודה‎.

Commentary on the Mishnah, Keritot 1:2: Maimonides cites Lev. 4:27 as ‏ועשה אחת מכל מצות ה'‎. Yet the verse reads: ‏בעשותה אחת ממצות ה'‎. The words Maimonides cites appear in Lev. 4:22 in a different context.

Commentary on the Mishnah, Meilah 4:3: Maimonides cites Lev. 11:29 as ‏בכל השרץ‎. Yet the verse reads ‏בשרץ‎.

---

84. The standard text of Mishnah, *Bekhorot* 8:1, also has the error, but the Mishnah text written in Maimonides' own hand, and published in Kafih's edition, cites the verse accurately.

Commentary on the Mishnah, Meilah 6:1: Maimonides cites a verse as
וחטאת הנפש ההיא. Yet there is no such biblical verse. He presumably
intended Lev. 5:15, וחטאה בשגגה.

Commentary on the Mishnah, Tamid 2:3: Maimonides cites Lev. 6:5 as
וערך עליה הכהן עצים בבקר בבקר. Yet the verse reads: ובער עליה הכהן.

Commentary on the Mishnah, Middot 3:1: Maimonides cites I Chron.
22:1 as בית ה' א-להינו. Yet the verse reads בית ה' א-להים.

Commentary on the Mishnah, Kelim, Introduction (p. 16):
Maimonides cites Lev. 11:37 as וכי יפול מנבלתם על כל זרע זרוע אשר יזרע
טמא הוא. Yet in the verse, the word טהור appears instead of טמא. Citing
from memory, Maimonides was no doubt confused by either Lev.
11:35, וכי יתן מים על זרע, or Lev. 11:38, וכל אשר יפול מנבלתם עליו יטמא,
ונפל מנבלתם עליו טמא הוא לכם.

Commentary on the Mishnah, Kelim 1:2: Maimonides cites a verse as
חשקת נפשי משחת. This is a corruption of Is. 38:17, חשקת נפשי משחת.
Yet in context, the verse from Isaiah has no relevance. Kafih suggests
that Maimonides intended Job 33:18: יחשך נפשו מני שחת.

Commentary on the Mishnah, Kelim 1:9: Maimonides cites Lev. 21:18
as כל אשר בו מום לא יקרב. Yet the verse reads: כל איש אשר בו.

Commentary on the Mishnah, Kelim 13:1: Maimonides cites Gen.
41:14 as ויספר ויחלף שמלותיו. Yet the verse reads: ויגלח ויחלף שמלתיו.

Commentary on the Mishnah, Ohalot 1:2, 24: Maimonides cites Num.
19:16 as כל הנוגע בחלל חרב. Yet the verse reads: וכל אשר יגע על פני
השדה בחלל חרב.

Commentary on the Mishnah, Negaim 6:8: Maimonides cites Lev. 13:2
as והיה בעור בשרם. Yet the verse reads בשרו.

Commentary on the Mishnah, Toharot 1:1: Maimonides cites Lev.
17:15 as והנפש אשר תאכל. Yet the verse reads וכל נפש.

Commentary on the Mishnah, Toharot 4:8: Maimonides cites Lev.
11:29 as בכל השרץ השורץ. Yet the verse reads בשרץ השורץ. This verse
is also cited incorrectly in the standard texts of *Nazir* 64a, and *Hullin*
64a, 67a, 67b. If these were Maimonides' texts as well, they no doubt
contributed to his confusion

Commentary on the Mishnah, Niddah 9:8: Maimonides cites Ps.
119:120 as סמר בשרי. Yet the verse reads: סמר מפחדך בשרי.

Commentary on the Mishnah, Zavim 1:1: Maimonides cites Lev. 15:2

as אדם כי יהיה זב מבשרו זובו טמא הוא. Yet the verse reads: איש כי יהיה.

Commentary on the Mishnah, Zavim 1:1: Maimonides cites Lev. 15:25 as ימי זובה. Yet the verse reads: ימי זוב טומאתה.

Commentary on the Mishnah, Yadayim 3:5: Maimonides cites Prov. 9:1 as חכמות נשים בנתה ביתה חצבה עמודיה שבעה. Yet the verse reads: חכמות נשים בנתה ביתה. Prov. 14:1 reads: חכמות בנתה ביתה ואולת בידיה תהרסנו, and this undoubtedly led to the confusion.

Sefer ha-Mitzvot, shoresh 4: Maimonides cites Lev. 18:4 as ואת משפטי תעשו. Yet the verse reads את, without the initial *vav*. Maimonides was perhaps confused by Lev. 25:18, ואת משפטי תשמרו.

Sefer ha-Mitzvot, pos. com. 11: Maimonides cites a verse as ולמדתם ועשיתם. Yet there is no such biblical verse. In some Yemenite *Mishneh Torah* manuscripts this verse is also quoted in *Talmud Torah* 1:3, and according to Kafih, this appeared in the first version of the *Mishneh Torah*.[85] Perhaps Maimonides was misled by *Yevamot* 109b, which also quotes the nonexistent verse: אמר קרא ולמדתם ועשיתם.

Sefer ha-Mitzvot, pos. com. 225: Maimonides cites Num. 35:25 as וישב שם עד מות הכהן הגדול. Yet the verse reads: וישב בה.[86] This error also led Maimonides to misquote the *Sifrei*: וישב שם: אינו יוצא משם לעולם שנאמר שם, שם תהא דירתו שם תהא מיתתו שם תהא קבורתו. Yet the *Sifrei's* interpretation is built on the words אשר נס שמה, which are also found in Num. 35:25.[87]

Sefer ha-Mitzvot, neg. com. 77: Maimonides cites Num. 19:13 as מקדש ה'. Yet the verse reads משכן ה'.

Sefer ha-Mitzvot neg. com. 122: Maimonides cites Ex. 12:46, ועצם לא תשברו בו, as the source for the commandment not to break any of the bones of the Second Passover offering. Yet this verse deals with breaking the bones of the main Passover offering—the immediately preceding commandment in *Sefer ha-Mitzvot*, where this verse is also cited—and thus is not relevant. Maimonides should have cited Num.

---

85. See Kafih, Commentary to *Talmud Torah* 1:3.

86. In the Oxford ms. and most other mss. the verse is cited incorrectly in the List of Commandments at the beginning of the *Mishneh Torah*, pos. com. 225. Yet Kafih's edition cites the verse correctly. See also Heller's note in his edition of *Sefer ha-Mitzvot* for places where Maimonides cites the verse correctly.

87. See *Sifrei* to Deut. 19:4.

9:12, ‏ועצם לא ישברו בו‏. Seeing how similar the verses are, it is easy to see how he was confused.[88]

Sefer ha-Mitzvot, neg. com. 253: Maimonides cites a verse as ‏לא תונו איש את אחיו‏. Yet there is no such biblical verse. Lev. 25:14 reads: ‏אל תונו איש את אחיו‏, and Lev. 25:17 reads: ‏ולא תונו איש את עמיתו‏. Since Maimonides states that the verse is used as a proof text in *Bava Metzia*, it is obvious that Lev. 25:17 is meant, since it appears as such in *Bava Metzia* 58b. Considering that Lev. 25:17 is quoted correctly just prior to this in neg. com. 251, it appears that we have a slip of the pen on Maimonides' part, rather than forgetfulness.[89]

Sefer ha-Mitzvot, neg. com. 286: Maimonides cites Deut. 19:16 as ‏לא יקום עד חמס באיש‏. Yet the verse reads ‏כי יקום‏. The verse immediately preceding this reads: ‏לא יקום עד אחד באיש‏, and no doubt this led to the confusion.

List of Commandments at the beginning of the *Mishneh Torah*, neg. com. 312 and the concluding paragraph, *Kilayim* 10:29, *Mamrim* 1:2: Maimonides cites Deut. 17:11 as ‏לא תסור מכל הדבר‏. Yet the verse reads: ‏מן הדבר‏.[90]

List of Commandments at the beginning of the *Mishneh Torah*, pos. com. 43, *Sefer ha-Mitzvot*, *shoresh* 13 and pos. com. 43: Maimonides cites Lev. 23:36, ‏שבעת ימים תקריבו אשה לה'‏, as the appropriate verse for the additional Passover offering.[91] However, this verse is stated with

---

88. Heller's edition of *Sefer ha-Mitzvot* cites the verse correctly, and he states that this version is found in some Arabic mss. Yet this doesn't seem to be what appeared in the original. See also the note in the Frankel edition.

89. Maimonides also quotes the verse correctly in *Avadim* 8:11. It is possible that there is also an error in the citation of a verse in *Sefer ha-Mitzvot*, neg. com. 279, as is suggested by Kafih in his note, *ad loc.* The contrary view can be found in Heller's note in his edition.

90. Kafih's edition cites the verse accurately in the Introduction to the *Mishneh Torah* and in *Kilayim*. His mss. have almost certainly been corrected. Maimonides cites the verse correctly in *Sefer ha-Mitzvot*, neg. com. 312, *Shabbat* 26:23.

91. One might have assumed that the error in the List of Commandments is due to the fact that Maimonides was simply copying from *Sefer ha-Mitzvot*. Yet there are times when the List of Commandments has an error and the verse is cited correctly in *Sefer ha-Mitzvot*. Another difference between the List of Commandments and *Sefer ha-Mitzvot* is that they have a different enumeration for a few of the commandments. See pos. com. 17–18, 76–77, neg. com. 81–82, 148–149 (the difference with the last two only appears in some mss., see Heller's note, *ad loc.*).

reference to Sukkot. Lev. 23:8, which is the relevant verse for Passover, reads: והקרבתם אשה לה' שבעת ימים. It is possible that Maimonides was misled by the *Sifrei*, which also quotes the incorrect verse with reference to Passover.[92]

List of Commandments at the beginning of the *Mishneh Torah*, pos. com. 70: Maimonides cites as his proof texts: ולא ידע ואשם וכו' והביא את אשמו. The first verse appears in Lev. 5:17, but the second verse appears prior to this, in Lev. 5:15, and refers to a different law. He intended to cite Lev. 5:18, and this is what is found in *Sefer ha-Mitzvot*, pos. com. 70: והביא איל תמים מן הצאן בערכך לאשם.

List of Commandments at the beginning of the *Mishneh Torah*, pos. com. 167: Maimonides cites Lev 23:36 as וביום השמיני מקרא קודש. Yet the verse reads ביום, without the initial *vav*.

List of Commandments at the beginning of the *Mishneh Torah*, pos. com. 239: Maimonides cites Ex. 21:37 as וכי יגנוב. Yet the verse reads כי, without the initial *vav*.

List of Commandments at the beginning of the *Mishneh Torah*, pos. com. 213: As a proof text for the commandment לבעול בקידושין, Maimonides cites Deut. 22:13: כי יקח איש אשה ובא אליה [ושנאה]. Yet this verse deals with a man who falsely accuses his wife of lack of virginity. He should have cited Deut. 24:1, כי יקח איש אשה ובעלה, which is the verse he quotes in *Sefer ha-Mitzvot*, pos. com. 213.

List of Commandments at the beginning of the *Mishneh Torah*, neg. com. 85, *Sefer ha-Mitzvot*, neg. com. 85: Maimonides cites Ex. 30:37 as ובמתכנתה לא תעשו. Yet the verse reads במתכנתה, without the initial *vav*.[93]

List of Commandments at the beginning of the *Mishneh Torah*, neg. com 136: Maimonides cites Lev. 22:4 as איש מזרעך וכו' בקדשים לא יאכל. Yet the verse reads: איש איש מזרע אהרן. The words איש מזרעך appear in the previous chapter, Lev. 21:17.[94]

---

92. See *Sifrei: Bamidbar*, ed. Horovitz (Jerusalem, 1992), p. 194; Heller's note in his edition of *Sefer ha-Mitzvot*. Rabinovitch, *Yad Peshutah, Sefer Zemanim* (2), p. 234, is willing to acknowledge an error on Maimonides' part with regard to the citation in the List of Commandments and the parallel citation in *Sefer ha-Mitzvot*, but he attempts to explain the use of Lev. 23:36 in *Sefer ha-Mitzvot*, *shoresh* 13.

93. The word appears correctly in Heller's edition of *Sefer ha-Mitzvot* and in *Kelei ha-Mikdash* 2:9.

94. Maimonides cites the verse correctly in *Sefer ha-Mitzvot*, neg. com. 136, *Terumot* 7:1. In the List of Commandments at the beginning of the *Mishneh Torah*, concluding

Yesodei ha-Torah 1:8: Maimonides cites the following verse: כי ה'
א-להיכם הוא הא-להים בשמים ממעל ועל הארץ מתחת. This is apparently a
citation from Josh. 2:11, but there the fifth word appears as א-להים,
lacking the initial *heh*. Kafih quite reasonably sees this as an example
of Maimonides' forgetfulness, although we can't discount the possibility that the copyist omitted the letter. Interestingly, in the Oxford
manuscript a later reader placed dots over the word א-להיכם, meaning
that it should be deleted. Missing this word, the verse is identical with
Deut. 4:39.[95]

Yesodei ha-Torah 5:4, *Sefer ha-Mitzvot*, neg. com. 63: With reference
to the prohibition to offer one's children to Molech, Maimonides cites
the following verse: ונתתי אני את פני באיש ההוא. Yet there is no such
biblical verse.[96] Maimonides intended one of the two verses that deal
with this issue: Lev. 20:3, ואני אתן את פני באיש ההוא, or Lev. 20:5, ושמתי
אני את פני באיש ההוא. (The *Sifra*, which is the source for this halakhah,
offers its exegesis on Lev. 20:3.) It is also likely that Maimonides was
misled by Lev. 20:6, which, although dealing with a different prohibition, states: ונתתי את פני בנפש ההוא. In fact, in *Guide* 3:46, Maimonides
mistakenly cites this last verse as referring to offerings to Molech.

Yesodei ha-Torah 9:1: Maimonides cites Deut. 13:1 as תשמרון
לעשות. Yet the verse reads תשמרו, and is cited correctly in
Maimonides' Introduction to the *Mishneh Torah*. Surprisingly, neither
Rabinovitch nor Kafih note the error (which might, in fact, be due to
the copyist).

Yesodei ha-Torah 10:4: Maimonides cites Jer. 28:7 as אך שמע נא את
הדבר הזה. Yet the verse reads: אך שמע נא הדבר הזה, omitting the word
את. It is surprising that Rabinovitch does not call attention to this.
Kafih has no reason to do so, for his text is based on Yemenite manuscripts which cite the verse accurately.[97] In fact, since all Yemenite

---

paragraph, all mss. except for the Oxford ms. cite Deut. 4:7 as ומי גוי גדול. The Oxford
ms. cites the verse correctly: כי מי גוי גדול.

95. See Havlin, ed., *Mishneh Torah*, p. 35, who believes that Maimonides changed his
mind about which verse to cite.

96. Contrary to Heller who, in his edition, refers to Lev. 20:5.

97. As a general rule, Kafih completely ignores the Oxford ms., the accuracy of
which is attested to by Maimonides, in favor of the Yemenite mss. in his possession. See
his commentary to *Sefer Ahavah*, pp. 708–709, *Sefer Kinyan*, p. 9, and see Havlin's rejection
of this view in *id.*, ed., *Mishneh Torah*, pp. 20–21, 26–27. Because he ignores it, he is led to

manuscripts used by Kafih and Frankel cite the verse accurately, we cannot discount the possibility that the Oxford manuscript contains a copyist's error.

Talmud Torah 6:10: Maimonides cites Hos. 8:10 as מלך ושרים. Yet the verse reads מלך שרים. Perhaps Maimonides was misled by *Bava Batra* 8a—assuming his text was the same as ours—for it, too, has מלך ושרים.[98]

Deot 4:19: Maimonides cites Prov. 31:3 as אל תתן לנשים חילך ושנותיך למחות מלכין. Yet the verse reads: ודרכיך למחות מלכין.[99]

Avodah Zarah 4:2: Maimonides cites Deut. 13:16 as אנשי העיר.[100] Yet the verse reads: יושבי העיר.

Avodah Zarah 5:4: Maimonides cites Deut. 13:12 as וכל ישראל ישמעו וייראו[101] ולא יוסיפו לעשות. Yet the verse reads ויראון.[102] Citing

---

certain errors. For example, in his note to the List of Commandments at the beginning of the *Mishneh Torah*, neg. com. 207, Kafih discusses Maimonides' incorrect use of a verse. Yet the Oxford ms. shows that Maimonides indeed cited the correct verse, although elsewhere he did err in this regard. See above p. 18, s.v. *Commentary on the Mishnah, Nazir* 6:5. See also Kafih's notes to the List of Commandments at the beginning of the *Mishneh Torah*, neg. com. 67 and 210, where, had he used the Oxford ms., he would not have assumed that Maimonides erred. In *Avodah Zarah* 4:13, the Oxford ms. reads שורפין אותן, while Kafih has אותה. In his note, Kafih states that his version is what appears in "all" mss. (meaning all the ones in his possession), and does not even mention the Oxford ms. There is no question that in all these cases the Oxford ms. is superior to the Yemenite mss. used by Kafih. In fact, in the examples mentioned in this note, none of the Yemenite mss. used by Frankel agree with Kafih's version, thus showing that the mss. used by Kafih were not as reliable as he thought.

98. This is a real textual variant, as the extra *vav* is found in some biblical mss., and is also reflected in Targum Jonathan's translation as well as in other ancient versions. See C. D. Ginsburg, *Esrim ve-Arba'ah Sifrei ha-Kodesh* (London, 1908), *ad loc.* Thus, perhaps this is not an example of Maimonides' forgetfulness.

99. The mistaken reading appears in the Oxford ms. as well as in one Yemenite ms. and two other medieval mss. used in the Frankel edition. The other Yemenite mss. used by Frankel (and Kafih) cite the verse accurately, but these have probably been corrected and thus do not reflect the original reading. In *Deot* 5:11, Maimonides cites three biblical verses out of order, but in that famous case, unlike others I discuss in this chapter, I assume Maimonides did so intentionally.

100. All of the mss. used by Frankel, with one exception (a Spanish ms.), cite the verse incorrectly. Kafih cites the verse correctly, but his mss. have presumably been corrected.

101. In the Oxford ms. this word is spelled with two *yuds*, although in Rabinovitch's edition, which is supposed to transcribe this manuscript exactly, there is only one *yud*.

102. The same mistake appears in the Vilna edition of the Talmud, *Sanhedrin* 63b, yet the entire verse is missing from the Munich edition and virtually all early printings. See *Dikdukei Soferim, ad loc.*

from memory, Maimonides confused this verse with Deut. 17:13: וכל העם ישמעו ויראו.[103] It is also possible that Maimonides' version of *Sanhedrin* 63b was the same as ours; it, too, contains the error and perhaps Maimonides simply copied it without realizing that it was inaccurate.

Teshuvah 3:3: Maimonides cites Ez. 33:12 as וצדקת הצדיק לא תצילנו ביום רשעו. Yet the verse reads: צדקת הצדיק לא תצילנו ביום פשעו. In addition to adding a *vav* at the beginning of the verse, Maimonides has substituted רשעו for פשעו, probably remembering the next section of the verse: ורשעת הרשע לא יכשל בה ביום שובו מרשעו. It is also possible that Maimonides had the inaccurate verse in his text of *Kiddushin* 40b,[104] and Tosefta, *Kiddushin* 1:15,[105] and this might explain his error.

Teshuvah 5:4, *Guide* 3:12: Maimonides cites Mal. 1:9 as מידכם היתה זאת לכם. Yet the word לכם does not appear in the verse. No doubt the error arose from a confusion of this verse with Is. 50:11: מידי היתה זאת לכם.

Teshuvah 6:1: Maimonides cites Deut. 24:16 as איש בחטאו יומת. Yet the final word should read יומתו. It is likely that Maimonides was confused by II Kings 14:6: איש בחטאו ימות [קרי: יומת].[106]

Teshuvah 6:3: Maimonides cites a verse as ואני אחזק את לב פרעה. There is no such biblical verse, but there are three similar ones: Ex. 4:21, ואני אחזק את לבו, Ex. 7:3, ואני אקשה את לב פרעה, and Ex. 14:4, וחזקתי את לב פרעה. It seems clear that Maimonides, because he was citing from memory, mistakenly combined two of these verses. Rabinovitch assumes that Maimonides, in citing Ex. 4:21, intentionally changed the verse's ending.[107] Yet this strikes me as most unlikely,

---

103. Kafih's edition, based on Yemenite mss., does not contain this mistake.

104. See *Minhat Shai* on Ez. 33:12, who notes that רשעו appears in *Kiddushin*. (There is no mistake in the Vilna edition of the Talmud, and the Bomberg Talmud [Venice, 1520–1523], has רשעתו.) A Bar Ilan Responsa CD-Rom search reveals five other medieval authors who make this mistake, including R. Isaac Alfasi, *Rosh ha-Shanah* 3b (in the Alfasi pages), and R. Asher ben Jehiel, *Rosh ha-Shanah* 1:5.

105. See *Tosefta* ed. Lieberman (New York, 1973), *Kiddushin* 1:15, where the word רשעו appears. Ginsburg, *Esrim ve-Arba'ah Sifrei ha-Kodesh, ad loc.*, lists no biblical mss. that have this reading.

106. Since the source of Maimonides' halakhah is *Sifrei* to Deut. *ad loc.*, there is no doubt that it is the verse in Deuteronomy that he had in mind.

107. Presumably, this is also what the editors of the Frankel edition believe, for they too cite Ex. 4:21 as the source for the verse, without even alerting the reader to the problem with the quotation.

and Kafih agrees that this is an example of carelessness on the part of Maimonides.

Teshuvah 9:2: Maimonides cites Jer. 31:33 as ולא ילמדו איש את אחיו ואיש את רעהו. Yet the verse reads: ולא ילמדו עוד איש את רעהו ואיש את אחיו. It should be noted that a number of the oldest Yemenite manuscripts of the *Mishneh Torah* cite the verse correctly. This means that we can't discount the possibility that the Oxford manuscript contains a copyist's error.

Tefillah 15:3: Maimonides writes: כהן שהרג את הנפש אפילו בשגגה ואע"פ שעשה תשובה לא ישא את כפיו שנ' ידיכם דמים מלאו וכתיב ובפרשכם כפיכם וכו'. Both biblical citations actually come from the same verse, Is. 1:15, and ובפרשכם כפיכם comes before ידיכם דמים מלאו. When recording this halakhah, Maimonides mistakenly thought that they came from two separate verses.

Tefillin 4:10: Maimonides cites Ex. 13:9 as והיו לך לאות.[108] Yet the verse reads: והיה לך לאות.[109]

Lulav 8:15: Maimonides cites 2 Sam. 6:16 as והמלך דוד מפזז. Yet the verse reads המלך, without the initial *vav*.[110]

Ishut 1:1: Maimonides cites Deut. 22:13 as כי יקח איש אשה ובא אליה. It would appear that this is an error, and Maimonides should have cited Deut. 24:1, כי יקח איש אשה ובעלה, which is the verse that appears in the Talmud.[111]

Gerushin 1:13: Maimonides cites Deut. 19:15 as על פי שנים עדים וכו' יקום הדבר. Yet the verse reads שני עדים. Citing from memory, Maimonides was confused by Deut. 17:6: על פי שנים עדים . . . יומת המת.[112]

Na'arah Betulah 1:13: Maimonides cites Lev. 24:21 as מכה נפש בהמה ישלמנה ומכה אדם יומת. Yet the verse reads: ומכה בהמה ישלמנה. The word נפש added by Maimonides comes from Lev. 24:18: ומכה נפש

---

108. The word לך was at first omitted from the Oxford ms., but later inserted in the margin.

109. The error also appears in Kafih's edition, yet he does not note this.

110. Kafih and Frankel neglect to note this.

111. *Kiddushin* 4b, 9b, 11b, 51a. See above, p. 27, s.v. List of Commandments at the beginning of the *Mishneh Torah*, pos. com. 213.

112. Frankel neglects to note this. Kafih cites the verse correctly, but his mss. have presumably been corrected.

בהמה ישלמנה נפש תחת נפש. Citing from memory, he confused the two verses. [113]

Na'arah Betulah 2:7: Maimonides cites Ex. 22:16 as ואם מאן ימאן אביה. Yet the verse reads אם מאן, without the initial *vav*.[114]

Na'arah Betulah 3:2: Maimonides writes: המוציא שם רע על הקטנה או על הבוגרת פטור מן הקנס ומן המלקות ואינו חייב עד שיוציא על הנערה שנאמר והוציאו את בתולי הנערה נערה מלא דבר הכתוב. Yet in the verse Maimonides quotes, Deut. 22:15, the word נער appears without a final *heh*. In *Ketubot* 40b and 44b, this halakhah is derived from Deut. 22:19, ונתנו לאבי הנערה, and this is the only place in the Torah where נערה is spelled with a final *heh*. Citing from memory, Maimonides confused the two verses.[115]

Sotah 4:2: Maimonides writes: ואין משקין שתי שוטות כאחת שנ' והעמיד אותה. Yet there is no such biblical verse. A few rabbinic texts derive this law from Num. 5:16, והקריב אותה,[116] and this is undoubtedly what Maimonides intended. The complete verse reads: והקריב אותה הכהן והעמידה לפני ה'. Num. 5:18, two verses later, reads: והעמיד הכהן את האשה. It is easy to see how, citing from memory, Maimonides could have been confused and substituted והעמיד for והקריב.[117]

Issurei Biah 7:1: Maimonides writes: שנאמר בזבה דם יהיה זובה בבשרה מפי השמועה למדו זובה מחמת עצמה ולא מחמת ולד. Yet this verse, Lev. 15:19, actually refers to a *niddah*, not a *zavah*. Maimonides should have cited Lev. 15:25, כי יזוב זוב דמה, which is the verse cited in *Niddah* 36b to derive the halakhah to which Maimonides refers. That Maimonides was citing the talmudic text from memory can also be seen from the last part of the quotation given above. While

---

113. Rabinovitch neglects to note this.

114. Kafih and Rabinovitch cite the verse accurately, but their mss. have presumably been corrected.

115. R. Joshua ha-Nagid, Maimonides' great-great-grandson, was asked about this example. See *Teshuvot R. Yehoshua ha-Nagid*, no. 36. Karo, *Kesef Mishneh, ad loc.*, was quite blunt about Maimonides' choice of verse: וזה שלא בדקדוק.

116. See Rabinovitch, *Yad Peshutah, ad loc.*

117. Rabinovitch's text reads: והעמיד אותה הכהן, yet this version is certainly an attempt to correct the original, and only appears in one ms. used by Frankel. Even if one accepts this version, there is still no verse that reads as such, and Rabinovitch therefore inserts an ellipsis between והעמיד and אותה, assuming that the conclusion of the "verse" is Num. 5:19: והשביע אותה הכהן. Yet this is clearly not what Maimonides had in mind.

Maimonides writes זובה, the Talmud reads: דמה מחמת עצמה ולא מחמת
ולד.[118]

Ma'akhalot Asurot 2:14: Maimonides writes: "In the case of such
species as originate in fruit and food, the rule is that once they come
out and reach the ground, even if they subsequently return inside the
food, whoever eats an olive's bulk of them is liable to a flogging." The
source for this is *Sifra, Shemini* 12:3. As a proof text, Maimonides cites
Lev. 11:42: לכל השרץ השורץ על הארץ. In *Sefer ha-Mitzvot*, neg. com. 178,
he also cites the same verse and the *Sifra*'s exegesis, referring to the
Sifra by name. Nahmanides already pointed out that the verse
Maimonides cites is not the one found in the *Sifra*.[119] The verse cited
there is Lev. 11:43: בכל השרץ השורץ.[120]

Shevuot 9:14: Maimonides cites Lev. 5:4 (or 5:5) as לאחת מהנה. Yet
the verse reads: לאחת מאלה.[121]

Nedarim 1:2,[122] *Ma'aseh ha-Korbanot* 11:1,[123] *Meilah* 1:3[124]:

---

118. In *Issurei Biah* 12:6, the best mss. cite Mal. 2:11 as כי חלל יהודה את קדש ה'. Yet
the word את does not appear in the verse.

119. See his *hasagah* to Maimonides' Introduction to *Sefer ha-Mitzvot*, shoresh 9 (p. 107
in Chavel's edition). See also Chavel's note, *ad loc.*, and Heller's note to *Sefer ha-Mitzvot*, neg.
com. 175, discussing the textual problems in Nahmanides' text.

120. The standard version of the *Sifra* adds the words על הארץ, yet this is an error as
these words do not appear in the verse.

121. The verse is cited incorrectly by all the mss. used by Frankel, including Yemenite
mss. Kafih cites the verse accurately, but his mss. have presumably been corrected.

122. Frankel does not note that the verse is cited inaccurately. I have found a number
of problems with the Frankel edition that need to be corrected, and here is another
such example from *Hilkhot Nedarim*: In *Nedarim* 12:21, the citation from Num. 30:12
appears in Frankel as לא הניא אביה אותה. Yet the editors note that *all* Yemenite mss. used
by them cite this verse in its correct form, omitting אביה. The question must therefore be
asked, why didn't the editors follow suit? In general, it is often hard to determine why the
Frankel edition picks one version over another. In *Nezirut* 5:21, the Frankel edition cites
Num. 6:9 as וטמא את ראש נזרו. Yet the editors inform us that some Yemenite mss. omit
את (as does Kafih's edition), and this is how the verse appears in the Torah. In a case like
this, shouldn't we assume that Maimonides cited the verse correctly?

123. The verse is cited incorrectly in all the mss. used by Frankel, including the
Yemenite mss. Yet Frankel published the verse in its corrected form, once again giving us
a faulty *Mishneh Torah* text. See Barukh Oberlander, "Iyyun be-Mahadurot ha-Hadashot
shel ha-'Mishneh Torah' le-ha-Rambam," *Or Yisrael* 23 (Nisan 5761), pp. 223–224. Kafih
cites the verse accurately, but his mss. have presumably been corrected.

124. With one Yemenite exception (that presumably has been corrected), the verse is
cited incorrectly by all the mss. used by Frankel. The verse is cited accurately by Kafih,

Maimonides cites Deut. 12:17 as ונדריך. Yet the verse reads וכל נדריך.[125]

Arakhim ve-Haramim 7:1: Maimonides cites a verse as ונתן את הכסף. Although there is no such verse in the Torah—Lev. 27:23 reads: ונתן את הערכך—the Talmud cites this "verse" a number of times (always omitting the word את),[126] and no doubt this is what misled Maimonides. In *Arakhim ve-Haramim* 7:12 and *Ma'aser Sheni* 8:7, Maimonides again cites the incorrect verse and adds the words וקם לו (from Lev. 27:19), which is how the "verse" often appears in the Talmud.

Mattenot Aniyim 4:22: Maimonides cites Deut 24:21 as וכי תבצר כרמך. Yet the verse reads כי, lacking the initial *vav*.[127]

Mattenot Aniyim 10:3: Maimonides cites a verse as שועת עניים אתה תשמע. Yet there is no such biblical verse. This text does, however, appear in the Sephardic version of the *Nishmat* prayer, and this is no doubt is what led to his confusion.[128] It is also possible that he intended to cite Job 34:28, וצעקת עניים ישמע, or Ps. 22:25, ובשועו אליו שמע.

Terumot 1:26, *Teshuvot ha-Rambam*, no. 129: Maimonides connects the biblical expression כי תבואו to the laws of *terumah*. In *Teshuvot ha-Rambam*, no. 440, he connects it to both *terumah* and *hallah*. There are a few different verses that have these words (Lev. 23:10, 25:2, Num.

---

but his mss. have probably been corrected. The verse is also cited accurately in the Oxford ms. List of Commandments at the beginning of the *Mishneh Torah*, neg. com. 146, but Kafih and most of the mss. used by Frankel cite the verse incorrectly. Frankel also cites the verse incorrectly in *Sefer ha-Mitzvot*, neg. com. 146, but Heller and Kafih cite it correctly.

125. In *Arakhim ve-Haramim* 6:7, the best mss. cite Lev. 25:34 as אחוזת עולם היא. Yet the verse reads הוא.

126. The "verse," in its various forms, is cited in *Berakhot* 47b, *Shabbat* 128a, *Eruvin* 31b, *Pesahim* 35b, *Kiddushin* 5a, 11b, 29a, 54b, *Bava Metzia* 54a, *Bekhorot* 11a, 50b, and *Arakhin* 33a. According to *Tosafot*, *Shabbat* 128a s.v. *ve-natan*, the Talmud was purposely citing the "verse" in a shortened form. This is certainly possible, as it is hard to believe that a nonexistent verse could have been repeated so often without being corrected.

127. With one Ashkenazic exception (that presumably has been corrected), the verse is cited incorrectly by all the mss. used by Frankel. The verse is cited accurately by Kafih, but his mss. have presumably been corrected.

128. In Maimonides' *siddur*, found at the end of *Sefer Ahavah*, he does not record the entire *Nishmat* prayer. However, what he does record is virtually identical to what appears in R. Amram Gaon's *siddur*, and R. Amram cites שועת עניים אתה תשמע. See *Seder Rav Amram ha-Shalem*, ed. Frumkin (Jerusalem, 1912), vol. 2, p. 48. There can be no doubt that these words were also in Maimonides' liturgy.

15:2), yet none of them are relevant. Although attempts have been made to explain Maimonides,[129] it is possible, as suggested by both Heller[130] and R. Zev Wolf Jehiel Landau,[131] that Num. 15:18, בבאכם אל הארץ, is the verse Maimonides intended. It is true that this verse is stated with reference to *hallah*,[132] not *terumah*. Yet it is likely, as *Kesef Mishneh* points out,[133] that Maimonides believed halakhot of *terumah* are derived from *hallah*.[134]

Terumot 15:20: Maimonides writes: תרומה גדולה ותרומת מעשר והחלה והבכורים כולם נקראו תרומה בתרומת מעשר הוא אומר והרמותם ממנו תרומת ה' ואומר כתרומת גורן. The first verse he cites, Num. 18:26, is correct. Yet the second verse, Num. 15:20, refers to *hallah*. Citing from memory, he confused this verse with the correct one, Num. 18:30, כתבואת גורן.[135]

Ma'aser Sheni 2:5,[136] *Bekhorot* 1:16:[137] Maimonides cites Deut. 12:17 as מעשר דגנך תירושך ויצהרך. Yet the verse reads ותירושך. The words Maimonides quotes appear in Deut. 14:23.

Ma'aser Sheni 2:6: Maimonides writes: אינו לוקה מן התורה עד שיאכל אותו אחר שנכנס לחומת ירושלם שנ' לא תוכל לאכול בשעריך וגו' ואכלת לפני ה' א-להיך. The source of this halakhah is *Makkot* 19b. The first verse Maimonides cites comes from Deut. 12:17, and is also found in *Makkot*. However, the second verse quoted in *Makkot* is לפני ה' א-להיך תאכלנו (Deut. 12:18). Citing from memory, Maimonides mistakenly cited Deut. 14:23 as the second verse.

Bikkurim 3:3: Maimonides cites a verse as: והנחתו לפני מזבח ה'

---

129. See, e.g., R. Hayyim Soloveitchik, *Hiddushei Rabbenu Hayyim ha-Levi* (Warsaw, 1936), *Shemitah ve-Yovel* 12:16.

130. *Sefer ha-Mitzvot*, p. 16 n. 28. Heller assumes that we have a copyist's error, but since the error appears in two places, it seems more likely that the mistake originates with Maimonides.

131. *Zekhuta de-Avraham* (Jerusalem, 1965), pp. 93–94.

132. Maimonides cites it in this regard in *Issurei Biah* 20:3 and *Bikkurim* 5:5.

133. *Terumot* 1:26.

134. וסובר רבינו דילפינן תרומה מחלה דחלה נמי תרומה היא. See also R. Moses of Coucy, *Sefer Mitzvot Gadol*, pos. com. 133 (end).

135. See Kanievsky, *Kiryat Melekh*, ad loc.

136. Kafih has מעשר דגנך וגו', but this is a later correction.

137. The verse is cited incorrectly in virtually all of the mss. used by Frankel, including Yemenite mss. Kafih cites the verse accurately, but his mss. have presumably been corrected.

א-להיך. Yet there is no such biblical verse.[138] He intended either Deut. 26:10, והניחו לפני מזבח ה' א-להיך, or Deut. 26:4, והנחתו לפני ה' אלהיך.

Bikkurim 4:9: Maimonides cites Deut. 26:10 as את ראשית כל פרי האדמה. Yet the verse does not have the word כל.[139]

Bikkurim 9:17: In codifying a halakhah concerning the portions of a sacrifice given to the priest, Maimonides cites Deut. 18:4, תתן לו, as a proof text. Yet this verse concerns the agricultural gifts and the first fleece of the sheep given to the priest. Maimonides should have cited the immediately preceding verse (Deut. 18:3), ונתן לכהן, which does refer to the sacrificial portions.[140]

Bikkurim 9:22: Maimonides cites Ex. 29:29, למשחה בהם. Yet this verse has no relevance to the halakhah he is discussing. He should have cited Num. 18:8, למשחה, which is the verse cited in *Hullin* 132b.[141]

Bikkurim 11:10, 13, *Bekhorot* 4:3[142]: Maimonides cites a verse as פטר רחם בישראל. In *Bikkurim* 12:15, he cites a verse as פטר רחם בבני ישראל.[143] Yet there are no such biblical verses. Ex. 13:2 reads: כל פטר רחם בבני ישראל, and Num. 3:12 reads: פטר רחם מבני ישראל. The standard version of *Bekhorot* 46a also mistakenly has פטר רחם בישראל. If Maimonides had this text, no doubt it contributed to his confusion.

Bikkurim 12:18: Maimonides cites Ex. 13:1 as ופטר חמור. Yet the verse reads: וכל פטר חמור. The standard version of *Bekhorot* 9a also cites the verse as Maimonides does. If Maimonides had this text, no doubt it contributed to his confusion.

Shemitah ve-Yovel 11:3: Maimonides cites Lev. 25:25 as וכי ימוך אחיך. Yet the verse reads כי, without the initial *vav*.

Beit ha-Behirah 1:11: Maimonides cites Ezra 9:9 as ולרומם את בית א-להינו. Yet the verse reads לרומם, without the initial *vav*.

---

138. Neither Kafih nor Frankel note this.

139. All Yemenite mss. used by Frankel cite the verse incorrectly. Kafih cites it accurately, but his mss. have presumably been corrected.

140. See Kafih's commentary, *ad loc.*; Heller, ed., *Sefer ha-Mitzvot*, p. 16 n. 28.

141. The standard printed versions of the *Mishneh Torah* have substituted the correct verse. The Frankel edition does so as well, even though it notes that *all* mss. have the incorrect verse. Regarding Frankel's unreliability in this regard, see also below, p. 37 n. 144. Kafih cites the verse accurately, but his mss. have presumably been corrected.

142. Kafih cites Ex. 13:2, yet none of the mss. used by Frankel have this reading.

143. All mss. used by Frankel have this reading. Kafih cites the verse accurately, but his mss. have presumably been corrected.

Beit ha-Behirah 2:1: Maimonides cites a verse as ויבן שלמה את הבית
בהר המוריה. Yet there is no such biblical verse. He has combined I
Kings 6:14, ויבן שלמה את הבית, and II Chron. 3:1, ויחל שלמה לבנות את
בית ה' בירושלם בהר המוריה.[144]

Beit ha-Behirah 4:1: Maimonides cites a verse as עד עמוד כהן לאורים
ותומים. There is no such biblical verse, yet two are very similar. Ezra
2:63 reads ולתומים, and Neh. 7:65 reads הכהן. The "verse," as
Maimonides quotes it, actually appears incorrectly in a number of talmudic passages,[145] and this presumably contributed to his confusion.
In *Melakhim* 12:2, however, he cites Ezra 2:63 accurately.[146]

Beit ha-Behirah 8:2: Maimonides cites Num. 3:38 as והחונים
קדמה.[147] Yet the verse reads: והחונים לפני המשכן קדמה.

---

144. The standard printed versions of the *Mishneh Torah* substitute the verse in II
Chron. for Maimonides' "verse." Incredibly, the Frankel edition does so as well, and only
the reader who bothers to look at the notes in the back of the volume will learn that *all*
mss. cite the nonexistent verse. By publishing what they *know* to be a false text, the editors of the Frankel edition have betrayed their responsibility to both the readers and
Maimonides. (After writing this, I found that Oberlander, "Iyyun," pp. 222–223, also calls
attention to this example.) See also *Ma'akhalot Asurot* 14:15, where even though all mss.
used by Frankel have וכן הבריא שהריח, the text of this edition follows the standard (and
mistaken) printed version: וכן החולה שהריח. Similarly, in *Ma'aseh ha-Korbanot* 10:23, the
Frankel edition has מקריבין אותו, even though all mss. used by it have מקריבין בו. In *Parah
Adumah* 4:6, all mss. used by Frankel have כנגד פתח ההיכל, yet the text of this edition omits
the word פתח. In *Nizkei Mamon* 7:1, all mss. used by Frankel have ולא ישמרנו בעליו, yet the
text of this edition omits the word בעליו. In *Gezelah ve-Avedah* 15:13, none of the mss.
used by Frankel have the words נוטל ומכריז, yet they appear in the text of this edition.
This error is based on earlier printed editions., which go back to an emendation of *Maggid
Mishneh*. In *Hovel u-Mazik* 6:8, the Frankel edition has והזהיר לבעל החבית, even though all
mss. it uses have לבעל. בעל doesn't even appear in the earliest printings of the *Mishneh
Torah*. In *Rotzeah u-Shemirat ha-Nefesh* 8:8, the beginning of this halakhah in the Frankel
edition has no basis in any ms. See also *Shabbat* 19:6 and the Frankel ed. textual note, s.v.,
שלא יפסיעו, *Shevitat Asor* 3:2 and the Frankel ed. textual note, s.v. פת לתינוק, *Hametz u-
Matzah* 6:2 and the Frankel ed. textual note, s.v. בלע, *Parah Adumah* 3:2, and the Frankel
ed. textual note, s.v. עץ ארז, *Sheluhin ve-Shutafin* 8:1, and the Frankel ed. textual note, s.v.
הנותן. Many other examples can easily be cited. See also Rabinovitch's introductions to his
editions of *Sefer Zemanim, Sefer Nashim, Sefer Nezikin*, and *Sefer Mishpatim*, and Chaim
Rapoport, "Maimonides, *Mishneh Torah*, Manuscripts and Indices," *Jewish Action* (Spring
2005), pp. 38–44.

145. See *Ketubot* 24b, *Sotah* 48b, *Kiddushin* 69b, and Jerusalem Talmud, *Kiddushin* 4:1.

146. In *Beit ha-Behirah* 4:6, Kafih's edition cites Ez. 42:2 as השער הזה סגור יהיה, instead
of יהיה סגור. The Frankel edition cites the verse correctly and does not note any mss. that
contain the error.

147. The Frankel edition cites different *Mishneh Torah* manuscript versions of the
verse, all of which are inaccurate.

Kelei ha-Mikdash 2:1: Maimonides cites Ex. 30:34 as ואתה קח לך סמים. Yet in the verse the word ואתה does not appear. It does appear earlier in the chapter, in verse 23 (ואתה קח לך בשמים), and this is undoubtedly what misled Maimonides.[148]

Kelei ha-Mikdash 10:6: Maimonides cites a verse, על בשרו ולבשם, as the source for the halakhah that there can be nothing interposing between the flesh of the priest and his vestments. Yet there is no such biblical verse. Kafih suggests that Maimonides intended Lev. 6:3, ילבש על בשרו, as it is cited by both *Sifra, ad loc.* and *Zevahim* 19a as the source of Maimonides' halakhah. In fact, in the first version of his *Commentary on the Mishnah, Zevahim* 2:1, he cited this latter verse (mistakenly recording the first word as ילבשם). However, Maimonides later erased this and added the same "phantom verse" that appears in the *Mishneh Torah.* It is also possible that Maimonides was thinking of Lev. 16:4, and he neglected to place וכו' after the words על בשרו (ולבשם appears at the end of this verse). If this is so, then for some reason Maimonides must have thought that this verse was preferable to the one cited in the Talmud and *Sifra.*[149]

Biat ha-Mikdash 5:2, *Commentary on the Mishnah, Zevahim* 2:1: Maimonides cites Ex. 30:21 as חקת עולם לו ולזרעו. Yet the verse reads: חק עולם.

Biat ha-Mikdash 5:7: Maimonides cites Ex. 30:19 as ורחצו ממנו אהרן ובניו. Yet the verse reads: ורחצו אהרן ובניו ממנו.[150]

Biat ha-Mikdash 6:4, *Commentary on the Mishnah, Kelim* 1:9: Maimonides cites Lev. 21:18 as כל אשר בו מום. Yet the verse reads: כל איש אשר בו מום.[151]

---

148. The Frankel edition notes no manuscript, Yemenite or otherwise, that cites the verse correctly (although it is quoted accurately in Kafih's edition). Maimonides cites the verse correctly in *Sefer ha-Mitzvot, shoresh* 10. In *Kelei ha-Mikdash* 10:1, the best mss. cite Ez. 44:18 as ולא יחגרו. Yet the verse reads לא, without the initial *vav*.

149. See above, p. 21, s.v. *Commentary on the Mishnah, Zevahim* 2:1. In *Biat ha-Mikdash* 1:14 all mss. used by the Frankel edition cite Lev. 6:10 correctly, although most printed editions mistakenly have לא תפרעו for אל תפרעו. In what is probably a printer's error, Kafih also has the incorrect version. In *Biat ha-Mikdash* 3:8, Frankel has ולא יבוא אל תוך המחנה (Lev. 16:2); yet the verse reads אל, without the initial *vav*. Kafih has the correct reading.

150. Frankel cites the verse correctly, yet that is because the mss. evidence— including all Yemenite mss.— was ignored in favor of the standard printed text. Kafih cites the verse accurately, but his mss. have presumably been corrected.

151. Maimonides cites the verse correctly in *Commentary on the Mishnah, Hullin* 1:5 and *Sefer ha-Mitzvot,* neg. com. 71. In *Biat ha-Mikdash* 9:6, Frankel has a printer's error in the

Issurei Mizbeah 2:8: Maimonides cites Deut. 12:11 as מבכר נדריך.
Yet the verse reads נדריכם.

Ma'aseh ha-Korbanot 2:3: Maimonides cites Num. 15:3 as לפלא נדר
או נדבה. Yet the verse reads בנדבה.[152]

Ma'aseh ha-Korbanot 5:7: As a proof text for the law that the blood
of sin offerings that are eaten must be sprinkled upon the four cor-
ners of the outer altar, Maimonides cites a verse as על קרנות המזבח.
These words appear a number of times in the Torah, yet not with
regard to sin offerings that are consumed. Maimonides obviously
intended Lev 4:25 (30, 34), על קרנות מזבח העולה, which does refer to
sin offerings that are consumed.

Ma'aseh ha-Korbanot 5:9: Maimonides cites Lev. 4:6 as וטבל אצבעו
בדם. Yet the verse reads: וטבל הכהן את אצבעו בדם.[153]

Ma'aseh ha-Korbanot 5:10: Maimonides cites Lev. 4:18: ואת כל הדם
ישפך אל יסוד מזבח העלה. Yet this verse is irrelevant to the halakhah
Maimonides is discussing. He should have cited either Lev. 4:30, ואת
כל דמה ישפך אל יסוד המזבח (see *Kesef Mishnah*), or Lev. 4:25, ואת דמו
ישפך אל יסוד מזבח העלה. As these verses are all very similar, it is easy
to see how Maimonides could have been confused.

Ma'aseh ha-Korbanot 5:17: Maimonides cites Num. 18:17 as ואת
דמם תזרק על המזבח. Yet the verse reads את, without the initial *vav*.[154]

Ma'aseh ha-Korbanot 5:18: Maimonides cites a verse as את עורם
ואת בשרם. Yet there is no such biblical verse. He intended either Lev.
16:27, את עורותם ואת בשרם, or, less likely,[155] Lev. 8:17, ואת עורו ואת
בשרו.

---

citation of Lev. 1:13, והקריב הכהן את הכל והקטיר המזבחה, omitting the word הקטיר. (That
this is a printer's error can be determined by examining the *Yalkut Shinuyei Nushaot, ad loc.*)

152. With the exception of two Spanish mss., the verse is cited incorrectly by all the
mss. used by Frankel. Kafih cites the verse accurately, but his mss. have presumably been
corrected

153. The verse is cited incorrectly by all the mss. used by Frankel, including
Yemenite mss. Kafih cites the verse accurately, but his mss. have presumably been corrected.

154. With the exception of one Ashkenazic ms., the verse is cited incorrectly by all
the mss. used by Frankel. Kafih cites the verse accurately, but his mss. have presumably
been corrected.

155. See Frankel's textual note.

Ma'aseh ha-Korbanot 10:14: Maimonides cites a verse as המקריב אותה יאכלנה.[156] Yet there is no such biblical verse. He intended Lev. 7:9: לכהן המקריב אותה לו תהיה. Citing from memory, he presumably was confused by Lev. 6:19: הכהן המחטא אותה יאכלנה.

Ma'aseh ha-Korbanot 10:15: Maimonides cites Lev. 7:9 as כל המנחה אשר תאפה בתנור. Yet the verse reads: וכל מנחה.

Ma'aseh ha-Korbanot 11:8: Maimonides cites Ex. 29:33 as ואכלו אותם אשר כפר בהם וזר לא יאכל כי קדש הם. Yet he omits the words which appear in the middle of the verse: למלא את ידם לקדש אותם. Since he gives no indication that he is skipping any part of the verse, it appears that Maimonides was citing from memory and forgot the middle words.[157]

Ma'aseh ha-Korbanot 18:15: After recording a halakhah, Maimonides cites Lev. 17:9 as the proof text: ואל פתח אהל מועד לא יביאנו. Although it is not certain (see *Lehem Mishneh*), it appears that this is an error and Maimonides should have cited Lev. 17:4: ואל פתח אהל מועד לא הביאו.

Temidin u-Musafin 2:1: Maimonides cites Lev. 1:7 as ונתנו בני אהרן הכהנים אש על המזבח. Yet the verse reads: בני אהרן הכהן.

Pesulei ha-Mukdashin 1:2: Maimonides cites Lev. 16:11 as ושחט אהרן. Yet the verse reads: והקריב אהרן . . . ושחט.

Pesulei ha-Mukdashin 11:8: Maimonides cites a verse as את כל לבונתה.[158] Yet there is no such biblical verse. Maimonides intended either Lev. 2:2, על כל לבונתה, or Lev. 6:8, ואת כל הלבונה. The Talmud, *Menahot* 11b, derives the halakhah Maimonides refers to from the latter verse.

Pesulei ha-Mukdashin 15:3: Maimonides cites Num. 5:15 as כי מנחת קנאות היא. Yet the verse reads הוא. Num. 5:18 reads: מנחת קנאות הוא [קרי: היא], yet it is missing the word כי.

---

156. The verse is cited incorrectly by all the mss. used by Frankel, including Yemenite mss. Kafih's version, while different, is also incorrect: הכהן המקריב אותה יאכלנה.

157. In *Ma'aseh ha-Korbanot* 18:2, most mss. used by Frankel cite Lev. 17:9 as ונכרת מעמיו. The verse actually reads: ונכרת האיש ההוא מעמיו.

158. The verse is cited incorrectly by all the mss. used by Frankel, including Yemenite mss. Kafih has על כל לבונתה (Lev. 2:2), yet his mss. have presumably been corrected.

Pesulei ha-Mukdashin 18:10: Maimonides states: והיכן הזהיר הכתוב
על הפגול ועל הנותר במלואים שהרי נאמר שם לא יאכל כי קדש הם.
Maimonides cites the same proof text in *Sefer ha-Mitzvot*, neg. com.
131. This verse appears in Ex. 29:33, but is referring to the prohibition forbidding any but a priest to eat from the sacrifice mentioned
there. The verse immediately following this (Ex. 29:34), which deals
with the leftovers from a sacrifice, is what Maimonides had in mind;
but it reads: לא יאכל כי קדש הוא. Kafih[159] points out that Maimonides'
error is also found in some talmudic manuscripts, as well as in
Rashi.[160] Presumably, Maimonides' own text of the Talmud had this
version, and this is what misled him. This example is significant,
because in *Sefer ha-Mitzvot* Maimonides explains what is derived from
the word הם—even though this word does not appear in the verse.[161]

Shegagot 1:5: Maimonides cites Num. 15:29 as תורה אחת תהיה לכם.
Yet the verse reads יהיה.[162]

Tum'at Met 1:14: Maimonides cites Num. 19:18 as ועל כל הנפשות
אשר היו שם. Yet the verse is missing the word כל.

Tum'at Met 2:10, *Commentary on the Mishnah, Ohalot* 1:9:
Maimonides cites Num. 19:18 as וכל הנוגע בעצם. Yet the verse reads:
ועל הנוגע.

Tum'at Tzara'at 9:3: Maimonides cites Lev. 13:44 as טמא הוא וטמאו
הכהן. Yet the verse reads: טמא הוא טמא יטמאנו הכהן.

Metam'ei Mishkav u-Moshav 7:2, *Commentary on the Mishnah, Zavim*
2:4: Maimonides cites Lev. 15:6 as והיושב על הכלי אשר ישב עליו הזב
יטמא. Yet the verse does not contain the word יטמא. It is possible that
Maimonides was misled by *Sifra, ad loc.*, which also misquotes the
verse. In addition, if he was citing from memory, Lev. 15:4 could have
created confusion. It reads: וכל הכלי אשר ישב עליו יטמא.

She'ar Avot ha-Tum'ah 5:9: Maimonides writes: והוא שתהיה בת שלש
שנים ויום אחד שנ' אשר ישכב את אשה. The problem with Maimonides'

---

159. See his note to *Sefer ha-Mitzvot, ad loc.*, Commentary to *Sefer Avodah* (2), p. 117.

160. See *Meilah* 17b s.v. *ki, Keritut* 2a (first column).

161. See, similarly, Rashi, *Meilah* 17b s.v. *ki*: כי קדש הם: משמע דשניהן מצטרפין לאכילה.

162. See the textual note in the Frankel edition, stating that, unlike the Yemenite
mss., the correct reading appears in Ashkenazic and Spanish mss. Yet these appear to be
later corrections. Kafih has the incorrect reading, yet he does not alert the reader to this.

statement is that the verse (Lev. 20:20) he cites in support of this halakhah does not appear to be relevant. *Kesef Mishneh* suggests that Maimonides should have cited Lev. 15:18, ואשה אשר ישכב איש אתה, as it is based on this verse that the *Sifra, ad loc.*, and the Talmud, *Niddah* 32a, derive the halakhah Maimonides records.

Kelim 24:7: Maimonides cites Lev. 15:5 as והנוגע במשכבו. In *Commentary on the Mishnah, Kelim* 19:2, the verse appears as הנוגע במשכבו, without the initial *vav*. Yet the verse reads: ואיש אשר יגע במשכבו. Maimonides was presumably confused by Lev. 15:21: וכל הנוגע במשכבה.

Gezelah ve-Avedah 1:11: Maimonides cites Mic. 2:2 as וחמדו בתים וגזלו. Yet the verse reads: וחמדו שדות וגזלו ובתים ונשאו.[163]

Hovel u-Mazik 1:5: Maimonides cites Ex. 21:18 as וכי יכה איש את רעהו. Yet the verse reads: והכה איש את רעהו.[164]

Hovel u-Mazik 5:1: Maimonides cites Deut. 25:3 as לא יוסיף להכותו. Yet the verse reads: לא יוסיף פן יוסיף להכותו.

Rotzeah u-Shemirat ha-Nefesh 4:9: Maimonides cites I Kings 22:21[165] as ויצא הרוח ויעמוד לפני ה'. Yet the verse reads: ותצא הרוח ותעמוד לפני ה'.

Rotzeah u-Shemirat ha-Nefesh 5:3, 4: Maimonides cites Num. 35:15 as והיתה לבני ישראל. Yet the word והיתה does not appear in the verse.[166]

Mekhirah 14:12: Maimonides cites Lev. 25:17 as ויראת מא-להיך אני ה'. Yet the verse reads: כי אני ה'.

Avadim 3:14: Maimonides cites Deut. 15:14 as מצאנך מגרנך ומיקבך. Yet the verse reads ומגרנך.[167]

Sanhedrin 20:4: Maimonides cites Deut. 19:13 as ולא תחוס עינך ובערת דם הנקי. Yet the verse reads: לא תחוס עינך עליו.

---

163. Kafih neglects to note that Maimonides' quotation is incorrect. Rabinovitch cites the verse accurately, but his mss. have presumably been corrected. Maimonides cites the verse correctly in *Sefer ha-Mitzvot*, neg. com. 266.

164. Maimonides cites the verse correctly in *Sefer ha-Mitzvot*, pos. com. 236.

165. The verse also appears in I Chron. 18:20.

166. With one exception, the verse is cited incorrectly by all the mss. used by Frankel (though this is not reflected in Frankel's *Mishneh Torah* text). Kafih cites the verse accurately, but his mss. have presumably been corrected.

167. In *Malveh ve-Loveh* 22:16, the best mss. cite Deut. 6:18 as ועשית הטוב והישר. Yet the verse reads: ועשית הישר והטוב. Deut. 12:28 reads: כי תעשה הטוב והישר.

Mamrim 3:8: Maimonides cites Deut. 17:13 as וכל ישראל ישמעו
ויראו. Yet the verse reads וכל העם. It is easy to see how the confusion
arose, as the words Maimonides cites appear in Deut. 21:21, and Deut.
13:12 is also very similar: וכל ישראל ישמעו ויראון.

Evel 14:26: Maimonides cites Jer. 34:5 as המלכים ישרפו לך (some
mss. have הראשונים ישרפו לך). Yet the verse reads: המלכים הראשונים אשר
היו לפניך כן ישרפו לך.

Melakhim 1:2: Maimonides cites I Sam. 15:3 as ועתה לך. Yet the
verse reads עתה, without the initial *vav*.[168] He also cites II Sam. 7:2 as
ראה אנכי יושב בבית ארזים. Yet the verse reads: ראה נא אנכי.[169]

Melakhim 1:7: In quoting from Ps. 89, Maimonides cites verse 34
as וחסדי לא אסיר מעימו. This is actually how the verse appears in I Chr.
17:13, but in Psalms it reads: לא אפיר מעימו.[170]

Melakhim 1:8: Maimonides cites I Kings 11:38 as והיה אם שמוע
תשמע את כל אשר אצוך. Yet the verse reads: והיה אם אם תשמע.

Melakhim 2:6: Maimonides cites I Kings 12:7 as אם תהיה לעבד. Yet
the verse reads: אם היום תהיה עבד. Also in this halakhah, Maimonides
cites Ps. 78:71 as לרעות ביעקב עבדו. Yet the verse reads: לרעות ביעקב
עמו.

Melakhim 4:1: Maimonides writes: רשות יש למלך ליתן מס על העם
לצרכיו או לצורך המלחמות וקוצב לו מכס ואסור להבריח מן המכס שלו ויש לו
לגזור שכל מי שיגנוב המכס ילקח ממונו או יהרג שנאמר ואתם תהיו לו לעבדים
ו<u>להלן</u> הוא אומר יהיו לך למס ועבדוך מכאן שנותן מס וקוצב מכס ודיניו בכל אלו
הדברים וכיוצא בהן דין שכל האמור בפרשת המלך זוכה בו. The first verse
Maimonides cites is 1 Sam. 8:17 (he refers to this biblical chapter as
פרשת המלך), and the second verse is Deut. 20:11. Yet Maimonides mistakenly remembered this latter verse as also coming from 1 Sam. 8.

---

168. The verse is cited incorrectly by all the mss. used by Frankel. Kafih cites the
verse accurately, but his mss. have presumably been corrected

169. With one exception (a Spanish ms.), this verse is cited incorrectly by all the mss.
used by Frankel. Kafih cites the verse accurately, but his mss. have presumably been corrected. In *Melakhim* 2:5, most mss., including those used by Kafih, cite I Kings 1:23 as
וישתחו למלך על פניו ארצה. Yet the verse reads: על אפיו ארצה.

170. All mss. used by the Frankel edition have the error. Kafih cites the verse accurately, but his mss. have presumably been corrected.

Melakhim 4:7: Maimonides cites I Sam. 11:17 as וצאנכם יעשר. Yet the verse reads צאנכם, without the initial *vav*.[171]

Melakhim 5:12: Maimonides cites Jer. 27:22 as בבלה יבואו. Yet the verse reads יובאו.[172]

Melakhim 6:4: Maimonides cites Deut. 20:14 as והנשים והטף. While these words appear in Deut. 2:34, the verse Maimonides refers to reads: רק הנשים והטף. Also in this halakhah, Maimonides cites Josh. 11:19 as אשר השלימה את ישראל. Yet the verse reads: אל בני ישראל.

Melakhim 11:1: Maimonides cites II Sam. 8:14 as ותהי אדום לדוד לעבדים. Yet the verse reads: ויהי כל אדום עבדים לדוד.[173] Citing from memory, Maimonides was confused by an earlier verse in this chapter, II Sam. 8:6: ותהי ארם לדוד לעבדים.[174]

Melakhim 11:1: Maimonides cites Zeph. 3:9 as לקרא כלם בשם ה' ולעבדו שכם אחד. Yet the verse reads לעבדו, without the initial *vav*.

Melakhim 11:2: Maimonides cites Deut. 19:8 as כי ירחיב ה' א-להיך את גבולך. Yet the verse reads ואם ירחיב. The words Maimonides cites appear in Deut. 12:20.

Melakhim 11:4: Maimonides cites Dan. 11:35 as לצרוף בהן. Yet the verse reads בהם.

Guide 1:19: Maimonides cites a verse as מלא העמר לאחד. Yet there is no such biblical verse. Maimonides intended either Ex. 16:32, מלא העמר ממנו, or Ex. 16:33, מלא העמר מן. Citing from memory, Maimonides mistakenly combined one of these verses with Ex. 16:22: שני העמר לאחד. Also in this chapter of the *Guide*, Maimonides cites Ex. 35:35 as וימלא אותו חכמת לב.[175] Yet the verse reads: מלא אותם. The confusion arose because a few verses prior, in Ex. 35:31, וימלא אותו does appear.

---

171. With one exception (an Ashkenazic ms.), all mss. used by Frankel have the error. Kafih cites the verse accurately, but his mss. have presumably been corrected.

172. In Kafih's edition, the word יובאו appears instead of יבואו. This is a typo, as can be seen from Kafih's letter in R. Moshe Malkah, *Ve-Heshiv Moshe* (Lod, 1994), p. 127. There is also uncertainty about the rest of this verse quoted by Maimonides. See Kafih's edition and Frankel's textual note.

173. I Chron. 18:13, the parallel verse, reads ויהיו.

174. Most mss. also have another error in *Melakhim* 11:1, with Maimonides citing Josh. 11:19 as השלימה את ישראל, instead of השלימה אל בני ישראל.

175. This is how the verse appears in the manuscript written by Maimonides, published in David Yellin, "Shenei Dapim mi-Ketav Yado shel ha-Rambam," *Tarbiz* 1:3 (1930), p. 105. The verse appears correctly in other mss., and it is possible that Maimonides himself later corrected his error.

Guide 1:20: Maimonides cites Gen. 7:17 as ותרם התבה מעל הארץ.
Yet the verse reads: ותרם מעל הארץ. Also in this chapter, Maimonides
cites I Kings 16:2 as הרימותיך מתוך העפר.[176] Yet the verse reads מן
העפר. The confusion presumably arose because Maimonides also cites
I Kings 14:7: הרימותיך מתוך העם.[177]

Guide 1:36: Maimonides cites Nah. 1:2 as נוקם הוא לצריו ומשלם
הוא לאויביו. Yet the verse reads: נוקם ה' לצריו ונוטר הוא לאויביו.[178]

Guide 1:44, 46: Maimonides cites Zech. 4:10 as עיני ה' המה
משוטטות. Yet the verse reads משוטטים. Maimonides confused this
verse with II Chr. 16:9: כי ה' עיניו משוטטות.[179]

Guide 1:47: Maimonides cites a verse as אשר חשב ה'. Yet there is
no such biblical verse. Jer. 49:20 and 50:45 read אשר חשב; Lam. 2:8
reads חשב ה'. Maimonides mistakenly combined the two.

Guide 2:19: Maimonides cites a verse from Jeremiah as עשה
השמים. Yet there is no such biblical verse. Presumably, he intended Jer.
32:17: אתה עשית את השמים.

Guide 2:31: Maimonides cites Deut. 5:15 as וזכרת כי עבד היית
במצרים.[180] Yet the verse reads בארץ מצרים. Maimonides no doubt confused this verse with Deut. 16:12 and 24:18, which do read: וזכרת
כי עבד היית במצרים.

Guide 2:41: Maimonides cites Gen. 22:15 as ויקרא מלאך ה' לאברהם.
Yet the verse reads אל אברהם.[181]

Guide 2:44: Maimonides cites Zech. 4:5 as ויאמר אלי הלא ידעת מה
המה אלה ויען המלאך הדובר בי. Yet in the verse the order of the clauses
is reversed: ויען המלאך הדובר בי ויאמר אלי הלא ידעת מה המה אלה.

---

176. This is how the verse appears in the manuscript written by Maimonides, published *ibid.*, as well as in the eds. of Munk, Joel, and Schwartz. Kafih cites the verse correctly, and states that this is how it appears in all Yemenite mss. Because of the uniformity of the Yemenite mss., it is possible that Maimonides himself later corrected his error.

177. In Ibn Tibbon's translation, Maimonides cites I Kings 14:7 before 16:2, and this
is how it appears in the manuscript written by Maimonides, published in Yellin, "Shenei,"
p. 105. All other editions of the *Guide* have the order reversed.

178. In *Guide* 1:41, Munk notes that in most mss. Maimonides cites Ps. 41:3 as אל
תתנהו בנפש צריו. Yet the verse reads: בנפש אויביו. Kafih cites the verse correctly.

179. In *Guide* 1:44, Maimonides cites a verse as פקח עיניך וראה. Schwartz may be correct in identifying the verse as Dan. 9:18, even though the *ketiv* is פקחה. Yet Munk, Joel,
Pines, and Kafih assume that the citation is a corruption of II Kings 19:16: פקח ה' עיניך
וראה.

180. Schwartz' translation mistakenly cites the verse accurately.
181. Schwartz' translation mistakenly cites the verse accurately.

Guide 2:45: Maimonides cites Is. 6:8 as ראיתי את ה'. Yet the verse reads: ואראה את ה'.

Guide 2:45: Maimonides cites Is. 6:5 as ויאמר את מי אשלח. Yet the verse reads: אומר את מי אשלח.

Guide 2:48: Maimonides cites Is. 13:3, אני צויתי למקדשי גם קראתי גבורי לאפי, as referring to the tyranny of Nebuchadnezzar and his armies. Pines, *ad loc.*, writes: "As Munk remarks, following Ibn Kaspi,[182] this reference is not correct; for the verse of Isaiah quoted immediately after it seems to refer to the army of the Medes setting out to conquer Babylon."

Guide 3:17: Maimonides mistakenly cites Hab. 1:12 as appearing after Hab. 1:14-15.

Guide 3:32: Maimonides cites Jer. 7:10 as ובאתם אל הבית וכו'. Yet the verse reads: ובאתם ועמדתם לפני בבית הזה.

Guide 3:41: Maimonides cites Josh. 22:12 as ויאמרו כל העדה לעלות עליהם לצבא. Yet the verse reads: ויקהלו כל עדת בני ישראל שילה לעלות עליהם לצבא.

Guide 3:46: Maimonides cites Lev. 20:6, ונתתי את פני בנפש ההוא, as referring to offerings to Molech. Yet this verse deals with a different prohibition. Maimonides should have cited either Lev. 20:3, ואני אתן את פני באיש ההוא, or Lev. 20:5, ושמתי אני את פני באיש ההוא.[183]

Guide 3:46: Maimonides cites Deut. 14:22 as שנה בשנה. Yet the verse reads: שנה שנה. The words Maimonides cites are found in Deut. 15:20.

Guide 3:47: Maimonides cites Num. 35:34 as ולא תטמאו את הארץ. Yet the verse reads: ולא תטמא.

Guide 3:49: Maimonides cites Ruth 4:2 as ויקח בעז עשרה אנשים. Yet the verse reads: ויקח עשרה אנשים.

Guide 3:51: Maimonides cites Is. 41:10 as אל תירא כי אתך אני. Yet the verse reads: כי עמך אני. The confusion no doubt arose since the expression כי אתך אני appears seven times in Isaiah and Jeremiah, while כי עמך אני appears only once.[184]

---

182. Ibn Kaspi writes concerning Maimonides' error: אמר זה הר"ם בעיון גס.
183. See above, p. 28, s.v. *Yesodei ha-Torah* 5:4.
184. I owe this insight to Chaim Rapoport.

Letter to Yemen (ed. Sheilat, p. 107): Maimonides cites Lev. 27:28 as ‏ואם החרם יחרים‎. Yet the verse reads: ‏כל חרם אשר יחרים‎.

Letter to Yemen (ed. Sheilat, p. 109): Maimonides cites Dan. 8:10 as ‏ותפל ארצה מן‎ ‏ויפל מן הצבא ומן הכוכבים ארצה וירמסם‎. Yet the verse reads: ‏הצבא ומן הכוכבים ותרמסם‎.

Letter to Yemen (ed. Sheilat, p. 109[185]): Maimonides cites Ps. 38:14 as ‏ואהי כחרש לא שמע‎. Yet the verse reads: ‏ואני כחרש לא אשמע‎. Maimonides was confused by the verse immediately following this (Ps. 38:15): ‏ואהי כאיש אשר לא שומע‎.

Aside from errors in the citation of biblical verses, we can point to other inaccuracies in Maimonides' works. Some are simply careless, mere slips of the pen. For example, in *Melakhim* 2:5 Maimonides writes: "This is the way Asa the King of Judah acted. When he saw even the disciple of a scholar, he rose from his throne, kissed him, called him, 'my teacher, my master.'" Maimonides' source is *Ketubot* 103b and *Makkot* 24a, yet there the subject of the story is Jehoshaphat. Citing from memory, Maimonides simply confused the two kings.[186] Another such instance is found in *Guide* 1:32, where Maimonides states that the Sages applied Prov. 25:16 to Elisha ben Avuyah, when in fact it was applied to Ben Zoma.[187] A similar example is found in *Guide* 1:54, where Maimonides quotes the Sages as commenting on the words "Ye shall be holy" (‏קדושים תהיו‎; Lev 19:2): "He is gracious, so be you also gracious, He is merciful, so be you also merciful." Yet nowhere in rabbinic literature is the teaching of *imitatio Dei* derived from this verse. It is, however, found in *Sifrei* to Deut. 11:22, where it is derived from the words "to walk in all His ways" (‏ללכת בכל דרכיו‎). In *Shabbat* 133b it is derived from Ex. 15:2: "This is my God, and I will adorn him" (‏זה א-לי ואנוהו‎).[188]

---

185. In his Hebrew translation, p. 161, Sheilat includes the correct reading of the verse without alerting the reader that this is an emendation.

186. Maimonides' error was corrected in most editions, beginning with Amsterdam, 1702.

187. See *Hagigah* 14b (in the Jerusalem Talmud, *Hagigah* 2:1, the verse is applied to Ben Azzai). Abarbanel, Commentary to *Guide* 1:32 (answer to question 9), writes: ‏זה שאמר הרב משל על אלישע אחר כשגגה היוצאת מלפני השליט ועם היות הרב המורה אב בתלמוד‎ ‏עליו אין להוסיף ממנו אין לגרוע [עכ"ן] עבר הקולמוס ובשגגה אמר שדרשו זה על אלישע אחר.‎

188. In *Sefer ha-Mitzvot*, pos. com. 8, which is the commandment of *imitatio Dei*, Maimonides cites both ‏ללכת בכל דרכיו‎ (Deut. 10:12, 11:22) and ‏והלכת בדרכיו‎ (Deut. 28:9) as the source. In *Deot* 1:5–6 only Deut. 28:9 is given. Use of this verse seems to be orig-

Other examples of careless errors are when he mistakenly writes "a hundred" instead of "two hundred,"[189] "three" instead of "a third"[190] (or omits "three" entirely[191]), "five" instead of "six,"[192] "tent" instead of "touch,"[193] and תקנו מזונות תחת מעשה ידיה instead of תקנו מעשה ידיה תחת מזונותיה.[194] In *Guide* 3:40, Maimonides remembered Lev. 27:3 as stating that the valuation of a man is sixty shekels, when in fact it is fifty shekels (a number stated correctly in *Arakhim ve-Haramim* 1:3).[195] Citing from memory explains other errors; for example, when Maimonides refers to something as appearing in *Keritut* when it is actually found in *Meilah*,[196] or *Beitzah* when it is found in *Megillah*,[197] or *Shevi'it* when it is found in *Terumot*,[198] or *Sanhedrin* when it is found in *Makkot*,[199] or *Bereishit Rabbah* when it is found in *Hagigah*;[200] when he refers to something as appearing in the last chap-

---

inal to Maimonides, as nowhere in earlier rabbinic literature is the teaching מה הוא נקרא חנון אף אתה היה חנון וכו' (or variations) connected to this verse. R. Abraham Maimonides discusses his father's use of this verse in *Teshuvot Rabbi Avraham ben ha-Rambam*, ed. Freimann (Jerusalem, 1937), no. 63. (For R. Abraham's own use of the verse, see *ibid.*, p. 67 n. 13.) See also Yitzhak (Isadore) Twersky, "On Law and Ethics in the *Mishneh Torah*: A Case Study of *Hilkhot Megillah* II:17," *Tradition* 24 (Winter, 1989), pp. 142–143; Menachem Kellner, *Maimonides on Human Perfection* (Atlanta, 1990), pp. 43–45 (CR), *id.*, *Maimonides' Confrontation with Mysticism* (Oxford, 2006), pp. 100–101.

189. See *Commentary on the Mishnah*, vol. 1, p. 255 n. 14.

190. See *ibid.*, vol. 4, p. 105 n. 49.

191. See *ibid.*, vol. 4, p. 105 n. 47.

192. See *Sefer ha-Mitzvot*, pos. com. 37, neg. com. 166, and the accompanying notes in the Heller, Kafih, and Frankel editions.

193. See *Commentary on the Mishnah*, vol. 4, p. 193 n. 56.

194. See *ibid.*, vol. 3, p. 58 n. 8. For other such examples, see *ibid.*, vol. 4, pp. 210 n. 66, 215 n. 3, vol. 5, pp. 156 n. 16, 166 n. 5, vol. 6, p. 350 n. 9. See also *ibid.*, vol. 3, p. 68 n. 14, that Maimonides corrected his text in one place, but neglected to do so subsequently. See also *ibid.*, p. 70 n. 29, vol. 5, pp. 66 nn. 21–22, 211 n. 10, 307 n. 12.

195. See R. Abraham Isaac Kook, *Iggerot ha-Re'iyah* (Jerusalem, 1977), vol. 1, nos. 300, 302, who offers forced solutions, and concludes (p. 339): והנה כל אלה הדברים הם בגדר תירוצים, אשר לא סכנו לאוהבי אמת, ויותר נח להם לומר שאיזה תלמיד הוסיף הערה זו ונכנסה בתוך דברי הספר, ושגיאות מי יבין. מ"מ ראוי לנו ליתן כבוד לכל מה שנקרא על שם רבנו אור ישראל ז"ל, ולישב הדברים אפילו באופן רחוק.

196. See *Commentary on the Mishnah*, vol. 1, p. 258 n. 30.

197. See *ibid.*, vol. 5, p. 189 n. 8.

198. See *ibid.*, vol. 5, p. 116 n. 13.

199. See *ibid.*, vol. 4, p. 108 n. 18.

200. See *Guide* 2:30. See also *Guide* 3:45, where he mistakenly claims that an otherwise unknown rabbinic passage is found in *Yoma*.

ter of *Bikkurim* when he means the second chapter,[201] the fifth chapter of *Eruvin* when he means the sixth,[202] the third chapter of *Yoma* when he means the second,[203] or the seventh chapter of *Shabbat* when he means the sixth;[204] when he mistakenly states that he explained something in the *Commentary on the Mishnah*,[205] in *Sefer ha-Mitzvot*,[206] and in the *Mishneh Torah*;[207] and when he claims that he explained something a few times when he only did so once.[208] On one occasion he also seemingly errs in stating that a certain halakhah does not appear in the *Mishneh Torah*.[209] Although he caught certain errors of this sort and incorporated his corrections in subsequent versions of his works,[210] not surprisingly, many still remain.[211]

---

201. See *Commentary on the Mishnah*, vol. 3, p. 125 n. 17.

202. See *ibid.*, vol. 4, p. 130 n. 19.

203. See *ibid.*, vol. 5, p. 83 n. 18.

204. See *Sefer ha-Mitzvot*, ed. Kafih, pp. 199 n. 83, 200 n. 92.

205. See *Commentary on the Mishnah*, vol. 1, p. 207 n. 24, vol. 5, pp. 52 n. 16, 77 n. 44.

206. See *Iggerot ha-Rambam*, vol. 2, p. 452 (in Sheilat's note).

207. See *Korban Pesah* 8:15.

208. See *Commentary on the Mishnah*, vol. 4, p. 242 n. 18, and *Commentary on the Mishnah*, *Avodah Zarah*, ed. Fixler, p. 177. In *Commentary on the Mishnah*, *Kiddushin* 4:5, Maimonides states that he will explain a certain point in his *Commentary* to *Sanhedrin*, yet he never did.

209. See *Iggerot ha-Rambam*, vol. 1, p. 287 n. 18. I say "seemingly" because Shlomo Zalman Havlin, *Alei Sefer* 15 (1988–1989), p. 156, rejects Sheilat's view that this is indeed an error. See also David Henshke, "Kelum Ne'eman ha-Rambam le-He'id al Nusah Sifro," *Sinai* 109 (1989), pp. 76–80. In *Teshuvot ha-Rambam*, no. 367, Maimonides writes: ואמרה המשנה שזה האחרון מוליך מזונותיה אצל אמה. Yet, as David S. Shapiro, *Ha-Darom* 4 (1957), p. 71, points out, there is no such Mishnah.

210. See, e.g., *Commentary on the Mishnah*, vol. 1, pp. 7 n. 17, 13 n. 12, 220 n. 15, 249 n. 5 (one error still remains), vol. 2, p. 182 n. 22, vol. 3, pp. 129 n. 32, 180 n. 8, 191 n. 17, vol. 4, p. 102 n. 13, vol. 5, pp. 46 n. 42, 90 n. 34, 138 n. 10, vol. 6, pp. 25 n. 9, 198 n. 2, 293 n. 2. In a later addition to the Introduction to the *Commentary on the Mishnah*, vol. 1, p. 28 n. 69*, Maimonides noted that R. Judah the Prince's father was R. Simeon. Yet right after this (p. 29 n. 90), he wrote that R. Judah's father was R. Gamaliel, and this was never corrected. See also *ibid.*, vol. 5, pp. 189 n. 10, 190 n. 27, 192 nn. 35–36, 198 n. 10.

211. See *Commentary on the Mishnah*, vol. 1, pp. 6 n. 10 (there is no evidence that the correction found here, as well as in some of the following examples, was made by Maimonides), 45 n. 5, 82 n. 53, 99 n. 26, 107 n. 27, 139 n. 7, 150 n. 18, 167 n. 13, 249 n. 5, vol. 2, pp. 109 n. 15, 129 n. 12, vol. 3, pp. 51 n. 32, 176 n. 12, 209 n. 16, vol. 4, p. 47 n. 24, vol. 5, pp. 13 n. 67, 100 n. 45, 180 n. 37, 189 n. 8, vol. 6, pp. 19 n. 81, 55 n. 10, 134 n. 28, 153 n. 27, 157 n. 20, 361 n. 2, 371 n. 47, 413 n. 38, 418 n. 19; *Tikkun Mishnah*, ed. Sheilat, p. 140 n. 12; *Sefer ha-Mitzvot*, ed. Kafih, pp. 202 n. 8, 231 n. 84, 250 n. 58, 253 n. 84, 265 n. 81, 310 n. 72, 314 n. 1, 344 n. 50; see also Appendix, Kafih's letter to Carmiel Cohen, and Cohen's additional references in "'Yosef ha-Kohen Hevi Bikurav Yayin ve-

Maimonides' meticulousness is revealed by his careful editing; yet even he occasionally overlooked things, leading to what Davidson has termed "inadvertent inconsistencies."[212] Throughout Kafih's notes to the *Commentary on the Mishnah*, he calls attention to differences between the words of the Mishnah quoted in the *Commentary* and the Mishnah text itself, both of which are in Maimonides' own hand. According to Kafih, one reason for this is that when Maimonides copied the Mishnah together with his *Commentary*, he used a different version of the Mishnah than when he originally composed the *Commentary*, and certain minor discrepancies escaped his notice.[213] Also in the *Commentary*, there are times when Maimonides made a correction in one place, but neglected to update a related passage, thus creating an internal contradiction in the work.[214] To give an example from the *Mishneh Torah*, in *Avodah Zarah* 3:3, Maimonides cites one verse as a

---

Shemen ve-Lo Kiblu Mimenu': Hearah al Keta mi-Mahadurah Kama shel Perush ha-Mishnah le-Rambam she-Nishkah ve-Lo Nimhak be-Mahadurah Batra," *Mealiyot* 20 (1999), pp. 93–94, nn. 18–20. While some of the examples from the *Commentary on the Mishnah* have been corrected in various manuscripts, unless the correction appears in the manuscript written by Maimonides—of which Kafih has identified four "editions" (cf. *Tikkun Mishnah*, ed. Sheilat, p. 28)—we have no way of knowing if Maimonides was responsible for it. Unlike the other five orders, Maimonides' manuscript of his *Commentary* to *Toharot* does not survive, and when dealing with this order there is always the possibility that we are confronted with scribal errors. See, e.g., *Commentary on the Mishnah*, vol. 6, p. 10 n. 24. Yet as Kalman Kahana points out, "Perush ha-Mishnah (1)," p. 57, this reference appears correctly in the Introduction to *Toharot* from Maimonides' own hand, published by Joshua Blau and Alexander Scheiber, *Otograf ha-Rambam me-Osef Adler u-mi-Genizat Leningrad* (Jerusalem, 1981), p. 12. Another relevant issue is that in the Introduction to the *Commentary on the Mishnah*, he tells us that he will list those *tannaim* in whose name only one halakhah appears in the Mishnah. Many subsequent scholars pointed to apparent errors in this regard, yet almost all of these can be explained. See R. Reuven Margaliot, *Peninim u-Margaliyot* (Jerusalem, 2006), pp. 185–196. According to Kafih, Maimonides erred in his explanation of a certain mitzvah; see his edition of *Sefer ha-Mitzvot*, p. 283 n. 32. See also his commentary to *Sefer ha-Mada*, p. 75. Another interesting problem is Maimonides' drawing of the Temple menorah; see *Commentary on the Mishnah*, vol. 5, p. 78 n. 54*. At first, Kafih thought that Maimonides erred, but he later retracted this view; see his commentary to *Sefer Avodah* (1), pp. 54ff.

212. See *Moses Maimonides*, p. 389, where he also provides two examples of this from the *Guide*.

213. See his introduction to the *Commentary*, p. 15.

214. See Elhanan Samet, *Yad le-Rambam* (Jerusalem, 2006), pp. 64ff.

proof text while in *Sefer ha-Mitzvot*, neg. com. 5, he offers another verse. This in itself should not occasion any surprise, as there are any number of differences between the *Mishneh Torah* and *Sefer ha-Mitzvot*. What is significant, however, is that the proof text in *Sefer ha-Mitzvot* also appears in the List of Commandments at the beginning of the *Mishneh Torah*, neg. com. 5. This lack of uniformity within the *Mishneh Torah* itself is certainly not intentional.[215] Similarly, in the List of Commandments at the beginning of the *Mishneh Torah*, pos. com. 127, Maimonides cites one verse as a proof text, while in the *Mishneh Torah* itself, *Ma'aser* 1:1 and *Mattenot Aniyim* 6:2, he offers another verse (which happens to also be the verse given in *Sefer ha-Mitzvot*, pos. com. 127).

Maimonides also shows a lack of consistency when it comes to grammar. Thus, while the word אש is a feminine word, and is treated as such numerous times in the *Mishneh Torah*, on at least one occasion Maimonides treats it as a masculine word.[216] Similarly, he sometimes treats the word מים as a singular word,[217] and on a few occasions treats לילה as a feminine word.[218] I assume that these are examples of Maimonides' carelessness. To argue otherwise—namely, that these words were not written carelessly, but with full cognizance of what he was doing—is to conclude that Maimonides consciously introduced grammatical inconsistencies into the *Mishneh Torah*.

While scholars of recent generations might be troubled by the evidence that we have examined so far, which shows Maimonides'

---

215. See Kafih, *Commentary* to *Sefer ha-Mada*, p. 63 n. 58, who notes another lack of consistency between the *Mishneh Torah* and the List of Commandments. In this case as well, *Sefer ha-Mitzvot*, neg. com. 65, agrees with the List of Commandments.

216. *Yesodei ha-Torah* 4:2.

217. See *ibid.* and *Yalkut Shinuyei Nushaot* in the Frankel ed., *ad loc.*

218. *Talmud Torah* 3:14 (there is uniformity on this among all the Yemenite, Spanish, and Ashkenazic mss. used by Frankel, so Kafih's version, which has the word used correctly in this case, must be based on more recent corrected mss.), *Issurei Biah* 7:14, 8:3. It is interesting to note that unlike Maimonides, whose treating לילה as feminine is simply a slip of the pen, R. Isaiah Horowitz, *Sha'ar ha-Shamayim* (Amsterdam, 1802), p. 500a (s.v *ma'aseh be-Rabbi Eliezer*), and the Vilna Gaon, Commentary on the Passover Haggadah (Jerusalem, n.d.), p. 30, s.v. *mah nishtanah*, actually offer explanations as to why לילה is feminine. This is so despite the fact that, throughout the Bible and tannaitic literature, it is a masculine word.

memory as less than perfect, his great follower, Joseph Ibn Kaspi, did not find this disconcerting:

> Is it necessary that he [i.e., Maimonides] always remember all these details without error? . . . How can anyone who knows what it takes to write a book, one in which the author cites hundreds and even thousands of verses and sayings, think that the author will not [unintentionally] omit or add or make minor changes? Does one expect that while deeply involved in his book, every time he wishes to cite a verse he will take out the Bible and trouble himself to find it? This is wondrous only for those imbeciles who do not know what it takes to author a book.[219]

Similarly, R. Yair Hayyim Bacharach notes that "forgetfulness is part of human nature affecting all people . . . and who is greater than Moses our teacher of blessed memory, choicest of the prophets, who overlooked two things in his anger."[220]

However, there is no question that it is the view of Azulai mentioned above, which negates the possibility of positing Maimonidean errors in order to answer perplexities, that was the dominant approach, even in the eighteenth century and certainly in subsequent years. Yet although it is always preferable to find interpretive solutions to problems, academic scholars cannot ignore the possibility that at times Maimonides forgot things, was careless, or overlooked rabbinic texts. As previously noted, Maimonides himself famously tells us that he once temporarily forgot the source of a halakhah.[221] Elsewhere, he mentions that he cannot recall if a certain law was given a scriptural connection by the Sages.[222] I have already noted that in his

---

219. Commentary to *Guide* 1:19. See also *ibid.*, 1:36 and R. Samuel Tzartza, *Mekor Hayyim* (Mantua, 1559), p. 98b: וכתב ז' כספי שהיה זה שכחה מהרב ז"ל עם רוב טירדת לבו ומצוקת עיוניו בחברו ס' המורה האם אין שכחה לפני כסא כבודו ז"ל והנה משה רבינו ע"ה שכח עצמו במי מריבה אבל האמת אין איש אשר לא יחטא וכל יתרון החכמים הוא במיעוט תעיותיו[!].

220. *Hut ha-Shani* (Jerusalem, 1970), no. 18, s.v. *teshuvah le-gadol ehad*. He then provides some examples of what he regards as Maimonides' forgetfulness from the Introduction to the *Commentary on the Mishnah*. R. Judah Leib Maimon, ed., *Sefer ha-Gra* (Jerusalem, 1954), p. 103, notes that Bacharach himself overlooked some apparent errors of Maimonides. Regarding what Moses forgot, see Rashi, Num. 31:21, citing *Sifra, ad loc.* (but here it states that Moses forgot *three* things, showing that Bacharach's memory was also not perfect).

221. *Iggerot ha-Rambam*, vol. 2, pp. 444–445.

222. See *Commentary on the Mishnah*, *Orlah* 2:1. Maimonides overlooked *Pesahim* 48a, Jerusalem Talmud, *Orlah* 2:1, and *Sifrei: Bamidbar* 121. This example led R. Jehiel Jacob

letter to the sages of Lunel, Maimonides writes that in his old age, he too suffers from forgetfulness.[223]

These passages and others in which Maimonides acknowledges the possibility that he erred and overlooked things,[224] while of comfort to the academic scholar, were not enough to also embolden the typical traditionalist commentator to point to examples where Maimonides was less than perfect. Traditionalists certainly did not argue that Maimonides *misinterpreted* rabbinic texts, a line of argument that assumes that the commentator understands the matter better than Maimonides himself. What the traditionalist commentators have done is to show why Maimonides' words are difficult to comprehend; if they can find no solution, matters are left at that. It is very rare to find a traditionalist scholar who will take the next step and actually attempt to refute Maimonides' understanding of a rabbinic passage; that is, to show that it is incorrect and based on a misinterpretation, rather than being simply "difficult."[225]

The only time that it has been somewhat acceptable among traditionalists to say that Maimonides erred was when the commentators felt that they were "saving" Maimonides, as it were. That is, they acknowledged that Maimonides erred, but not in his first statement, only in his second. There are times when Maimonides changed what he originally wrote, and we find traditionalists concluding that what Maimonides first wrote was correct and that he was wrong to move

---

Weinberg to declare: לפעמים רחוקות שר של שכחה שלט גם ברמב"ם. See *Kitvei ha-Gaon*, vol. 1, pp. 90–91. See also *ibid.*, p. 121: ונעלמו דברי הירושלמי מהרמב"ם ז"ל.

223. *Iggerot ha-Rambam*, vol. 2, p. 503.

224. See also his conclusion to the *Commentary on the Mishnah* and *Iggerot ha-Rambam*, vol. 1, pp. 286, 306, 394.

225. One such example is Hirschenson, *Malki ba-Kodesh*, vol. 2, pp. 192ff., who argues that Maimonides misunderstood a passage in the *Sifrei*, and was thus led to forbid women from holding any positions of authority. On p. 194, he writes: ורק פלא לנו איך נעלם דבר זה מעינו הבדולח של הרמב"ם ז"ל, אות הוא כי זה משה איש הוא ובכל חכמתו הגדולה, ודעתו הרחבה לא נמלט משגיאה אשר הוליכה גם גדולים אחרים לשגות אחריו, ובלי ספק סמך הרמב"ם ז"ל על זכרונו בהמאמר, ולא הספיק לעיין עוד הפעם פנימה וכל הבאים אחריו נמשכו אחרי דברו ויצא הטעות הזה. See also R. Ben Zion Uziel, *Mishpetei Uziel* (Jerusalem, 1947), second series, *Orah Hayyim* no. 19, with reference to a responsum of Maimonides, and the criticism of R. Ovadiah Yosef, *Yabia Omer* (Jerusalem, 1986), vol. 6, *Orah Hayyim* no. 26:5. Also with reference to a Maimonidean responsum, see R. Dov Ber Anushiski, *Matzav ha-Yashar* (Vilna, 1886), vol. 2, p. 84b: והרמב"ם קם מדעת עצמו ללמוד מהם גם לענון סתם קטלנית דעלמא אע"פ שאין לה שום שייכות למצות יבום ובזה שגג לגמרי.

away from it. It appears that R. Solomon ben Adret was the first to argue in this fashion.[226] We also find traditionalists who, in a very modern (even post-modern) fashion, believed that they understood Maimonides' words better than the master himself. Thus, they offered interpretations of the *Mishneh Torah* without considering that which Maimonides wrote in his other works. On occasion, they even ignored the explanations Maimonides himself later gave for his halakhot. Similarly, traditionalist scholars found sources for rulings in the *Mishneh Torah* that appeared more reasonable than those sources pointed to by Maimonides in his responsa.[227] This approach was justified by R. Nahum Ash, who wrote: "In his old age Maimonides forgot the source of many things, and those who came after him probed and pointed to their source."[228] A different justification, with a more

---

226. *She'elot u-Teshuvot ha-Rashba*, vol. 1, no. 4.

227. Concerning this approach, see R. Mathias Strashun, *Mivhar Ketavim* (Jerusalem, 1969), pp. 310ff; R. Reuven Margaliot's introduction to his edition of R. Abraham Maimonides, *Milhamot ha-Shem* (Jerusalem, 1959), p. 13 n. 3. Margaliot cites a number of examples where *aharonim* provided what they believed to be better proofs for Maimonides' decisions than what he himself was able to supply. See Kalman Kahana, "Al 'Hazarotav' shel ha-Rambam ve-Siboteihen," *Ha-Ma'ayan* 17 (Tamuz 5737), pp. 5–26, who shows that the *aharonim* who adopted this approach erred in almost every example. See also R. Moses Shalom Stoll, *Darkhei Shalom* (Riga, 1930), pp. 259–260. However, for my purposes it is not important whether these *aharonim* erred or not, only that they thought that this line of reasoning—that is, preference for *their* explanation of the *Mishneh Torah* over Maimonides' own explanation—was an acceptable approach. In line with this, see also Margaliot's *Nefesh Hayah* (Tel Aviv, 1954), *Orah Hayyim* 209, where he brings examples from the Talmud in which one sage interprets another sage's words differently than the explanation offered by the latter sage himself. With regard to Maimonides, see also R. Solomon of Chelm, *Mirkevet ha-Mishneh* (Jerusalem, 2000), *Nedarim* 12:1, where, after referring to Maimonides' own explanation of a halakhah in the *Mishneh Torah*, he proceeds to explain the halakhah differently. R. Jacob Joshua Falk, *Penei Yehoshua* (Jerusalem, 1998), *Ketubot* 35b, writes: אלא . . . "כתבתי ישוב מספיק על מה שהקשו הקדמונים על שיטת הרמב"ם שהרמב"ם גופא תירץ בענין אחר ועכ"ז הנראה לענ"ד כתבתי (CR). R. Moses Sofer, *She'elot u-Teshuvot Hatam Sofer* (Jerusalem, 1989), vol. 6, no. 101, explains a formulation in the *Mishneh Torah*, and then adds: אך הרמב"ם בעצמו לא תי' כן לחכמי לוניל (CR). Similarly, R. Reuven Katz writes: אפשר לתרץ דברי הרמב"ם בהלכה, לא כמו שמתרץ לחכמי לוניל, אלא כפי שפירש בפירוש המשניות. See *Degel Reuven* (Petah Tikvah, 1976), vol. 3, no. 38. See also Shraga Abramson's notes to *Teshuvot ha-Rambam*, vol. 3, p. 177, vol. 4, p. 51.

228. *Tziyunei Maharan, Nizkei Mamon* 4:4 (found in the Frankel edition, p. 205). R. Moses Margaliot makes the same point. See *Mar'eh ha-Panim* to Jerusalem Talmud, *Shabbat* 24:1. In support of this approach, R. Reuven Margaliot, *Nefesh Hayah, Orah Hayyim* 209, cites *Bava Metzia* 44a–44b. It is stated here that Rabbi Judah the Prince taught his son that "gold acquires silver." His son replied, "Master, in your youth you did teach us silver

modern appeal, is quoted in the name of R. Naphtali Zvi Judah Berlin: "All the works of our teachers, the *rishonim*, until the era of the *Penei Yehoshua*,[229] were written with *ruah ha-kodesh*, and obviously Maimonides' Code is in this category. What Maimonides wrote in a responsum is Maimonides' explanation of what he wrote in his Code, but there is still room for other explanations, for there are 70 facets to the Torah."[230] In fact, even after Maimonides wrote to the sages of Lunel—who had asked about a difficulty in the *Mishneh Torah* (*Nizkei Mamon* 4:4)—informing them that their text of this halakhah was mistaken,[231] we still find R. Hayyim Soloveitchik[232] and others[233] offering analyses of the mistaken text!

Old Questions, Modern Answers

While even academic scholars should be hesitant to assume that Maimonides erred, there are times—in particular when it is a question of Maimonides overlooking a source—that this option must remain open. This will create a clear divergence between the academic scholar and the traditionalist, who will eschew this approach even as a last resort, despite the indisputable evidence that Maimonides did not

---

acquires gold; now, advanced in age, you reverse it and teach, gold acquires silver." After the Talmud explains why Rabbi Judah changed his view, it states: "R. Ashi said: 'Reason supports the opinion held in his youth.'" See also R. Netanel Weil, *Korban Netanel* to *Shabbat* 153b and R. David Fraenkel, *Shirei Korban* to Jerusalem Talmud, *Yoma* 3:6, who each offer an example to show that Maimonides forgot the source of a halakhah in the *Mishneh Torah*. Incidentally, in seeking to explain the contradictions in the *Shulhan Arukh*, both R. Jacob Castro and R. Hayyim Vital point to the fact that it was written in Karo's old age. See Castro, *Oholei Yaakov* (Livorno, 1783) no. 20 (p. 35), and Vital's letter published in *Asupot* 3 (1989), p. 273.

229. R. Jacob Joshua Falk (1680–1756).

230. *Ve-ha-Ish Moshe* (Kiryat Sefer, 2001), p. 161 (CR).

231. *Teshuvot ha-Rambam*, no. 433.

232. *Hiddushei Rabbenu Hayyim ha-Levi, Nizkei Mamon* 4:4, 11. See Shlomo Zalman Havlin, "Ha-Yahas li-'She'elot Nusah' be-Sifrei Hazal," in Yoel Catane and Eliyahu Soloveitchik, eds., *Beit ha-Va'ad* (Jerusalem, 2003), p. 27 n. 28.

233. See Malbim, Commentary on *Mekhilta*, Ex. 21:29 (note 106); R. Moses Avigdor Amiel, *Ha-Middot le-Heker ha-Halakhah* (Tel Aviv, 1942), vol. 2, p. 294. All were aware of Maimonides' responsum, as it is mentioned in *Kesef Mishneh, Nizkei Mamon* 4:4. For what seems to be another contradiction between the responsa of Maimonides and R. Hayyim's *hiddushim*, see R. Isser Yehudah Unterman, *Shevet mi-Yehudah* (Jerusalem, 1994), vol. 3, pp. 340–341.

have a perfect memory. We have already seen that Maimonides cited biblical verses from memory, and this led him to make errors. It is also clear that at times he did not examine the relevant talmudic texts when citing these verses, and this, too, contributed to mistakes. Even when not dealing with biblical verses, one is safe in assuming that there were times when Maimonides cited talmudic texts from memory, which undoubtedly brought about some additional errors.[234]

A good deal has been written about Maimonides' use of the expression "it appears to me,"[235] especially since there are times when it seems that Maimonides' ostensibly novel ruling is actually explicit in an earlier rabbinic text. Traditionalist commentators have offered all sorts of explanations for these cases, but from an academic perspective, it would seem that one cannot discount the possibility that in at least some of these cases, Maimonides simply overlooked the rabbinic text; had he recalled it, he would not have asserted that his ruling was original.[236] In short, academic scholars should approach Maimonides' writings in the same way they approach, for example, the writings of Aristotle. If there is a contradiction between two of Aristotle's books, or two chapters in the same book, and all attempts at harmonization are unsuccessful, scholars will be forced to conclude that there is a real inconsistency and Aristotle was not as careful as he should have been. If such an approach is suitable when studying Aristotle, only hagiographic sensibilities can render it invalid when applied to Maimonides.[237] I say this even though Maimonides, in speaking about

---

234. For two such examples, where it is clear that Maimonides is citing talmudic texts incorrectly from memory, see *Commentary on the Mishnah*, vol. 6, pp. 36 n. 33, 48 n. 28.

235. See, e.g., R. Eliyahu Rabinowitz-Teomim, *Teshuvah mi-Yir'ah* (Jerusalem, 1906); R. Yosef Hayyim Haberman, *Samahti be-Omrim Li* (Elad, 2007).

236. See above, p. 11 n. 58, where I refer to one such case where R. Abraham Maimonides offered this approach.

237. Herbert Davidson, in his discussion of Maimonides' view of creation, has already noted the damaging effect of this assumption on the esoteric reading of Maimonides. "On the alternative portrait the various contradictions we discovered in his discussion of creation would not be deliberate and intended to conceal an esoteric belief. They would be inadvertent; and Maimonides would have been less immune to error and carelessness than he and his readers through the centuries have imagined." See "Maimonides' Secret Position on Creation," in Isadore Twersky, ed., *Studies in Medieval Jewish History and Literature* (Cambridge, 1979), p. 36. See also Davidson, *Moses Maimonides*, p. 369.

the reasons for contradictions, holds authors up to a very high standard: "If, however, the two original propositions are evidently contradictory, but the author has simply forgotten the first when writing down the second in another part of his compilation, this is a very great weakness, and that man should not be reckoned among those whose speeches deserve consideration."[238] The more charitable path is to conclude that even the greatest of authors, Maimonides among them, sometimes fall victim to forgetfulness or carelessness.

Let me offer some other examples to illustrate the options that I believe must remain open to academic scholars, but that are not acceptable to most traditionalists. I will begin with the issue of exactitude in language. For the typical traditionalist commentator, every alternative expression and change of word in the *Mishneh Torah* is of significance, just as if one was interpreting the Mishnah. (Ironically, before the new editions of the last generation, these commentators were forced to work with faulty Maimonidean texts, although most were unaware of this limitation and how it could affect what they were writing.[239]) Jacob Levinger, in his classic study of the *Mishneh*

---

238. *Guide*, Introduction (sixth cause of contradictions).

239. It is worth noting that the faulty texts are not only due to the typical errors of copyists. There are times when the commentators themselves were responsible. For example, in *Terumot* 11:3, *Kesef Mishneh*, troubled by the word ושמן, and unaware that not only do all mss. have this word, but that it also appears in Maimonides' *Commentary on the Mishnah, Terumot* 11:1, insisted that it was a mistake and should be deleted. In accordance with his view, subsequent printings until our generation omitted the word. In *Temidin u-Musafin* 5:12, *Kesef Mishneh's* advocacy of the version לא נפסל הלחם (instead of נפסל הלחם, found in the best mss.) led to its adoption by subsequent printed versions. In *Korban Pesah* 7:8, *Kesef Mishneh* claimed that בטהרה (כטהור in most mss.) should read בטומאה, and this mistaken emendation appeared in subsequent printed versions. In *Tum'at Met* 17:4, all mss. have אפילו גבוהות מן הארץ אמה. *Kesef Mishneh* mistakenly insisted that it should read אלף אמה, and that is how it appeared in subsequent printings. For some other suggested emendations by *Kesef Mishneh*, many without any basis in mss., see *Avodah Zarah* 11:1, *Shabbat* 29:4, *Hametz u-Matzah* 2:11, *Ma'aser* 13:2 (and see Kafih's commentary, ad loc.), *Ma'aseh ha-Korbanot* 18:15, *Pesulei ha-Mukdashin* 10:3, 16:7, *Mehuserei Kaparah* 1:5, *Parah Adumah* 7:11, *Tuma't Tzara'at* 7:2, and *She'ar Avot ha-Tum'ah* 5:19. See also Frankel's note to *Ma'aseh ha-Korbanot* 2:10 and Moshe Assis, "Ma-Shehu al 'Kesef Mishneh' le-Sefer Zeraim ve-al Nusah Sefer Zeraim shel Mefarshei ha-Rambam bi-Zemano shel Maran," *Asupot* 3 (1989), pp. 275–322. Even Kafih occasionally suggests emendations without having any manuscript support. For example, *Ma'aser Sheni* 5:14 reads יצרף, and he believes it should be יפרוט; *Mikvaot* 4:8 reads: והיה ממלא ושואב חוץ למקוה, and he believes that ושואב should be replaced with ושופך; *Sekhirut* 9:2 reads ומשמנין, and he believes that it should be משמין.

Torah[240] has as one of his goals the refutation of this hagiographic assumption and the "humanizing," as it were, of Maimonides and the *Mishneh Torah*. Although Levinger cites numerous examples to support his approach, let me offer two that he does not mention that illustrate that Maimonides, for stylistic reasons, was not always exacting in his language.

In *Nedarim* 4:14 he writes:

האומר פירות אלו אסורין עלי היום אם אלך למקום פלוני למחר הרי זה אסור לאכל אותן היום היום גזרה שמא ילך למחר לאותו מקום ואם עבר ואכלן היום והלך למחר לוקה ואם לא הלך אינו לוקה.

The last five words do not teach us anything; indeed, they are entirely unnecessary. They are added simply to complete the thought—that is, for stylistic reasons. It is only the traditionalist commentator with hagiographic assumptions who will attempt to locate a significant teaching in these words, and regard the text as "difficult" if he cannot.

Similarly, in *Shevitat Asor* 2:6, Maimonides writes: ואלו הן לולבי גפנים כל שלבלבו בארץ ישראל מראש השנה ועד יום הכפורים. The words בארץ ישראל have no halakhic significance, as it doesn't matter where the vine shoots sprouted. Because of this, some traditionalist commentators have suggested that these words are a later interpolation; yet this is impossible, as they appear in all manuscripts. The most likely explanation is that Maimonides was merely copying what appeared in his version of the Talmud, and the phraseology is such not because it imparts any halakhic lesson, but simply because vines were common in the Land of Israel.[241]

While the previous examples are only stylistic, I believe that even when dealing with halakhic matters there are times when Maimonides' language and organization is simply not as careful as we've come to

---

(Unknown to Kafih, this latter example has ms. support; see *Yad Peshutah, ad loc.*). For an example from *Maggid Mishneh* that affected subsequent printed editions, see *Gezelah ve-Avedah* 15:13.

240. *Darkhei ha-Mahashavah*, and see especially his formulation on p. 16.

241. For the points made in this paragraph, see *Yalkut Shinuyei Nushaot* in the Frankel edition of the *Mishneh Torah, ad loc.* It is also noted there that Meiri seemed to have had the words בארץ ישראל in his version of the Talmud.

expect from him—meaning that any attempt to come up with a "solution" for these problematic texts is doomed to failure. For example, in *Yom Tov* 1:21, Maimonides writes, with reference to the nature of *yom tov sheni*: In שני ימים מנהג הוא זה שאנו עושין בחוצה לארץ כל יום טוב מאלו. *Yom Tov* 6:14, he writes: מן הספק אלא מנהג אבל היום שבני ארץ ישראל בלבד סומכין על החשבון ומקדשין עליו אין יום טוב שני להסתלק. In *Talmud Torah* 6:15, in speaking of those people placed under the ban, he writes: המחלל יום טוב שני של גליות[242] אע"פ שהוא מנהג.

Yet in *Kiddush ha-Hodesh* 5:6, he writes: יום טוב שני שאנו עושין בגליות בזמן הזה מדברי סופרים שתקנו דבר זה. In *Hanukkah* 3:5, he also refers to it in this fashion: ולמה מברכין על יום טוב שני והם לא תקנוהו אלא מפני הספק.[243] Traditionalist commentators have attempted all sorts of harmonization for these statements, and those with an academic perspective can offer similar solutions. However, one must not overlook the possibility that these contradictions are due to the fact that Maimonides himself was unsure on this point, had different ideas at different times, and never brought these various halakhot into line. After all, examination of *Mishneh Torah* manuscripts reveals that, as with the *Commentary on the Mishnah*[244] *Sefer ha-*

---

242. This is how the word appears in the Oxford ms.

243. Regarding Maimonides' view of *minhag* and *takanot*, see Yaakov (Gerald) Blidstein, *Samhut u-Meri be-Halakhat ha-Rambam* (Tel Aviv, 2002), pp. 54–56, index, s.v. *takanah*. In the Introduction to the *Mishneh Torah* and *Mamrim* 1:2–3, Maimonides speaks of three separate categories: תקנות, גזרות, מנהגות.

244. With reference to this work, Simon Hopkins has recently written: "Here before us we see Maimonides in the process of composition, and investigation of the textual changes which he introduced affords us a rare opportunity of studying his methods of work. Before our very eyes the text of the *Commentary on the Mishna* emerges, sometimes growing and gaining, sometimes shrinking and receding, yet always developing and in a constant state of change." *Maimonides's Commentary*, p. xx. See also Nissim Sabato and Ezra Shabet, "Teyutot ha-Rambam le-Ferush ha-Mishnah bi-Khtav Yad Kodsho," *Yeshurun* 15 (2005), pp. 15–30. In Kafih's edition of the *Commentary on the Mishnah*, he notes approximately two thousand corrections that Maimonides made to this work (on a number of occasions Maimonides corrected his text more than once). Kafih did not even have access to Maimonides' autograph commentary to the order *Toharot*, for it is not extant, nor to some other sections which do survive. See above, pp. 16 n. 72, 49 n. 202 (I have compiled a list of all the corrections noted by Kafih). See also *Hilkhot ha-Yerushalmi le-ha-Rambam*, ed. Lieberman (New York, 1948), pp. 6ff. To the corrections noted by Kafih must now be added the pages from the *Commentary* on *Shabbat*, in Maimonides' own handwriting, published by Hopkins and mentioned earlier in this note. In addition to sty-

Mitzvot,[245] and his commentary on the Talmud[246]—and, to the best of our knowledge, unlike the *Guide*[247]—the *Mishneh Torah* was a work in progress, waiting to be brought to final order by its author. As far as we know, this was never done.[248]

---

listic changes, there is also a halakhic correction (*Shabbat* 2:5). See Hopkins' introduction, p. xviii, for other autograph texts from the *Commentary on the Mishnah* that have appeared in print. Maimonides himself explains that one reason for all the changes in his later editions is that when he first wrote the *Commentary* he relied too heavily on the explanations of the geonim. See *Teshuvot ha-Rambam*, no. 217, *Iggerot ha-Rambam*, vol. 1, p. 305.

245. See R. Moses Ibn Tibbon's introduction to his translation of *Sefer ha-Mitzvot*; Heller's introduction to his edition of *Sefer ha-Mitzvot*, p. 18; Kafih's introduction to his edition of *Sefer ha-Mitzvot*, pp. 11ff., 266 n. 88.

246. See Israel M. Ta-Shma, *Keneset Mehkarim* (Jerusalem, 2004), vol. 2, pp. 309–316.

247. See Simon Rawidowicz, *Iyyunim be-Mahshevet Yisrael* (Jerusalem, 1969), vol. 1, pp. 185 n. 133, 292; Davidson, *Moses Maimonides*, p. 110. David Yellin, "Shenei," pp. 93–106, published two pages of the *Guide* in Maimonides' own handwriting. While these pages have a number of corrections, they appear to have been made while the author was writing, or when reviewing what he wrote. None of them seem to be from a later period of time. The differences between this ms., which was probably regarded by Maimonides as a first draft, and later mss. relate to matters of style, not substance, and there is no evidence that Maimonides continued over time to correct the *Guide* in any significant way.

248. See Samuel Atlas, *Ketaim mi-Sefer Yad ha-Hazakah* (London, 1940); Menahem M. Kasher, "Ha-Rambam bi-Defus u-ve-Khitvei Yad," *Sinai* 18 (1946), 152–162; Eleazar Hurvitz, "Seridim Nosafim mi-Sefer Mishneh Torah Ketuvim be-Etzem Ketav Yad Kodsho shel ha-Rambam," *Ha-Darom* 38 (1974), pp. 4–44; Isadore Twersky, *Introduction to the Code of Maimonides* (New Haven, 1980), p. 315; Eliav Schochetman, "Makat Mardut be-Mishnat ha-Rambam," in Moshe Ber, ed., *Mehkarim be-Halakhah u-ve-Mahshevet Yisrael Mugashim li-Khvod ha-Rav Menahem Emanuel Rackman be-Hagio li-Gevurot* (Ramat Gan, 1994), pp. 117–119; Havlin, ed., *Mishneh Torah*, pp. 375–407. Kafih calls attention to numerous examples of alternate readings which he regards as earlier versions of the *Mishneh Torah*. See the introduction to his edition of *Sefer ha-Mitzvot*, pp. 13–16, his commentary to *Sefer ha-Mada*, pp. 71, 246, 534, 548, 553, *Sefer Zemanim* (2), pp. 205–206, 258, 301–302, *Sefer Zemanim* (3), p. 158, *Sefer Nashim*, pp. 13–15, 17, 84, 199–200, 245, 356, 477, *Sefer Kedushah* (2), pp. 83–84, 106, 207, 244, *Sefer Hafla'ah*, p. 282, *Sefer Avodah*, p. 604, *Sefer Korbanot*, p. 182, *Sefer Taharah* (2), p. 137, *Sefer Nezikin*, pp. 105–106, *Sefer Shoftim* (1), p. 199, *Sefer Shoftim* (2), p. 222. (He is not entirely sure about a few of the preceding examples.) Kafih also calls attention to what he believes are examples of Maimonides' early teachings in the *Mishneh Torah*, which he neglected to update after changing his mind. See *Commentary on the Mishnah*, vol. 5, p. 117 n. 33, Kafih's commentary to *Sefer ha-Mada*, p. 650, *Sefer Ahavah*, pp. 395, 710, *Sefer Kedushah* (2), pp. 106, 207, 244, 796, *Sefer Zeraim* (2), p. 53, *Sefer Shoftim* (2), pp. 27, 353.

A separate study is needed to chart Maimonides' corrections to the *Mishneh Torah*, as well as divergent views in the *Commentary on the Mishnah*, *Sefer ha-Mitzvot*, and *Mishneh Torah*. Kafih often notes the changes and sometimes attempts to explain them,

Neriah Guttel recently noted another example of internal incon-sistency in the *Mishneh Torah*.[249] In *Ma'akhalot Asurot* 11:8, Maimonides states that whenever the term גוי is used without qualification, it refers to an idolator. Yet in *Issurei Biah* 12:1–10, the terms גוי and גויה clear-ly refer to all gentiles, including Muslims. As with the previous exam-ple, it is likely that Maimonides would have eventually brought the two sections into line, as there appears to be no way of harmonizing the texts other than positing that Maimonides was not careful in his lan-guage.

I now turn to an example that has been discussed by many recent commentators. In *Ma'aseh ha-Korbanot* 4:2, Maimonides writes:

> If that part of an offering which made it permitted for the altar [i.e., the blood] was offered by day, its other parts might be offered up on the altar all of the following night. How was this? The sacrificial por-tions of sacrifices whose blood was sprinkled by day were burnt upon the altar at night, until the rise of dawn. Likewise, the limbs of a burnt offering were burned at night until the rise of dawn. However, in order to avoid neglect [beyond their proper time], the Sages decreed that sac-rificial portions and the limbs of a burnt offering were to be burned only until midnight.

Yet in *Korban Pesah* 1:8, Maimonides writes: "The fat pieces of the Passover offerings may be burnt any time of the night until daybreak."

The reader is left perplexed, since according to the first source the sacrifice can only be burnt until midnight; according to the latter source, it can be done all night. (Also perplexing is the fact that none of the early commentators note the contradiction.) One who exam-ines this example without a presumption that Maimonides cannot err would probably be forced to conclude that he was somewhat careless in leaving two contradictory rulings in the *Mishneh Torah*. It is tempt-ing to say that Maimonides changed his mind and neglected to correct

---

yet not always. Since traditionalist commentators have not even been aware of many of Maimonides' corrections, we do not have a literature from them dealing with the issue

249. See Daniel Sperber, "Legitimacy and Necessity: Scientific Disciplines and the Learning of Talmud," *Robert M. Beren College Studies in Jewish Thought and Identity* 1 (2006), pp. 67–68.

one of the texts, an approach offered by both R. David Ibn Zimra and the Vilna Gaon concerning other contradictions.[250] Yet although his opinion in *Korban Pesah* is indeed shared by Rashi,[251] there is no record of any vacillation in Maimonides' view in his *Commentary on the Mishnah, Berakhot* 1:3, for which we have his own manuscript. Here he explains matters in accordance with what he writes in *Ma'aseh ha-Korbanot.* Since the *Commentary on the Mishnah* underwent significant revisions, lack of any evidence of this in our case would seem to be good, though not conclusive, proof that Maimonides did not change his mind. It must further be noted that elsewhere in the *Mishneh Torah, Temidin u-Musafin* 1:6, Maimonides reaffirms the ruling given in *Ma'aseh ha-Korbanot.*

One way of explaining the contradiction is that in *Korban Pesah* Maimonides is only speaking about Torah law.[252] That this is unsatisfying hardly needs to be stated. After all, we are discussing a law code; if it says that one can do something until dawn, then that is what the reader assumes the halakhah to be. The notion that Maimonides expects the reader to know that this passage does not record the actual halakhah as practiced, but rather a "pure" biblical perspective, is hardly tenable. His purpose was not to confuse the reader, and as Maimonides explained in the Introduction to the *Mishneh Torah*, his Code was to "consist of statements, clear and reasonable . . . so that the rules shall be accessible to young and old."[253] If Maimonides wanted to note the biblical law and how it was adjusted by the Sages, he could have easily done so in *Korban Pesah*, as he in fact did in *Ma'aseh ha-Korbanot.*[254]

It is true that on at least one occasion, for the sake of simplicity and to illustrate a certain point, Maimonides uses an example from

---

250. See above, pp. 6-7 nn. 26-27.

251. See *Berakhot* 2a s.v. *kedei.* See also *Tosafot Yom Tov, Berakhot* 1:1.

252. See R. Eleazar ben Samuel Schmelke Landau, *Arba'ah Turei Even* (Lvov, 1889), pp. 20b–21a; R. Meir Simhah ha-Kohen, *Or Sameah* (New York, 1946), *Korban Pesah*, 1:8.

253. Maimonides writes similarly in a number of other places. See Twersky, *Introduction*, pp. 20ff.

254. See also *Ma'aseh ha-Korbanot* 10:8, *Korban Pesah* 8:15, 10:14, where, with regard to sacrifices and midnight vs. daybreak, Maimonides explicitly notes the difference between Torah and rabbinic law.

rabbinic literature even though it is not exactly in accord with the settled halakhah. But this case is from *Sefer ha-Mitzvot*;[255] Maimonides, in explaining his approach, specifically distinguishes between this work, whose purpose is to provide general knowledge about the commandments, and the *Mishneh Torah*, whose purpose is to provide the correct halakhah.[256] Furthermore, in the case of *Korban Pesah* 1:8, Maimonides' omission of the time until which the sacrifice may be burnt has no didactic value. It certainly seems incorrect to posit, as Binyamin Ze'ev Benedikt does, that because the main point of this halakhah is stated correctly, Maimonides did not regard it as necessary to also cite correctly a secondary point that is recorded properly elsewhere in the *Mishneh Torah*.[257] Would not such an approach make a mockery of Maimonides' careful editing, since it would mean that any time there is a secondary halakhah there is no reason for Maimonides to cite it accurately?[258] Benedikt's approach also begs the question: Why would Maimonides diverge from the halakhah here, as it would have been just as easy for him to record the correct practice? Certainly, if one assumes that Maimonides intentionally recorded a false halakhah, one must provide a very good reason for him to have done so. Along these lines, it strikes me as very unlikely that the proper way to explain a seeming contradiction in the *Mishneh Torah* is, as R. Joseph Karo argues, by positing that Maimonides allowed himself to be less than careful in his language in one halakhah, on the assumption that the reader would understand that it should be explained in accordance with the apparently contradictory halakhah.[259] A similar criticism was actually lodged against R. Hayyim Soloveitchik by R. Abraham Isaiah Karelitz, the *Hazon Ish*.[260]

---

255. Neg. com. 321. There are undoubtedly other examples as well. See Kafih in his edition of *Sefer ha-Mitzvot*, p. 55 n. 50; Rabinovitch, *Yad Peshutah, Zemanim* (1), p. 787; Binyamin Ze'ev Benedikt, *Ha-Rambam le-lo Setiyah min ha-Talmud* (Jerusalem, 1985), pp. 123ff.

256. *Teshuvot ha-Rambam*, no. 310.

257. *Ha-Rambam*, p 25.

258. Cf. R. Moses Feinstein, *Iggerot Moshe* (Bnei Brak, 1985), *Hoshen Mishpat* 2, no. 69: ודברי הבל הם לומר שהרמב"ם לא דק וכתב טעם שקר שליכא כלל (CR).

259. *Kesef Mishneh, Na'arah Betulah* 2:17: וצריך לדחוק שסמך שם על מה שכתב כאן.

260. *Gilyonot* to *Ma'akhalot Asurot* 4:3 (printed in the back of the standard edition of *Hiddushei Rabbenu Hayyim ha-Levi*): כפי המקובל בידינו, אין להעמים דברים שהם בבחינת עיקר חסר מן הספר, שבעלי המסורה שקדו שהבאים אחריהם יבינו דבריהם באר היטב ומבחינה זו יפלא, איך יתכן שהר"ם איירי בנבילה מחיים ויכחד תחת לשונו הדבר וכאילו מכוין להעלים מהלומדים כונתו.

While the academic scholar must consider all conceivable solutions to problems such as this, he must also be open to the possibility that the halakhah in *Korban Pesah* was a short-lived assumption, a careless formulation, or even a copyist's error, and had Maimonides been asked about it, he would have acknowledged it as such and instructed his interlocutor to correct his text, as he did on other occasions.[261] As far as we know, Maimonides was not asked about this, so we can only speculate. Yet before this approach is dismissed out of hand, consider what would have happened had Maimonides not been asked, or had the responsa not survived, concerning the other difficulties regarding which he told his interlocutors to correct their texts. Since there is very little manuscript tradition—in a couple of cases, none at all—that reflects these responsa of Maimonides, post-Maimonideans would have had no way of knowing the truth, and the commentators would have struggled to come up with solutions. How many such texts requiring correction are there of which we are unaware?

In order to remove any confusion, let me restate my position. The academic scholar is well advised to examine the available commentaries to find answers to perplexities such as this. It can't be stressed enough that the traditional commentators, whose knowledge of the *Mishneh Torah* is so all encompassing, are an invaluable resource to any academic study of Maimonides. Their scholarship is not of the sort that is recorded on note cards "stored in boxes made for this purpose,"[262] and it stands ready to call attention to missed sources and nuances in the text. Use of these commentaries has been facilitated by the index of such writings on every halakhah in the *Mishneh Torah*, published by Makhon Halakhah u-Verur Halakhah in Jerusalem.[263] However, when the best the traditional commentaries can come up

---

261. See *Teshuvot ha-Rambam*, nos. 287, 302, 316, 354, 433.

262. Weinberg, *Kitvei ha-Gaon*, vol. 1, p. 191. See also Weinberg, *Seridei Esh* (Jerusalem, 1977), vol. 4, p. 250, where, in the same fashion, he contrasts the knowledge of R. Isaac Halevy and academic talmudists.

263. *Mafteah le-Ferushim al Mishneh Torah le-ha-Rambam* (Jerusalem, 1995). The most recent update of this book is found at www.halachabrurah.org. I recall how pleased my late teacher, Prof. Isadore Twersky, was when I showed him this work.

with is that Maimonides recorded an incorrect halakhah because he assumed the reader would know that this is only the biblical law, I think the academic scholar must look elsewhere. The contradiction between *Ma'aseh ha-Korbanot* (and *Temidin u-Musafin*) and *Korban Pesah* is, I think, a good example of where the academic scholar might feel comfortable in assuming that the divergence is due to Maimonides changing his mind and neglecting to correct the opposing text(s), or that *Korban Pesah* is a careless formulation or even a copyist's error. None of these answers satisfy, but they are more faithful to Maimonides' description of the purpose of his Code than positing that he would knowingly record an incorrect halakhah.

Let me offer one final example, also a famous case. In *Ma'akhalot Asurot* 9:3–4, Maimonides writes:

> According to the Torah, the prohibition applies only to the meat of a clean *behemah* [264] boiled in the milk of a clean *behemah*, as it is said, *Thou shalt not seethe a kid in its mother's milk* (Ex. 23:19). . . . Meat of a *hayah* and bird cooked in the milk of a *behemah* or of a *hayah* is not forbidden to be eaten according to the Torah, and for that reason both the cooking and the benefiting are permitted. The eating thereof is, however, forbidden on the authority of the Scribes.

Yet in *Mamrim* 2:9, Maimonides writes:

> Since the court is authorized to issue decrees prohibiting what is permitted and the prohibition is binding upon succeeding generations; and since it is empowered to permit provisionally what is forbidden in Scripture, how are we to understand the scriptural injunction *Thou shalt not add thereto, nor diminish from it* (Deut. 13:1)? [It is to be understood as an admonition] not to add to the precepts of the Torah nor to take any precept away from it. . . . To elucidate this point: The Bible says: *Thou shalt not seethe a kid in its mother's milk* (Ex. 23:19). We have it on tradition that this verse prohibits the cooking or eating of flesh with milk, be it the flesh of a *behemah* or of a *hayah*. . . . Should the court permit the flesh of a *hayah* with milk, it would be taking away [from the commands of the Torah].

---

264. A *behemah* is a domesticated animal, and a *hayah* is a wild animal.

In *Ma'akhalot Asurot* Maimonides says that it is permitted to cook meat of a *hayah* in milk and there is a rabbinic prohibition forbidding its consumption, while in *Mamrim* he says that there is a Torah prohibition forbidding both the cooking and eating of it. As I mentioned, this is a famous problem. R. Levi ben Habib,[265] R. Joseph Karo,[266] R. Abraham di Boton,[267] R. David Ibn Zimra,[268] and R. Samuel de Medina[269] claim that since, in *Mamrim*, Maimonides was trying to best illustrate a principle, he was prepared to use an example that is not in accord with the halakhah, and that contradicts what he writes elsewhere. Di Boton states that "we are forced to explain thus, and there is apparently no other way." Among modern scholars, this approach was also adopted by Benedikt[270] and Levinger,[271] and is akin to what Maimonides terms the fifth cause for contradictions in the Introduction to the *Guide*.[272] Although this certainly solves the immediate problem, it opens a host of others, for it means that the *Mishneh Torah* contains halakhically incorrect material whose purpose is didactic. Couldn't Maimonides find an example that was in accord with the halakhah? Despite what di Boton writes, is there really no other way to explain the contradiction?

The approach mentioned in the previous paragraph would be problematic if it was simply an instance of Maimonides using an example for illustrative purposes that is not in accord with the halakhah. Yet in this case, we even have an internal halakhic contradiction in the *Mishneh Torah*. I find it most unlikely that Maimonides would consciously allow such a thing given his intention in writing his

---

265. *She'elot u-Teshuvot ha-Ralbah*, no. 87.

266. *Kesef Mishneh, Mamrim*, 2:9.

267. *Lehem Mishneh, Mamrim*, 2:9. He offers an alternative explanation in his commentary to *Ma'akhalot Asurot*, ad loc.

268. Commentary to *Mamrim*, ad loc., *She'elot u-Teshuvot ha-Radbaz*, vol. 6, no. 2141.

269. *She'elot u-Teshuvot Maharashdam* (Lemberg, 1862), *Orah Hayyim* no. 2.

270. *Ha-Rambam*, pp. 28ff.

271. *Darkhei ha-Mahashavah*, pp. 24–25. Levinger does not note any of the traditionalist scholars who earlier offered this explanation.

272. See Twersky, *Introduction*, p. 316.

Code, as stated in the Introduction to the *Mishneh Torah*.[273] In fact, contrary to di Boton, there is another way to explain the contradiction, and that is to assume that there was an element of carelessness on Maimonides' part, in that he did not establish complete halakhic unity throughout the *Mishneh Torah*. In this case, there is even some solid evidence to support this assumption.

In the first version of the Introduction to his *Commentary on the Mishnah*,[274] Maimonides stated that cooking and eating *hayah* in milk are biblical prohibitions. There is no didactic element here that could lead one to say that Maimonides was not precise with halakhic truth in order to make a larger point. Maimonides was explaining decrees of the Sages, and in doing so, he carefully distinguished between what the Torah prohibits and what the Sages forbid. As mentioned, this was in the first version of his *Commentary*, and he later crossed out "*hayah*" so that it agrees with *Ma'akhalot Asurot*. What this reveals is that Maimonides held this view at one time in his life; I assume, therefore, that the passage in *Mamrim* is an example of this early teaching. This makes much more sense than positing that Maimonides intentionally included an incorrect halakhah for didactic purposes.

In fact, it is likely that we should not even describe matters in terms of "early" vs. "late" teachings, since in his *Commentary on the Mishnah, Hullin 8:4*, Maimonides decides in accordance with what he later writes in *Ma'akhalot Asurot*, and there is no sign of a change in ruling in the manuscript (which is from Maimonides' own hand). In other words, Maimonides appears to have gone back and forth about the parameters and severity of this prohibition. Is it far-fetched to assume that when Maimonides finally corrected the Introduction to the *Commentary on the Mishnah*, he neglected the passage in *Mamrim*, at least for a while, and that the contradiction is a result of editor-

---

273. וראיתי לחבר דברים . . . <u>כולו בלשון ברורה</u> ודרך קצרה עד שתהא תורה שבעל פה כולה סדורה בפי הכל בלא קושיא ולא זה אומר בכה וזה אומר בכה, אלא <u>דברים ברורים קרובים נכונים</u> . . . עד שיהיו כל הדינין <u>גלוים לקטן ולגדול</u> . . . לפי שאדם קורא תורה שבכתב תחלה ואחר כך קורא בזה וידע ממנו תורה שבעל פה כולה ואינו צריך לקרות ספר אחר ביניהם. With reference to the last words quoted, if the reader of the *Mishneh Torah* does not need to refer to any other works, how would he even know that a certain halakhah is problematic, which in turn would lead him to conclude that it is only serving a didactic purpose?

274. P. 12 n. 91.

ial oversight?[275] I say "for a while," because we actually have the testimony of R. Joshua ha-Nagid, Maimonides' great-great-grandson, that in a copy of the *Mishneh Torah* from Maimonides' own hand,[276] the word "*hayah*" did not appear at all in *Mamrim*.[277] This means that Maimonides corrected this section as well.[278] This further illustrates that, contrary to all the authorities cited above, Maimonides did not intend a contradiction between *Ma'akhalot Asurot* and *Mamrim*, not even for didactic purposes.[279] I believe it also bolsters my assumption that any blatant contradictions in the *Mishneh Torah* were the result of careless or incomplete editing, and that Maimonides intended to correct such matters.

Maimonidean Scholarship: Some Methodological Issues

In discussing the need to study the *Mishneh Torah* in the context of all of Maimonides' writings, Isadore Twersky wrote:

> [This] does not mean automatic transfer from one work to another, but it does mean imposing limits upon speculation and hypothetical reconstruction when Maimonides makes explicit statements about his method, motivation or meaning. . . . Now in completely ahistorical and systematic study, transcending time, space, and personality, various statements of Maimonides, retractions or reformulations, may be treat-

---

275. Kafih claims that the use of the term "*hayah*" in *Ma'akhalot Asurot* 9:27 is a remnant from when *Ma'akhalot Asurot* also stated that a *hayah* cooked in milk is forbidden from the Torah, and that although 9:3–4 was corrected, Maimonides overlooked this text. See his commentary to *Ma'akhalot Asurot* 9:27. There is no manuscript evidence to support this supposition, and it is rejected by Yitzhak Sheilat, *Hakdamot ha-Rambam* (Jerusalem, 1992), p. 97 n. 13.

276. See *Teshuvot R. Yehoshua ha-Nagid*, no. 26 (p. 74), that all his citations are from this manuscript.

277. *Ibid.*, no. 45. R. Joseph Karo, *Avkat Rokhel* (Jerusalem, 1960), no. 38, and R. David Ibn Zimra, *She'elot u-Teshuvot ha-Radbaz*, vol. 5, no. 1382, also cite this version, with Karo specifically referring to R. Joshua's responsum and Ibn Zimra referring to a ספר שהוגה מספרו של הרב ז"ל (שהיה בחלב).

278. In this case as well, there is no manuscript tradition attesting to the change. Were it not for R. Joshua's responsum, the halakhah in *Mamrim* would simply be another "difficult Rambam."

279. After completing this section, I found that Ta-Shma made a number of the same points. See *Keneset Mehkarim*, vol. 2, pp. 324–325.

ed as so many competing, unrelated views. The early Maimonides and the later Maimonides need not be unified, may indeed be treated as individual, halakic or philosophic, personae. In the abstract and systematic categories of jurisprudence or metaphysics an earlier view may be more attractive or persuasive than the late one. Chronology or even author's preference are not binding considerations. Historically, however, the authentic and final Maimonidean view should be precisely identified, for his own judgment and assent are certainly determinative.[280]

Twersky is speaking historically, but the issue has also been debated in the ahistorical world of the traditional commentators and halakhists.[281] The question is: What does one do with a contradiction in Maimonides' works? From Twersky's perspective, one must assume that Maimonides' final statement represents the authentic Maimonidean position. Yet many traditionalists did not agree with this. I have already cited examples of those who believed that Maimonides' corrections to the *Mishneh Torah* were not to be granted the same authority as his original formulation. For the most part, these scholars were discussing issues of rabbinic interpretation rather than practical halakhah. In purely theoretical matters, they were prepared to defend Maimonides' first formulation, even after Maimonides himself had abandoned it. It is much less common to find one who was willing to decide a practical matter in accordance with the *Mishneh Torah* in the face of an explicit and authentic retraction; that is, when Maimonides tells his questioner to ignore what appears in the *Mishneh Torah*.[282] It is true that R. Abraham Maimonides quotes his father as

---

280. *Introduction*, pp. 93–94.

281. See Yaakov S. Spiegel, *Amudim be-Toledot ha-Sefer ha-Ivri: Ketivah ve-Ha'atakah* (Ramat Gan, 2005), pp. 275ff.

282. I have already referred to R. Solomon ben Adret, *She'elot u-Teshuvot ha-Rashba*, vol. 1, no. 4. Among more recent authorities who were prepared to ignore a retraction by Maimonides was the Vilna Gaon; see *Beur ha-Gra, Orah Hayyim* 301:42: האמת יורה דרכו שדברים הראשונים ברורים וקיימים ולא טעה כלל. See also R. Hayyim Soloveitchik's view as recorded in R. Moshe Sternbuch, *Teshuvot ve-Hanhagot* (Jerusalem, 1989), vol. 2, no. 49. In advancing his opinion, R. Hayyim ignored the fact that Maimonides retracted what he wrote in the *Mishneh Torah*. There is no doubt that R. Hayyim was aware of this retraction, since it is mentioned by a number of *rishonim* and recorded in *Kesef Mishneh, Tefillah* 7:17. This shows that R. Yaakov Hayyim Sofer is mistaken when he writes that the numerous discussions about whether we accept Maimonides' view in his Code or in his

saying that in contradictions between the *Mishneh Torah* and his other writings, one relies on the *Mishneh Torah*, for it is a more exacting work.[283] However, when Maimonides is known to have explicitly retracted a *Mishneh Torah* ruling, R. Abraham leaves no doubt that it must no longer be followed.[284]

The question of which Maimonidean work has primacy is an important one for halakhists, for there are a number of contradictions between the *Mishneh Torah* and the responsa—real contradictions, as opposed to Maimonides' occasional statements that the *Mishneh Torah* contains an error. Furthermore, it is often not clear which came first, the responsa or the *Mishneh Torah* (although one would be inclined to assume that it was the *Mishneh Torah*, since it was his fame as a halakhist that led people to ask him questions). To give an example, in the *Mishneh Torah*[285] Maimonides states that one cannot publicly read from a Sefer Torah that is *pasul*, yet in a responsum he says that one may.[286] A further example is that in the *Mishneh Torah* Maimonides writes: "Another decree of the Sages forbade the playing of musical instruments and the enjoyment of melody and song of any kind, on account of the destruction of the Temple. Even vocal singing over wine is forbidden, in accordance with the verse, *they drink not wine with a song* (Is. 24:9)."[287] Yet in a responsum Maimonides takes an even stricter position, forbidding all singing, even when not accompanied by wine and instruments.[288]

---

responsa are only applicable when we don't know what his final decision was, but when we do know this, all agree that it is the final ruling which binds us. See "Al Sefarim ve-Soferim," *Tzefunot* 19 (1993–1994), p. 77. Sofer's position is strange, since in his *Berit Yaakov* (Jerusalem, 1985), p. 306, he himself quotes the Vilna Gaon's comment referred to at the beginning of this note.

283. See *Ma'aseh Nissim* (Paris, 1867), no. 7 (p. 82).

284. See *Teshuvot R. Avraham*, no. 113, *Sefer ha-Maspik le-Ovdei ha-Shem*, ed. Dana (Ramat Gan, 1989), p. 199.

285. *Sefer Torah* 10:1.

286. *Teshuvot ha-Rambam*, no. 294.

287. *Ta'aniyot* 5:14.

288. *Teshuvot ha-Rambam*, no. 224. For an analysis of this responsum, see Boaz Cohen, *Law and Tradition in Judaism* (New York, 1959), ch. 8. For another contradiction, compare *Edut* 12:1 to *Teshuvot ha-Rambam*, no. 3. Regarding this last responsum, see S. H. Kook, *Iyyunim u-Mehkarim* (Jerusalem, 1959), vol. 1, p. 319.

There are halakhists who, in cases such as these, give primacy to the responsa over the *Mishneh Torah*, seeing the former as part of the real world and the *Mishneh Torah*, by comparison, as a somewhat theoretical construct. This is so despite the fact that Maimonides is absolutely clear in his Introduction to the *Mishneh Torah* that he regards his Code as the practical halakhic work *par excellence*. Thus, R. David Ibn Zimra states that if there is a contradiction between the responsa and the *Mishneh Torah*, preference is given to the responsa, since these rulings were actualized in the real world (*halakhah le-ma'aseh*).[289] He does not mean that the *Mishneh Torah* was not intended for practical application; rather, that when the question actually came up, Maimonides ruled differently. R. Naphtali Zvi Judah Berlin repeats this notion with reference to all *poskim*, positing that, when there is a contradiction between responsa and *pesakim*, the responsa have priority since they were written in response to actual cases. It is not merely a functional concern motivating Berlin, for he states that a certain divine assistance is present when one is issuing a practical halakhic ruling, as opposed to simply recording one's opinion in a code.[290]

On the other hand, R. Joseph Trani states that when it comes to Maimonides or any other figure who authored a book as well as responsa, the law as recorded in the book—either a code, as with Maimonides, or a halakhic compilation, as with R. Asher—always takes precedence and reflects the author's final view.[291] Since the author did not correct his book, we assume that the responsum is a one-time decision that is trumped by the book, which was the focus of a lifetime. According to Trani, it is not the nature of the book itself, as the author's greatest achievement, which gives it precedence; it is the assumption that this was his final word on the subject. However, if one is able to determine otherwise, one must follow the responsum. The inherent problem in Trani's approach is that there was no way for

---

289. *She'elot u-Teshuvot ha-Radbaz*, vol. 7, no. 25 (p. 11a).

290. *Meshiv Davar* (Jerusalem, 1994), vol. 1, no. 24.

291. *She'elot u-Teshuvot Maharit* (Lemberg, 1861), *Hoshen Mishpat* no. 7. See, similarly, R. Joseph Karo, *She'elot u-Teshuvot Beit Yosef* (Jerusalem, 1987), *dinei yibbum ve-halitzah*, no. 4: אפילו אם היה הרב עצמו ז"ל חותם באותה תשובה עצמה והיינו מכירים חתימתו היינו אומרי' בילדותו סבר הכי ובזקנותו דהיינו בחיבור הדר ביה.

him to be sure that his version of the *Mishneh Torah* was indeed
Maimonides' final word on any subject, as the work went through a
number of changes. Today, after we have collated numerous manuscripts and responsa, we have a better grasp of the different versions
of the *Mishneh Torah*. Yet there is still no reason to assume that a
responsum that contradicts even the final version of the *Mishneh Torah*
must precede it in time.[292]

While Trani's reason for preferring the *Mishneh Torah* is functional, others simply assume that the *Mishneh Torah* is decisive because of
its unquestioned standing as Maimonides' masterpiece.[293] The justification for this approach is provided by R. Dov Ber Anushiski, who
states that the *Mishneh Torah* is primary because it was written after
great thought, that is, it is his halakhic work *par excellence*. The responsa, he suggests, may have been written in a haphazard manner, and
without much care.[294] I think that this latter sentiment has been com-

---

292. As I mention, dating the responsa is often difficult. In this regard, see Kafih,
Commentary to *Sefer Ahavah*, p. 186, where he disputes with R. Abraham Maimonides
concerning one responsum (*Teshuvot ha-Rambam*, no. 313). R. Abraham regarded the
responsum as later than the *Mishneh Torah*, and thus a revision to the Code, while Kafih,
citing the Yemenite tradition, regards the responsum as prior to the *Mishneh Torah*. One
wonders how a Yemenite tradition, even one that goes back many hundreds of years, can
possibly be regarded as more trustworthy than R. Abraham, especially when R. Abraham
testifies that he heard this opinion *directly from his father*, and this was *after* the writing of
the *Mishneh Torah*. (R. Abraham wasn't born until 1186 and the *Mishneh Torah* was com-
pleted around 1180.) See *Sefer ha-Maspik*, p. 199. R. Abraham's testimony is quoted by R.
Aaron of Lunel, *Orhot Hayyim* (Jerusalem, 1956), *kiddush meyushav*, no. 1 (p. 24). Regarding
the issue under dispute (*kedushah de-yotzer* for an individual), see Ruth Langer, *To Worship
God Properly* (Cincinnati, 1998), pp. 224ff. For other examples where Kafih rejects R.
Abraham's testimony, see *Commentary on the Mishnah*, vol. 2, p. 108 n. 6, Kafih's commentary to *Sefer Ahavah*, pp. 700–701, *Sefer Zemanim* (2), pp. 333, 335. See also Oberlander,
"Iyyun," pp. 216ff. Cf. *Kesef Mishneh, Ishut* 1:2, where Karo rejects the testimony of R.
Abraham, and Kafih, Commentary *ad loc.*, finds this rejection quite strange. While I
believe that R. Abraham must be regarded as the most authoritative halakhic interpreter
of Maimonides, this does not mean that he was infallible. See, e.g., *Birkat Avraham*, no. 34
and *Teshuvot R. Avraham*, no. 114, where his explanation of Maimonides includes the
notion that the one reading the Scroll of Esther does not have to have in mind to fulfill
his religious obligation. Yet this is directly contradicted by Maimonides, *Megillah* 2:5.

293. I presume this is the reason R. Shlomo Zalman Auerbach prefers the *Mishneh
Torah*. See *Minhat Shlomo* (Jerusalem, 1986), vol 1, no. 37 (p. 203; CR).

294. *Matzav ha-Yashar*, vol. 2, p. 79 (Hebrew numerals). This text, and the one quoted above, p. 53 n. 225, were cited by Shraga Abramson in his notes to *Teshuvot ha-Rambam*,
vol. 4, pp. 51, 54. (Cf. Anushiski, *Matzav ha-Yashar*, vol. 2, pp. 22a–b, for another approach

mon among traditionalist scholars, many of whom devote their lives to the *Mishneh Torah*, but pretty much ignore the responsa, even as a tool to better understand the Code. For example, there is a tradition in the Soloveitchik family that R. Hayyim Soloveitchik did not "like" the twenty-four responsa of Maimonides to the sages of Lunel.[295] This is not surprising. These responsa were written by Maimonides in order to explain a number of rulings in the *Mishneh Torah*. Had he thought along the lines of R. Hayyim, we would have expected learned answers in accordance with the latter's analytic approach. Yet Maimonides gives short, non-analytic answers. In a number of these responsa, he tells the sages of Lunel that there are mistakes in their copy of the *Mishneh Torah*, or that he has abandoned his earlier opinion.[296]

According to the approach described in the previous paragraph, it appears that the *Mishneh Torah* has a life of its own, apart from its author, and can be explained without reference to Maimonides' own explanations in his responsa.[297] A good example of this is the many explanations that have been offered over the centuries for Maimonides' view of *"divrei sofrim."* Many of these explanations have been collected by J. J. Neubauer in his book *Ha-Rambam al Divrei Sofrim*.[298] There is no doubt that Neubauer is correct when he writes

---

to reduce the significance of Maimonides' responsa.) Anushiski's qualitative distinction between the *Mishneh Torah* and the responsa was raised as a possibility by R. Menahem Mendel Schneersohn, but he did not decide definitively. See *Kovetz Ginat ha-Melekh* (n.p., 1987), pp. 5–8. See also R. Mordekhai Winkler, *Levushei Mordekhai* (Budapest, 1928) third series, *Orah Hayyim* no. 15.

295. See Twersky, *Introduction*, p. 94 n. 171. (According to the version told to me by Prof. Haym Soloveitchik, it was R. Moses Soloveitchik who expressed himself this way.) R. Moses Sofer is said to have held a similar view, and is quoted as saying that while the *Mishneh Torah* was written with *ruah ha-kodesh*, this was not the case with the responsa to the sages of Lunel (or the *Guide*); see Aaron Marcus, *Keset ha-Sofer* (Cracow, 1912), p. 124a. To give another example, R. Moses Feinstein did not use the published collections of Maimonides' responsa (he does cite a few responsa that appear in *rishonim* and the *Kesef Mishneh*). Apparently, in his eyes, Maimonides' responsa did not have the same importance for practical halakhic decision-making as did other collections of responsa, such as those by R. Asher ben Jehiel and R. Solomon ben Adret. See also the responsum of R. Zvi Hirsch Grodzinski published in *Yeshurun* 2 (1997), p. 203.

296. See above, p. 64 n. 261.

297. See above pp. 54–55.

298. (Jerusalem, 1957).

that "the idea of explaining Maimonides in accordance with Maimonides himself remained foreign to the authors, the halakhic authorities. If, on rare occasion, we do find this tendency, it is no more than an isolated phenomenon" (p. 79).[299]

This approach—of reading the *Mishneh Torah* in what amounts to almost a historical vacuum—was a feature of R. Hayyim Soloveitchik's Brisker "school," which was always ahistorical in its orientation.[300] Not for naught was this approach criticized by such figures as the *Hazon Ish*[301] and R. Jehiel Jacob Weinberg. Weinberg wrote:

> While the ideas of R. Hayyim Soloveitchik are true from the standpoint of profound analysis, they are not always so from a historical standpoint, that is, with regard to the true meaning of Maimonides, whose

---

299. See also José Faur, *Iyyunim ba-Mishneh Torah le-ha-Rambam* (Jerusalem, 1978), p. 1. R. Moses Sofer, *She'elot u-Teshuvot Hatam Sofer*, vol. 7, no. 21, writes: ואם לא היתה זאת דעת הרמב"ם, מכל מקום אם הדברים אמתיים יש לנו לפסוק הדין כך, מפני הטעמים שכתבתי אני, רק שדרכינו בדור הזה לתלות באילן גדול (CR). R. Solomon ha-Kohen's responsum in R. Hayyim Berlin, *Nishmat Hayyim* (Bnei Brak, 2002), no. 67, quotes R. Hayyim of Volozhin as follows: שיש לומר פירוש בלשון הרמב"ם והשו"ע אם הוא עולה ע"פ ההלכה אף שבודאי לא כוונו לזה משום שרוח הקודש נזרקה על לשונם.

300. See my "The Brisker Method Reconsidered," *Tradition* 31 (Spring, 1997), pp. 78–102. For more on the Brisker method, see Moshe Lichtenstein, "What Hath Brisk Wrought: The Brisker Derekh Revisited," *Torah u-Madda Journal* 9 (2000), pp. 1–18; Shlomo Tikochinski, "Darkhei ha-Limud bi-Yeshivot Lita ba-Meah ha-Tesha Esreh" (unpublished masters dissertation, Hebrew University, 2004); Shai Akiva Wosner, "Hashivah Mishpatit bi-Yeshivot Lita ba-Re'i ha-Rav Shimon Shkop" (unpublished doctoral dissertation, Hebrew University, 2005), ch. 2.

301. See Lawrence Kaplan, "The Hazon Ish: Haredi Critic of Traditional Orthodoxy," in Jack Wertheimer, ed., *The Uses of Tradition* (New York, 1992), p. 155. Kaplan quotes one observer's interesting remark, that the *Hazon Ish* judged R. Hayyim's interpretations of Maimonides "by the wrong criterion; he wanted to determine if they were true!" See also Binyamin Brown, "Ha-Hazon Ish: Halakhah, Emunah ve-Hevrah bi-Fesakav ha-Boltim be-Eretz Yisrael (5693–5714)" (unpublished doctoral dissertation, Hebrew University, 2000), pp. 79ff., appendix, pp. 28, 45ff. R. Hayyim's explanations found a defender in R. Hayyim Dov Ber Gulevski (a grandson of R. Simhah Zelig Rieger, the *dayan* of Brisk), *Lahat ha-Herev ha-Mithapahat* (Brooklyn, 1976). See also the anonymous volumes of *Hiddushei Batra al Hiddushei R. Hayyim ha-Levi* (Jerusalem, 1978–1995). In order to answer one of the criticisms of the *Hazon Ish*, R. Shlomo Fisher points to a source in Ibn Ezra's Torah commentary. See *Derashot Beit Yishai* (Jerusalem, 2004), p. 400. Quite apart from the unproven assumption that R. Hayyim studied Ibn Ezra, I have no doubt that neither R. Hayyim nor the *Hazon Ish* regarded him as an authoritative source. I have already noted that R. Hayyim ignored Maimonides' responsum to the sages of Lunel concerning *Nizkei Mamon* 4:4. In contrast, the *Hazon Ish*, *Gilyonot* to *Nizkei Mamon*

way of study was different than that of R. Hayyim Soloveitchik. This does not detract from the value of this intellectual genius who is worthy of being called a "new Rambam," but not always as an interpreter of Maimonides. Yet R. Hayyim, by means of his brilliance, arrived at the same conclusions Maimonides reached through his own method of study.[302]

Returning to the issue of determining the halakhah when there is a contradiction between a scholar's halakhic composition or code and his responsa, this is, of course, a problem not unique to Maimonides. It applies to all halakhists who authored these different types of work, and has been discussed in detail with regard to both R. Asher ben Jehiel and R. Joseph Karo (and the logic of these discussions has been transferred to the case of Maimonides). For example, R. Judah ben Asher, when asked about a contradiction in his father's writings between a responsum and his halakhic composition, gave precedence to the latter, for it was written last.[303] His brother, R. Jacob ben Asher, offers the same justification.[304] Yet in a responsum, R. Hayyim Joseph David Azulai writes that responsa have precedence since they are examples of actual case law.[305]

To complicate matters, and to show how difficult it is to find consistency when dealing with prolific halakhists (a point we must also bear in mind when dealing with Maimonides), I must note the follow-

---

4:4, 11, *Hazon Ish: Hoshen Mishpat* (Bnei Brak, 1965), *Bava Kamma* 7:7, sees no reason not to accept Maimonides' responsum.

302. *Seridei Esh* (Jerusalem, 1977), vol. 2, no. 144. See my *Between the Yeshiva World and Modern Orthodoxy* (London, 1999), pp. 194–195. This passage, and a number of other relevant texts from Weinberg, are found in the Hebrew appendix. For a strong criticism of R. Hayyim which has not been noted in the scholarly literature, see R. Yaakov Avigdor, *Haskel ve-Yadoa* (Mexico City, 1962), pp. 299–317.

303. *Zikhron Yehudah* (Berlin, 1846), no. 15. This responsum is quoted in *Beit Yosef, Hoshen Mishpat* 110:11. In *She'elot u-Teshuvot Beit Yosef, dinei kidushin,* no. 2, Karo also says that the *pesakim* of R. Asher ben Jehiel take precedence over his responsa.

304. *Tur, Hoshen Mishpat* 72:35. Regarding R. Judah ben Asher's view, see R. Hayyim Benveniste, *Keneset ha-Gedolah* (Jerusalem, 1988), *Hoshen Mishpat* 72, *hagahat ha-Tur*, no. 68. Regarding R. Jacob ben Asher, see Spiegel, *Amudim*, p. 279. See also R. Hayyim Palache, *Kol ha-Hayyim* (Izmir, 1874), 10:57 (with reference to R. Asher ben Jehiel): דהפסקים עיקר יען הפסקים הם כולו אורייתא דיליה שחיברו בכונה מכוונת לברר הדינים לפי מה שהוא הלכה פסוקה, אז עדיף כחו יותר מתשובות שהיה [!] לפרקים.

305. *Hayyim Sha'al*, vol. 1, no. 74:11. Azulai adds, however, that with regard to Karo this might not be so, for the *Shulhan Arukh* has a special binding status.

ing: The same Azulai, in his commentary on the *Shulhan Arukh*, discusses Maimonides, and here he states just the opposite; namely, that the halakhic composition has precedence.[306] We must therefore ask which work of Azulai, his responsa or his halakhic commentary, is to be preferred?

When dealing with contradictions between Maimonides' responsa and the *Mishneh Torah*, there has often been a concern that perhaps certain responsa are not authentic. As R. Solomon ben Simeon Duran put it, with regard to one such contradiction: "How can we set aside the explicit teaching from the mouth of Maimonides in his great Code based on what appears in a responsum bearing his name, which he might or might not have written."[307] R. Joseph Karo also cites this concern in rejecting Maimonides' responsa when they conflict with the *Mishneh Torah*.[308]

R. Joseph Kafih went so far as to deny Maimonides' authorship of any of the responsa to the sages of Lunel.[309] Prior to this, R. Solomon of Chelm denied the authenticity of some of these responsa,[310] and the Yemenite scholar, R. Yahya al Abyad (1864-1935), anticipated Kafih's view that they are all forgeries.[311] As has already been pointed out by many, any attempt to impugn the authenticity of these responsa is completely without basis, and there is no need to rehash the arguments here. Let me simply note that Maimonides' own son, R.

---

306. *Birkei Yosef, Orah Hayyim* 118:2.

307. *She'elot u-Teshuvot ha-Rashbash*, ed. Sobel (Jerusalem, 1998), no. 11.

308. *She'elot u-Teshuvot Beit Yosef, dinei goy masiah lefi tumo*, no. 5, *dinei yibbum ve-halitzah*, no. 4. In the last source, Karo makes the following amazing statement: ולכן כשנראה איזו תשובה בשם אדם גדול שאין הדעת נוחה הימנה יש לנו רשות לומר שלא אמרה הגדול ההוא מעולם.

309. "She'elot Hakhmei Lunel u-Teshuvot ha-Rambam—Kelum Mekoriyot Hen?" *Sefer Zikaron le-ha-Rav Yitzhak Nissim* (Jerusalem, 1985), vol. 2, pp. 235–252. Kafih has no real proofs and simply follows the approach set out by Karo (see previous note) that if a responsum seemingly makes no sense, this is reason enough to question its authenticity. See the responses to Kafih by Yitzhak Sheilat, *ibid.*, pp. 253ff.; Shlomo Zalman Havlin in *Alei Sefer* 12 (1986), p. 14; Ta-Shma, *Keneset Mehkarim*, pp. 321, 325–327; and R. Eliezer Waldenberg, *Tzitz Eliezer* (Jerusalem, 2007), vol. 18, no. 20:4. I vividly recall how, in one of his graduate seminars, Prof. Isadore Twersky expressed his great disdain for Kafih's position.

310. See *Mirkevet ha-Mishneh, Shabbat* 19:24, *Nizkei Mamon* 4:4.

311. See Kafih, Commentary to *Sefer Ahavah*, p. 31.

Abraham, discusses a number of these responsa,[312] and this alone is certainly sufficient to squelch even the most ingenious objections. I must also point out that at the conclusion of his letter to Samuel Ibn Tibbon, Maimonides uses the uncommon expression ישע יקרב.[313] This same expression is also found at the conclusion of his responsa to the sages of Lunel[314] and the conclusion of his Letter on Astrology,[315] both of which pre-date the letter to Ibn Tibbon. According to Kafih, who also denies the authenticity of the Letter on Astrology,[316] we must assume that all this is a coincidence.

From here I turn to the question of Maimonidean originality. In this area, as well, I think that we can see a divergence between the academic approach and the traditional approach—not all traditionalists, to be sure, but enough of them that it is worth calling attention to. From the standpoint of modern scholarship, showing the originality

---

312. *Birkat Avraham*, nos. 40–43. See also *Milhamot ha-Shem*, ed. Margaliot (Jerusalem, 1959), p. 52.

313. *Iggerot ha-Rambam*, vol. 2, p. 554. Prior to Maimonides, the expression was used by R. Nathan ben Abraham (d. circa 1053), *av beit din* of the Palestinian academy in Jerusalem. See El. Dov Shapira, "Mikhtav me-Ramleh Lirushalayim," in Michael Ish-Shalom, *et al.*, eds., *Yerushalayim* 4 (1953), p. 119. R. Abraham Maimonides also used the expression, probably picking it up from his father. See *Teshuvot Rabbenu Avraham*, nos. 3, 75, 107, 124, *Milhamot ha-Shem*, p. 129. For one of Maimonides' contemporaries who used the expression, see *Teshuvot ha-Rambam*, vol. 2, p. 490.

314. *Teshuvot ha-Rambam*, vol. 3, p. 43, *Iggerot ha-Rambam*, vol. 2, p. 510.

315. *Iggerot ha-Rambam*, vol. 2, p. 490.

316. See *Iggerot ha-Rambam*, vol. 2, p. 476 n. 6. Davidson has recently referred to this work as being "of questionable authenticity." See *Moses Maimonides*, pp. 119, 494ff. For an earlier attempt to deny the authenticiy of one passage in the Letter, see Moses Hayyim Ephraim Bloch, "Iggeret ha-Rambam le-Hakhmei Marseilles," *Ha-Pardes* 34 (April 1960), pp. 39–42, *id.*, "Od al Teshuvat ha-Rambam le-Hakhmei Tzarfat," *Ha-Doar*, 17 Shevat 5721, pp. 230–231 (and see the response of David S. Shapiro, *Ha-Pardes* [July 1960], pp. 33–34, *id.*, *Orahim* [Jerusalem, 1977], pp. 76–79). Regarding other Maimonidean works whose authenticity has been questioned, see J. L. Teicher, "Maimonides' Letter to Joseph b. Jehudah—A Literary Forgery," *JJS* 1 (1948), pp. 35–54, and *id.*, "Ziyyuf Sifruti: Ma'amar Tehiyat ha-Metim," *Melilah* 1 (1944), pp. 81–92 (and see the devastating response by Isaiah Sonne, "A Scrutiny of the Charges of Forgery against Maimonides' 'Letter on Resurrection,'" *PAAJR* 21 [1952], pp. 110–117); Lea Naomi Goldfeld, *Moses Maimonides' Treatise on Resurrection: An Inquiry into Its Authenticity* (New York, 1986); Herbert A. Davidson, "The Authenticity of Works Attributed to Maimonides," in Ezra Fleischer, *et al.*, eds., *Me'ah She'arim: Studies in Medieval Jewish Spiritual Life in Memory of Isadore Twersky* (Jerusalem, 2001), pp. 111–133, *id.*, *Moses Maimonides*, pp. 313ff., 470ff., 501ff. In addition to the Letter on Astrology, Davidson casts doubt on five other works, including *Iggeret ha-Shemad* and *Milot ha-Higayon*.

of Maimonides' formulations in the *Mishneh Torah* remains an important goal. This is not to say that modern scholarship has not made any contributions to the age-old quest for rabbinic sources of passages in the *Mishneh Torah*. There is no question that Maimonides made use of rabbinic works that were not available to the standard traditional commentators, a point recognized by them.[317] Since, until recently, these texts were published almost exclusively by scholars with an academic orientation, this gave them the opportunity to contribute in this area.[318]

In general, it is obvious that the further away from Maimonides we get, the less likely it is that we can actually point to new sources, not noted by earlier scholars, that serve as the basis for Maimonides' rulings. Most of the true sources were already noted by the standard commentaries, and more recent scholars have often pointed to texts with only a limited connection to Maimonides' words, or to midrashim of which Maimonides was unaware. Yet there remained sources that the standard commentaries missed, even when these were found in classical rabbinic literature. For example, in *Teshuvah* 3:14,[319] Maimonides includes "he who glorifies himself by disgracing his friend" in a list of twenty-four who do not have a share in the world to come. R. Joseph Karo wrote that he did not know the origin of this halakhah.[320] A glance at the Frankel edition of the *Mishneh Torah* reveals that since Karo's time, many scholars have pointed to the Jerusalem Talmud, *Hagigah* 2:1, and *Bereishit Rabbah* 1:5, where this exact statement is found.[321]

---

317. *Migdal Oz*, *Sanhedrin* 8:2 writes, with some exaggeration, of ספרים ישרים קדמונים וישנים כאשר הגיעו ליד ר"מ ז"ל מימות בית שני.

318. See, e.g., Michael Guttmann, "Zur Quellenkritik des Mischneh Thora," *MGWJ* 79 (1935), pp. 148–159. R. Menahem M. Kasher, whose *Ha-Rambam ve-ha-Mekhilta de-Rashbi* is devoted to identifying sources of the *Mishneh Torah* in a newly published rabbinic work, cannot be easily categorized. While he certainly approached classical rabbinic texts from a traditionalist perspective, his wide-ranging knowledge of both recently published texts and modern scholarship was, until recently, quite uncommon among traditionalist scholars.

319. See also *Deot* 6:3.

320. *Kesef Mishneh*, ad loc.

321. In *Deot* 6:3, Karo gives the source as *Avot* ch. 2. Yet what appears in *Avot* is המלבין פני חבירו, not המתכבד בקלון חבירו, and these two are listed separately in *Teshuvah* 3:14.

As mentioned, modern scholarship is focused, to a large extent, on showing the originality of the *Mishneh Torah*. To quote one illustrative example, Gerald J. Blidstein has noted that there are *"thousands of instances where, rooted in the text, Maimonides interprets from his own perspective."*[322] While traditionalist commentators have not been as quick to see originality as modern scholars, and would prefer to assume that a Maimonidean formulation has a rabbinic source, they too have recognized that the originality found in the *Mishneh Torah* exceeds the numerous instances where Maimonides mentions that he is offering his own opinion.[323] Thus, it was traditionalist commentators who long ago recognized that Maimonides would sometimes substitute his own biblical proof texts for the ones offered by the Sages, or even use a proof text offered by a sage whose opinion is rejected in the Talmud.[324]

---

322. "Where Do We Stand in the Study of Maimonidean Halakhah?" in Isadore Twersky, ed., *Studies in Maimonides* (Cambridge, 1990), p. 5 (emphasis added).

323. For example, in *Evel* 14:7, Maimonides writes: "It appears to me." He does not include this expression immediately prior to this, in 14:5, and yet R. David Ibn Zimra has no compunctions about writing, with regard to this halakhah: ורבינו חידש טעם אחר לפי בקיאותו בחלאים. In his commentary to *Ishut* 2:17, *Lehem Mishneh* offers the following possibility to explain a troubling Maimonidean formulation: ואולי הסברא הכריח לרבינו לומר כן. See, similarly, *Lehem Mishneh*, *Talmud Torah* 1:12, *Shabbat* 2:16, 15:14, *Sanhedrin* 2:7, *Mamrim* 3:8. Many more such comments can easily be cited. See, e.g., Twersky, *Introduction*, p. 474 n. 293; R. Solomon of Chelm, *Mirkevet ha-Mishneh*, *Shabbat* 11:17 (CR); R. Joseph Raphael Hazzan, *Hikrei Lev* (Jerusalem, 1998), *Orah Hayyim* no. 16 (p. 91); R. Jehiel Mikhel Epstein, *Arukh ha-Shulhan, Orah Hayyim* 578:2: ודע שדין זה . . . לא נתבאר בש"ס בשום מקום רק הרמב"ם מסברא דנפשיה קאמר (CR); Feinstein, *Iggerot Moshe, Orah Hayyim* 4, no. 77 (CR). Let me point to an example which, as far as I know, has not been noted by modern scholars seeking to discover societal influences on Maimonidean halakhah. *Tefillah* 5:4 reads: תקון הגוף כיצד . . . ומניח ידיו על לבו כפותין הימנית על השמאלית. R. Joel Sirkes, *Bayit Hadash, Orah Hayyim* 95:3, rejects Karo's suggested source for this (*Beit Yosef, ibid.*, and see also *Kesef Mishneh, Tefillah* 5:4), and writes: נראה שכך היה מנהג מקומו כשמדברים עם המלך. Sirkes' assumption is shared by R. Shneur Zalman of Lyady, *Shulhan Arukh ha-Rav* (Vilna, 1905), *Orah Hayyim* 95:4 (CR).

324. See Ha-Kohen, *Yad Malakhi*, p. 182b; Kasher, *Ha-Rambam*, pp. 27–28; Palache, *Kol ha-Hayyim*, p. 22b; Kanievsky, *Kiryat Melekh*, p. 287; Sofer, *Berit Ya'akov*, p. 228 n. 2; Blidstein, "Where Do We Stand," p. 7 n. 16; Guttel, "Derekh," p. 127 n. 86; R. Pinhas Zevihi, *Mi-Zahav u-mi-Paz* (Jerusalem, 1993), pp. 179–180. See also David Sykes, "Setiyotav shel ha-Rambam mi-Mekorotav be-Halakhah," *Dine Israel* 13–14 (1986–1988), pp. 115ff.; Yitzhak Gilat, *Perakim be-Hishtalshelut ha-Halakhah* (Ramat Gan, 1992), pp.

This is all well known, and there is no need to discuss it further. Yet it is not so commonly known that there is a strand of traditional scholarship that completely denies any substantive Maimonidean originality in the *Mishneh Torah*, regarding the work as nothing more than a great summation of rabbinic teachings. In other words, while Maimonides' input can be seen by which rabbinic opinion he chooses to codify when there is no clear guidance in earlier sources, everything that actually appears in the *Mishneh Torah* is believed to have an explicit source in earlier rabbinic literature. The only exception to this is when Maimonides states that he is offering his own opinion. In fact, this view can actually be supported by Maimonides himself, for he says as much in his letter to R. Pinhas of Alexandria.[325]

The following are some quotations that testify to this approach.[326]

382ff. In the *Commentary on the Mishnah*, one also finds that Maimonides prefers his own biblical proof text to that offered in the Talmud. See *Commentary*, vol. 3, p. 88 n. 23; Guttel, "Derekh," p. 126. For two commentaries—not mentioned in the sources noted above—that understand Maimonides to be creating his own *derashot*, see *Maggid Mishneh*, *Yibbum ve-Halitzah* 2:6: ורבינו פירש פשט הפסוק דרך המדרש; R. Menahem Nahum Trebitsch's commentary to *Yibbum ve-Halitzah* 6:14 (found in the Frankel edition): ובגמרא מצינו דרשא אחרת ורבינו הוסיף דרש זה מדעתו. (With reference to *yibbum*, see also *Commentary on the Mishnah*, vol. 3, p. 10 n. 14, for a *derashah* whose origin is unknown.)

325. *Iggerot ha-Rambam*, vol. 2, pp. 442–443: וזה שאמרת שתמצא בחבור דברים הנסתרים, מפני שהם בלא ראיה, ואין דעתך צלולה, לא היה לך לומר כן אלא אלו היו בחבור דברים שהוצאתי אותן מפלפולי ודעתי, וכתבתי אותן סתם, ולא הבאתי עליהן ראיה, וזה לא עשיתי אותו מעולם. גלה אזן חכמתך ודע, שכל הדברים הסתם שבו תלמוד ערוך הוא בפרוש בבבלי או בירושלמי או מספרא וספרי או משנה ערוכה או תוספתא. על אלו סמכתי ומהן חברתי. ודבר שהוא מתשובת הגאונים אמר בפרוש הורו הגאונים או תקנת אחרונים היא וכו' וכיוצא בזה. ודבר שהוא מפלפולי אמר בפרוש יראה לי שהדבר כך וכך או אני אומר מכאן אתה למד שהדבר כך וכך.

326. Most of these sources are cited in Sofer, "Al Soferim u-Sefarim," pp. 79–81, and R. Pinhas Zevihi, *Ateret Paz* (Jerusalem, 1995), vol. 2, pp. 399–400. The following additional sources were provided to me by Chaim Rapoport: R. Joel Sirkes, *She'elot u-Teshuvot Bayit Hadash* (New York, 1966), no. 18; R. Hayyim Shabbetai, *Torat Hayyim* (Jerusalem, 2004), vol. 1, no. 73; R. Yom Tov Lipmann Heller, *Tosafot Yom Tov, Shekalim* 2:1; R. Zvi Hirsch Ashkenazi, *Hakham Zvi* (Jerusalem, 2000), no. 77; Fleckeles, *Teshuvah me-Ahavah*, vol. 1, nos. 43, 198; Sofer, *She'elot u-Teshuvot Hatam Sofer*, vol. 2, *Yoreh Deah* no. 92, vol. 4, *Even ha-Ezer* 2, no. 2. Many other relevant sources can be found by searching the Bar Ilan Responsa CD-Rom using the phrase דרכו של הרמב"ם.

R. Shem Tov Ibn Gaon: כתבתי כמה פעמים כי ר"ם ז"ל אין עסק בחבור
משנה תורה זה אלא במה שמפורש בתלמוד אבל לא מה שנוכל לדקדק מן
התלמוד.327

Elsewhere, he writes: כי ר"ם ז"ל לא כתב במשנה התורה הזה מה שהוא
מתוך דקדוק אלא מה שהוא תלמוד ערוך ובלשונו השכילנו מאין הוציא דיניו
ופסקיו.328

R. Israel Isserlein: דכבר ידעינן דהרמב"ם כתב כל פסקיו רק מסוגיית
התלמוד לפי פשוטו ולא מתוך הדקדוקים כמו התוספות ושאר גאונים.329

R. Levi ben Habib: ככה דרכו ז"ל לכתוב הדינין כאשר הם בתלמוד אמנם
הדיני' הנלמדים מדיוק דברי התלמוד מניחו ועל המעיין ללומדם מדיוק דבריו.330

R. Samuel Kalai: שדרך הר"ם ז"ל בספ' משנה תורה שלא להביא רק
הדין הנמצא בגמרא מפורש.331

R. Elijah Alfandari: שהרמב"ם ז"ל קרא שם הספר הלזה משנה תורה מפני
שהוא מעתיק בו התורה כמו שנתנה מפי החכמי' בעלי המשנ' והבריתא
והתוספתא ומפי בעלי התלמוד, ומה שמצא מדברי' העתיק בצביונו ובקומתו
בלתי שינוי ותמורה כאשר יתאמת כל זה אצל הרגיל לקרות בספר זה וכמו
שכבר הודיעו לנו הבאים אחריו אשר קדמונו ועמדו עליו ופירשו את
דבריו.332

R. Abraham Yitzhaki: דאטו רבינו אמורא הוא לפרש שיטת הש"ס
כרצונו, ומעולם לא שמענו דמלאכת הרב ז"ל אינה אלא להעתיק דברים הנאמרי'
בש"ס לא לדחות פשט דברי הש"ס.333

---

327. *Migdal Oz, Ishut* 2:19. Blidstein, "Where Do We Stand," p. 11, cites this passage and comments: "This goes rather too far, as Maimonides frequently produces rulings based on inference and extrapolation." Let me point to one example that I have recently come across. Maimonides, *Milah* 2:1, writes: "The best method of fulfilling the precept is to use an iron instrument." *Kesef Mishneh* does not point to any source for this halakhah; but the Vilna Gaon, *Beur ha-Gra, Yoreh Deah* 264:17, commenting on the same language in the *Shulhan Arukh*, cites Mishnah *Shabbat* 19:1: "R. Eliezer said further, they may cut wood [on the Sabbath] to make charcoal to forge an instrument of iron [i.e., a circumcision knife]." According to the Vilna Gaon, Maimonides inferred that iron is the preferred instrument because, in an entirely different context, we see that it was used in rabbinic times and that its use impacted the Sabbath laws. This sort of inference, which is not prefaced by Maimonides informing the reader that he is now offering his own opinion, obviously contradicts the conservative approach which rejects the notion that Maimonides operates in this fashion.

328. *Migdal Oz, Ishut* 2:15.

329. *Terumat ha-Deshen* (Jerusalem, 1991), *Pesakim u-Khetavim*, no. 20.

330. *She'elot u-Teshuvot ha-Ralbah*, no. 33.

331. *Mishpetei Shmuel*, no. 91.

332. *Seder Eliyahu Rabbah ve-Zuta* (Constantinople, 1719), p. 47b.

333. *Zera Avraham* (Constantinople, 1732), vol. 1, p. 129b.

הלא ידוע שהרי"ף והרמב"ם אין מעתיקין :R. Aryeh Leib Gunzberg
אלא דברים המפורשים בש"ס בהדי'. אבל אין דרכם לכתוב כל חדושי דינים שיש
להוכיח מתוך דקדוקים ופלפולים מן הש"ס וזו רבו כמו רבו הרבה דינים שחדשו
הבאים אחריהם מתוך עיון ופלפול . . . ולא משום דלא ס"ל ז"ל השמיטום אלא
משום שאין דרכם להעתיק אלא דינים המפורשים בש"ס בהדיא.334

ומי שבקי בסדרו של הרמב"ם בספרו [יודע] שאין :R. Ezekiel Landau
דרכו להביא רק דין שמוזכר במשנה או בגמ' או בספרא וספרי ותוספתא וירושלמי
אבל להוציא דין מחודש שאינו מפורש אף שהדין דין אמת ומוכח מתוך פלפול
הש"ס בכמה הוכחות אין דרכו להביאו בספרו.335

וכן כתב באגרו' הר"ם דכל דבר שהוא :R. Hayyim Joseph David Azulai
מפורש במשנה ובגמרא בבלי וירושלמי וספרא וספרי ותוספתא הוא כותב בסתם,
ודבר שהוא חידש שאינו מפורש הוא כותב ויראה לי.336

שכבר ידענו שהרמב"ם אינו פוסק כי אם :R. Israel Moses Hazzan
הדיני' המבוארים בתלמוד ושאר הדינים הנלמדים מדיוק מניחם ועל המעיין
ללומדם . . . וכן כתב הרמב"ם עצמו באגרותיו לר' פינחס בן משולם דיין נא
אמון כי זה לא עשה מעולם בחיבורו כי אם לכתוב הדינים המבוארים בתלמוד.337

דאין דרכו של הרמב"ם לכתוב דבר חדש מדעתו :R. Jacob Meir Padua
אפילו דבר פשוט אם לא במה שמפורש בהדיא בבבלי וירושלמי או תוספתא
וכשכותב דבר חדש מדעתו כותב בלשון יראה לי כנודע דרכו בקודש.338

וידוע דהרמב"ם לא כתב דין מעצמו :R. Naphtali Zvi Judah Berlin
אלא מהמבואר בגמרא או בראשונים.339

דאין דרכו של הרמב"ם להביא בחבורו כי :R. Solomon Alfandari
אם רק מה שמפורש בהדיא בתלמוד בבלי וירושלמי ספרא ספרי וכו' אבל אם איזו
פעם רוצה ללמוד דבר מדבר אומר ונ"ל דוקא.340

ואין דרכו של הרמב"ם להוסיף מה שאינו :R. Judah Aryeh Leib Alter
מפורש בגמ'.341

אין דרכו של הרמב"ם לפסוק אלא בלשון :R. Mordekhai Winkler
"יראה לי" בכל היכא דאינו מפורש רק מחמת שקלא וטרי' בגמ' כידוע דרכו
בקדש.342

---

334. *Sha'agat Aryeh he-Hadashot* (Vilna, 1874), no. 3 (second numbering).

335. *Noda bi-Yehudah*, first series, *Yoreh Deah* no. 26. See also *ibid.*, first series, *Orah Hayyim* no. 36, first series, *Even ha-Ezer* no. 77, second series, *Even ha-Ezer* no. 54.

336. *Hayyim Sha'al*, vol. 2, no. 42:5.

337. *Kerakh shel Romi* (Livorno, 1876), p. 37a.

338. *Teshuvot Maharim* (Warsaw, 1854), p. 17a.

339. *Ha-Amek She'alah* (Jerusalem, 1961), 99:2.

340. *She'elot u-Teshuvot ha-Saba Kadisha* (Jerusalem, 1973), vol. 1, p. 152.

341. *Sefat Emet* (Jerusalem, 1996), *Keritot* 15b, s.v. *kiblah*.

342. *Levushei Mordekhai al Massekhet Nedarim* (Brooklyn, 1979), p. 15a.

R. Aryeh Zvi Frommer: ידוע שרבינו הרמב"ם ז"ל לא כ' שום דבר
של"ה לו מקור ע"ז מדברי חז"ל ואם ריק הוא מאתנו ריק.[343]

While the formulations are striking, I believe that most of these
scholars would grant that they were only expressing a general rule, and
would allow exceptions. We see this from R. Joseph Karo, who writes:
שכבר נודע דרכו של הרב ז"ל שאינו אלא מעתיק דברי הגמרא,[344] and similarly: אין דרכו לכתוב מה שלא הוזכר בגמרא בהדיא.[345] These two passages
come from the *Beit Yosef*, yet elsewhere in this work, Karo also writes:
שכבר נודע שאין דרכו של הרמב"ם ברוב המקומות לכתוב אלא הדינים הסדורים
בתלמוד אליבא דהלכתא.[346] In addition, there are places in the *Kesef
Mishneh* where Karo explicitly acknowledges Maimonides' originality.
In one such famous example, *Melakhim* 8:11, Karo writes: נראה לי
שרבינו אומר כך מסברא דנפשיה.[347] The scholars mentioned above are
also only referring to halakhic matters that appear in the *Mishneh
Torah*; they, too, would acknowledge that Maimonidean formulations dealing
with philosophy and medicine do not have a source in earlier rabbinic
literature.

A contemporary scholar, R. Pinhas Zevihi, provides a good illustration of the "conservative" approach. In *Sefer ha-Mitzvot*, neg. com.
65, Maimonides writes: "By this prohibition, we are forbidden to
break down houses of worship of the Lord or to destroy books of

343. *Eretz Hayyim* (Lublin, 1939), appendix to p. 36b. Many of the texts quoted
understand Maimonides' use of "it appears to me" to mean that even though there is a
rabbinic source for his ruling, it is not explicit. But see *Maggid Mishneh, Ishut* 22:19, regarding a halakhah where Maimonides adds "it appears to me": זו סברת רבינו בלא ראיה מן
הגמרא.

344. *Beit Yosef, Even ha-Ezer* 27:7-9.

345. *Beit Yosef, Orah Hayyim* 264:7.

346. *Beit Yosef, Yoreh Deah* 194:3 (CR).

347. *Kesef Mishneh, Melakhim* 8:11. Karo was actually mistaken in his example, as
Maimonides himself identifies his source: *Mishnat Rabbi Eliezer*, ed. Enelow (New York,
1934), p. 121. See *Teshuvot ha-Rambam*, no. 148, and Shraga Abamson's note, *ibid.*, vol. 3,
pp. 163–164. One problem is that according to *Mishnat Rabbi Eliezer*, a Gentile must
accept that the Noahide laws were given to Noah, while in *Melakhim* 8:11, Maimonides
states that a Gentile must accept the Mosaic revelation of these laws. Because of this
divergence, J. David Bleich assumes that the *Beraita shel Rabbi Eliezer* quoted by
Maimonides must refer to a different work. See "Judaism and Natural Law," in Martin
Golding, ed., *Jewish Law and Legal Theory* (New York, 1993), pp. 113–114. As far as I know,
Bleich is the only one to advocate this position.

prophecy, or to erase the Sacred Names and the like. This prohibition is contained in His words, *Ye shall not do so unto the Lord your God* (Deut. 12:4)." The basis for this halakhah is the *Sifrei*,[348] but Zevihi notes that there is no mention there of destroying houses of worship, that is, synagogues. In the *Mishneh Torah, Yesodei ha-Torah* 6:7, Maimonides follows the *Sifrei*, mentioning nothing about synagogues.[349] According to Zevihi, this illustrates that, while in the *Sefer ha-Mitzvot* and other works Maimonides would add his own insights and inferences, when it came to the *Mishneh Torah* he would not do so without adding a suitable comment (such as "it appears to me").

Yet despite such arguments, only the most stubborn will assert that there are *no* Maimonidean additions in the halakhic sections of the *Mishneh Torah*, and that the only reason they appear to be original is because we haven't yet found the source.[350] What then is one to do with Maimonides' statement in his letter to R. Pinhas of Alexandria, that unless he notes otherwise, everything in the *Mishneh Torah* has a source in earlier rabbinic literature?[351] For academically oriented scholars, it is a fundamental point that not everything Maimonides (or any writer for that matter) states must be taken at face value. In fact, this assumption is especially relevant in Maimonidean scholarship, since so much of it is based on the divergence between the exoteric and esoteric. In this case, it indeed appears that Maimonides was exaggerating in his formulation.[352] Leaving aside the numerous examples of Maimonidean originality in the *Mishneh Torah* pointed to over the last eight hundred years, Levinger also notes that Maimonides records a number of halakhot whose origin is geonic.[353] Yet he does

---

348. To Deut. 12:3.

349. As Zevihi notes, he does mention בתי כנסיות ובתי מדרשות in the List of Commandments at the beginning of the *Mishneh Torah*, but it is absent from the actual *Mishneh Torah* text.

350. See in particular ch. 2 of this book.

351. See above, p. 80 n. 325.

352. Already Samuel David Luzzatto claimed that Maimonides' letter to R. Pinhas of Alexandria was colored by apologetics, and thus did not reflect his true view. See *Kerem Hemed* 3 (1839), p. 290 (=Luzzatto, *Mehkerei ha-Yahadut* [Warsaw, 1913], vol. 1, p. 182). See also Twersky, *Introduction*, pp. 31–32: "Some apologetic overtones in this detailed rebuttal are obvious and not all emphases are readily integrated with earlier statements."

353. *Darkhei ha-Mahashavah*, p. 148.

not inform the reader of this, as he promises he will do in his letter to R. Pinhas of Alexandria.[354] It is far-fetched to assume that, in all of these examples, Maimonides was unaware of the geonic rulings.

Traditionalists, however, have a harder time accepting that some of what Maimonides writes could have educational or polemical value, but not reflect his true opinion. Yet as with much else in modern scholarship, traditionalists have not been entirely unaware of this option.[355] There is even medieval rabbinic precedent in this regard (as opposed to the post-Maimonidean philosophical tradition, which, from the beginning, interpreted Maimonides in this way). Haym Soloveitchik's argument that the Letter on Martyrdom is a work of rhetoric that doesn't reflect Maimonides' true view is well known. Less well known is the fact that the fifteenth-century R. Simeon ben Zemah Duran had already suggested pretty much the same approach in seeking to explain one of this work's difficulties.[356]

Maimonides and Kabbalah

Another clear divergence between at least some traditional scholars and academic scholars relates to Maimonides and Kabbalah. There is a well-known medieval legend that has Maimonides converting to Kabbalah late in his life.[357] Kabbalists confronted with Maimonides the rationalist were forced to either reject him or bring him over to

---

354. See *Iggerot ha-Rambam*, vol. 2, p. 443.

355. See below, pp. 109–110, where I cite R. Hayyim Eleazar Shapira, and my *Limits of Orthodox Theology* (Portland, 2004), p. 83. R. Joseph Kafih, a traditional interpreter, also recognizes that Maimonides wrote things that did not reflect his true view. In his note to *Guide* 2:46 (p. 268) he writes: וברור כי רבנו אמר את הדברים כאן על דרך הדרש וההטפה שדרך המטיף להגדיל ולהפריז בענין. In *Ketavim* (Jerusalem, 1989), vol. 2, p. 619, he writes: אמנם כתב הרמב"ם מה שכתב באיגרת תימן כדי להרתיע את מאמיני משיח השוא, וכדי להשקיט לבות החוככים אם להימין ואם להשמאיל. אבל באמת לא כן עמו.

356. *She'elot u-Teshuvot ha-Tashbetz*, vol. 1 no. 63: דילמא הרב ז"ל הפריז על מדותיו בזה למלאכת שמים לחזק ידי הנאחזים במצודה רעה להינצל מפח מוקשם ואל תעצרם אהבת בנים ובנות.

357. See Gershom Scholem, "Mi-Hoker li-Mekubal (Aggadat ha-Mekubalim al ha-Rambam)," *Tarbiz* 6 (1935), pp. 90–98; Michael A. Shmidman, "On Maimonides' 'Conversion' to Kabbalah," in Isadore Twersky, ed., *Studies in Medieval Jewish History and Literature* (Cambridge, 1984), vol. 2, pp. 375–386.

their side.[358] The assumption of those who adopted the latter approach is that since at the end of his life Maimonides found the truth, his halakhic works remain valid, but the same cannot be said for the *Guide* and the philosophical sections of the *Mishneh Torah*. These are now to be rejected, and Maimonides himself rejected them.[359] In line with this approach, it was asserted that subsequent to the widespread circulation of Kabbalah, there is no longer any excuse for one to regard philosophy as part of Torah, as Maimonides famously did.[360]

The legend of Maimonides abandoning philosophy for Kabbalah assumes that when he wrote the *Mishneh Torah*, he had not yet seen the light. Yet there have also been those who argued that Maimonides actually knew the Zohar, or at least portions of it, and he incorporated this into the *Mishneh Torah*. This is in line with the kabbalistic conception that the Zohar was a secret book passed down from mishnaic times until it was revealed by R. Moses De Leon. Obviously, this view of Maimonides is not a position that any academic scholar could take seriously, but it is somewhat popular in traditional rabbinic literature. In fact, quite apart from "saving" Maimonides for kabbalists,[361] the assumption that he was familiar with the Zohar also enables com-

---

358. See Alexander Altmann, "Maimonides' Attitude Toward Jewish Mysticism," in Alfred Jospe, ed., *Studies in Jewish Thought* (Detroit, 1981), pp. 200–219; Moshe Idel, "Maimonides and Kabbalah," in Twersky, ed., *Studies in Maimonides*, pp. 31–81, *id.*, "Maimonides' *Guide of the Perplexed* and the Kabbalah," *Jewish History* 18 (2004), pp. 197–226; Elliot R. Wolfson, "Beneath the Wings of the Great Eagle: Maimonides and Thirteenth Century Kabbalah," in Görge K. Hasselhoff and Otfried Fraisse, eds., *Moses Maimonides* (1138–1203): *His Religious, Scientific, and Philosophical Wirkungsgeschichte in Different Cultural Contexts* (Würzberg, 2004), pp. 209–238.

359. Unless, of course, the *Guide* itself was read as a kabbalistic work, as in the case of R. Abraham Abulafia and R. Samuel ben Mordechai of Marseilles. In addition to the sources cited in the previous note, see Gershom Scholem, *Origins of the Kabbalah*, trans. Allan Arkush (Princeton, 1987), p. 225.

360. See, e.g., R. Solomon Elyashiv, *Leshem Shevo ve-Ahlamah* (Petrokow, 1912), vol. 2, p. 80b: עתה אחר שכבר נתברר עניני מעשה בראשית הכלול בספר יצירה ועניני מעשה מרכבה הכלול בספד"צ בספרי הזוהר והתיקונים ע"פ עומק הדברים אשר בכל ספרי האר"י ז"ל . . . אי אפשר מעתה לטעות כלל לחשוב את חכמת הפילוסופיא לאיזה חלק מחלקי התורה ח"ו.

361. In doing so, kabbalists must reject an explicit statement by R. Hayyim Vital, a "canonical" figure in Kabbalah, that in contrast to the other great medieval Moses (Nahmanides), Maimonides was devoid of all kabbalistic knowledge. See *Sha'ar ha-Gilgulim* (Jerusalem, 1978), ch. 36 (p. 117), s.v. *ha-Rambam*.

mentators to find solutions to some of the great Maimonidean conundrums. That is, they can identify the sources of certain halakhot, which, as mentioned already, has been a focus of scholarship since the *Mishneh Torah*'s appearance.

I am not referring here to examples where Maimonides' position corresponds to that of the Zohar,[362] and one could argue that they both originated from the same source. For example, in *Yibbum ve-Halitzah* 4:6, Maimonides writes: "The levir should then place his foot firmly on the ground, whereupon she should sit down before him, extend her hand in the sight of the court, loosen the laces of the shoe off his foot, remove the shoe, and cast it to the ground." The standard commentators are unable to point to any rabbinic source that refers to the woman casting the shoe on the ground, and R. Joseph Karo assumes that Maimonides did not require this, but was simply expressing what was generally done.[363] The Vilna Gaon[364] is the first

362. Many examples of this are provided by R. Reuven Margaliot, *Ha-Rambam ve-ha-Zohar* (Jerusalem, 1954; reprinted in Margaliot, *Peninim Margaliyot*, pp. 9–87). Margaliot's list includes those examples earlier suggested by R. Meir Shapiro, *Or ha-Meir* (Petrokow, 1926), no. 31, and R. Nathan Neta Leiter, *Tziyun le-Nefesh Hayah* (Jerusalem, 1964), no. 105 (responsum of R. Ze'ev Wolf Leiter). One example omitted by Margaliot is the following: Maimonides excludes from *Sefer ha-Mitzvot* the commandment not to harass Moab. As he explains in the Introduction to this work, *shoresh* 3, this is because the commandment was not intended as a permanent prohibition, but only for Moses' generation (see Nahmanides' discussion of Maimonides' view at the end of his additions to the negative commandments, s.v. *od ahat*). This approach also appears in Zohar, vol. 3, p. 190a.

363. *Beit Yosef, Even ha-Ezer* 169:30. All of the early commentators were unaware that this same procedure is mentioned by R. Hai Gaon, *Otzar ha-Geonim* (Jerusalem, 2002), *Yevamot*, p. 210, and *Sefer ha-Ma'asim li-Venei Eretz Yisrael*, published by B. M. Lewin in *Tarbiz* 1 (1930), p. 101. This means that Maimonides was actually reflecting a geonic tradition. For R. Menahem M. Kasher's attempt to locate this view in a gloss on Targum Neophyti, see *Torah Shelemah* (Jerusalem, 1992), vol. 24, pp. 175–176. (Maimonides never mentions the targumic literature as a source for his halakhic views, yet it seems likely that there was at least some such influence. See R. Joseph Patsanovsy, *Pardes Yosef ha-Shalem al ha-Torah* [Jerusalem, 1995], vol. 3, pp. 246–247 [to Lev. 11:4]; Kasher, *Torah Shelemah*, vol. 25, pp. 20–22; Rabinovitch, *Yad Peshutah, Sotah* 3:22 [CR].)

364. *Beur ha-Gra, Even ha-Ezer* 169:82. R. Yeruham Leiner, *Ma'amar Zohar ha-Rakia*, p. 144 (published as an appendix to R. David Luria, *Kadmut Sefer ha-Zohar* [New York, 1951]), cites the Vilna Gaon's reference to the Zohar as if this indicates a source for Maimonides, which is certainly not the Gaon's intention. Kanievsky, *Kiryat Melekh, Yibbum ve-Halitzah* 4:6, also cites this reference, but see *ibid.*, p. 288, where he acknowledges that Maimonides never saw the Zohar (although he believes it possible that Maimonides had the *Midrash ha-Ne'elam*). See also R. Mordechai Eliyahu, *Imrei Mordechai* (Jerusalem, 2006), p. 37.

to point out that the same *halitzah* routine is recorded in the Zohar,[365] although he uses this reference only to show that it was an early practice (*minhag kadmonim*). He does not say that the Zohar is Maimonides' source—and indeed, he did not believe that Maimonides knew this work.[366]

I also do not have in mind those scholars who believed that despite Maimonides' ignorance of the Zohar, and Kabbalah in general, he was blessed with divine providence, even *ruah ha-kodesh*, that enabled his words to reflect kabbalistic truth.[367] For example, R. Hayyim Joseph David Azulai assumes that Maimonides never saw the Zohar. Yet, confronted with an example in which both of them have the same formulation, he notes: בא וראה תוקף גדול' הרמב"ם אשר רוח הקדש שורה עליו.[368] Referring to another such case, R. Jacob Joseph of Polonnoye writes as follows: כיון הרמב"ם לדעת חכמי האמת ברוח קדשו גם שלא ראה חכמה זו כשכתב ספרו.[369] This might also be what a third eighteenth-century figure, R. Masud Hai Rakah, has in mind when he notes regarding Maimonides and the Zohar: צ"ל דב' נביאים נתנבאו בסיגנון אחד.[370]

However, I am referring to those scholars who assume that Maimonides actually made use of the Zohar. Those who advocate this approach are obviously led to it by a need to establish that Maimonides was not ignorant of the basic text of Jewish mysticism. Their method is simple: find passages in the *Mishneh Torah* which have no source in rabbinic literature but do have a "source" in the Zohar. To my knowledge, the first to argue in this fashion was R. Shem Tov

---

365. Vol. 3, p 180a.

366. See *Beur ha-Gra, Yoreh Deah* 119:13, 246:18.

367. This is undoubtedly what R. Jacob of Karlin has in mind when he writes, with reference to Maimonides' above-mentioned ruling regarding *halitzah* and the Zoharic connection: ואני קורא קורא על הרמב"ם סוד ד' ליראיו. See *Mishkenot Yaakov* (Jerusalem, 1960), p. 105. Similarly, R. Aryeh Leib Zuenz says concerning Maimonides and this very example: ואני אומר על דברי הרמב"ם כי חכם עדיף מנביא ונצצה בו רוח הקודש שכוון לדברי הזוהר. See *Tiv Halitzah* (Cleveland, 1970), no. 83 (p. 98).

368. *Hayyim Sha'al*, vol. 2, no. 43. For similar language by Azulai, see *Mahazik Berakhah* (Livorno, 1785), *Orah Hayyim* 608:4, *Kise David* (Livorno 1804), p. 38a. In *Yosef Ometz*, no. 51, Azulai specifically rejects the notion that Maimonides used the Zohar.

369. *Toledot Yaakov Yosef* (Jerusalem, 1966), *parashat Yitro*, 49a, s.v. *ve-hineh*.

370. *Ma'aseh Rakah* (Jerusalem, 1976), *Avodat Yom ha-Kippurim* 2:7.

ben Abraham Gaon (thirteenth-fourteenth centuries), who offers as a source for Maimonides' enumeration of the angelic ranks (*Yesodei ha-Torah* 2:7) a work he calls "Midrash Bereshit."[371] This is none other than the *Midrash ha-Ne'elam* which is printed in *Zohar Hadash*,[372] and it has the identical enumeration as that given by Maimonides. I have not found anyone who argues similarly until a few hundred years later, when R. Joseph Ergas leaves open the possibility that Maimonides might have seen the Zohar; but, not having received a kabbalistic tradition, he was unable to understand it.[373]

It is only in the nineteenth century that we find the first detailed assertions that Maimonides indeed made use of the Zohar. While R. Judah Najar (d. 1830) suggested that Maimonides "possibly" had access to the work,[374] R. Moses Kunitz (1774-1837) was much more emphatic. Early in the century he published his book *Ben Yohai*,[375] one of the purposes of which was to refute R. Jacob Emden's criticisms of the Zohar. Kunitz attempts to prove, with numerous citations, that geonim and medieval authorities such as Rashi,[376] R. Asher ben Jehiel, and the Tosafists received by tradition much of the material later writ-

---

371. *Migdal Oz, Yesodei ha-Torah* 2:7. This text should be read in conjunction with his commentary to *Yesodei ha-Torah* 1:10, which, according to Scholem, provides the earliest example of the legend of Maimonides discovering Kabbalah. See Scholem, "Mi-Hoker," p. 92.

372. Ed.. Margaliot (Jerusalem, 1994), p. 6a. See Scholem, "Mi-Hoker," p. 93.

373. *Shomer Emunim* (Jerusalem, 1965), vol. 1, pp. 12–13.

374. *Shevut Yehudah, Kuntres Sheni* (Livorno, 1801), p. 9b. The issue is Maimonides' ruling, *Shabbat* 24:7, that lashes are not administered on the Sabbath. There is no explicit talmudic source for this law, but it is found in Zohar, vol. 3, p. 243b and *Tikkunei Zohar*, ed. Margaliot (Jerusalem, 1978), p. 85a. Rabinovitch, *Yad Peshutah, ad loc.*, offers the reasonable suggestion that Maimonides understood Jerusalem Talmud, *Sanhedrin* 4:6: שלא יהו דנין בשבת, as meaning that one does not punish the guilty on the Sabbath. *Mekhilta de-Rashbi* and *Midrash Tannaim* are also possible sources for this law. See Kasher, *Ha-Rambam*, pp. 134–138.

375. (Vienna, 1815).

376. I find it strange that R. Abraham ben ha-Gra (son of the Vilna Gaon), who had a real critical sense, also advocated this position with regard to Rashi. See *Rav Pealim* (New York, 1959), pp. 58–59, s.v. *Zohar Gadol*. While, for obvious reasons, Emden would never claim that Rashi knew the Zohar, he did believe that "more than R. Solomon the commentator was a talmudic sage, he was a faithful kabbalist." See *Amudei Shamayim* (Altona, 1745), p. 175b. See also R. Yaakov Hayyim Sofer, *Menuhat Shalom* (Jerusalem, 2002), vol. 4, pp. 64–68.

ten down in the Zohar. He also cites a few Maimonidean formulations that he believes originate in the Zohar, including *Yesodei ha-Torah* 2:7, which was mentioned above.[377]

In fact, it was *Yesodei ha-Torah* 2:7, 4:6, and 7:1 that led Emden[378] —and he was apparently the first—to suggest that the author of the Zohar actually used Maimonides as a source. He calls attention to the previously mentioned *Midrash ha-Ne'elam*, in which the term *ishim* is used to mean angels, and points out that nowhere in rabbinic literature does one find this usage.[379] Yet it does appear in the *Yesodei ha-Torah* passages mentioned at the beginning of this paragraph, leading to Emden's assumption that the Zohar took this from Maimonides.[380] Needless to say, those who start with different assumptions will use

---

377. *Ben Yohai*, pp. 120ff.

378. *Mitpahat Sefarim*, p. 53.

379. See Wilhelm Bacher, *Bibelexegese Moses Maimuni's* (Budapest, 1897), p. 69 n. 8. Samuel Ibn Tibbon writes that he does not know where Maimonides found this term, and assumes that its origin is a rabbinic work (בספרי המדרשות או זולתם בדברי החכמים ז"ל). See *Perush me-ha-Milot Zarot* (found at the end of the standard edition of the *Guide*), s.v. *sekhel ha-poel* (found under letter *samekh*). In fact, Ibn Tibbon's suspicion might be correct. See R. Reuven Rapoport, *Itur Soferim* (Lvov, 1871; printed as an appendix to this edition of Emden's *Mitpahat Sefarim*), pp. 47–48, who calls attention to *Midrash Mishlei*, ed. Visotsky (New York, 1990), ch. 8, where *ishim* means angels: אליכם אישים אקרא . . . אם זכיתם וקיימתם דברי תורה אתם נקראים אישים כמלאכי השרת ואם לאו אתם בני אדם. Maimonides presumably was aware of this work, as it is cited by geonim. See S. Buber's introduction to his edition (Vilna, 1893), pp. 20ff. Maimonides famously cites Prov. 8:4 (אליכם אישים אקרא) at the beginning of the *Guide*, and it is possible that there is a connection between his use of *ishim* there and in *Yesodei ha-Torah*. See Schwartz' note in his translation of the *Guide*, p. 9; David R. Blumenthal, "Maimonides on Angel Names," in A. Acquot, *et al.*, eds., *Hellenica et Judaica: Hommage à Valentin Nikiprowetzky* (Leuven, 1986), p. 366.

380. I don't know why Emden neglects to mention that the entire section in *Midrash ha-Ne'elam* is clearly copied from Maimonides. He also doesn't mention other examples where the Zohar uses the term *ishim* to mean angels. See Zohar, vol. 1, p. 81a, vol. 2, p. 43a. For other Zoharic passages that Emden believes originate with Maimonides, see *Mitpahat Sefarim*, pp. 29–30, 50. In general, there is a tendency among those who wish to harmonize Kabbalah and philosophy to identify the ten *ishim* (=intelligences) with the *sefirot*. See Aviezer Ravitzky, *Al Da'at ha-Makom* (Jerusalem, 1991), p. 196 n. 81; Elliot R. Wolfson, *Abraham Abulafia—Kabbalist and Prophet* (Los Angeles, 2000), pp. 152ff. Samuel David Luzzatto was perhaps the first to argue that the very notion of the *sefirot* was borrowed from the medieval conception of a ten-sphered universe. See *Vikuah al Hokhmat ha-Kabbalah* (Gorizia, 1852), p. 58. See also *ibid.*, p. 115, where he lists a number of terms found in the Zohar that originate in medieval philosophical works.

this example to reach exactly the opposite conclusion. Thus, R. Hayyim Palache writes: "From here you see that Maimonides knew the *Zohar Hadash*."[381]

Another attempt to use the Zohar to identify a Maimonidean source relates to *Deot* 2:3, where Maimonides writes: "The early wise men (חכמים הראשונים) said: 'He who yields to anger is as if he worshipped idolatry.'"[382] The traditional commentators give no source for this statement, and, as R. Zvi Hirsch Chajes was apparently the first to point out, it is not found in tannaitic or amoraic literature.[383] Upon reading this observation of Chajes, Rabbi Eleazar Horovitz of Vienna wrote to him, pointing out that Maimonides' quote is actually found in the Zohar.[384] Whereas Horovitz cited a source that is quite similar to Maimonides' statement, later scholars pointed out that in other Zoharic passages, Maimonides' exact quote actually appears in full.[385] It is not clear from Horovitz' comment if he actually believed the Zohar to be Maimonides' source or if he was only quoting it as a matter of interest. However, a number of later scholars used this exam-

---

381. *Hayyim u-Mazon* (Jerusalem, 2000), p. 7. See also Palache, *Birkat Moadekha le-Hayyim* (Izmir, 1868), p. 92b, *id., Hayyim u-Melekh* (Izmir, 1874), *Deot* 6:7: ול' רבינו יורה בתחילה כמימר קדישין של הזוה"ק. Palache's son, R. Isaac, also claims that Maimonides made use of the Zohar. See *Yafeh la-Lev* (Izmir, 1880), vol. 3, p. 110b, *Avot ha-Rosh* (Salonika, 1862), vol. 1, p. 111b. For others who argue in this fashion, see R. Aryeh Leib Trivish Ziskind in *Ha-Pisgah* 1 (1896), pp. 70–71; R. Zadok ha-Kohen, *Peri Tzadik* (Lublin, 1934), vol. 5, p. 98b (*Va-Yelekh-Shabbat Shuvah*, no. 10; CR); R. Isaac Safrin, *Zohar Hai* (Tel Aviv, 1971) vol. 1, p. 40b, *id., Netiv Mitzvotekha* (Jerusalem, 1983), p. 137; R. Ovadiah Hadaya, *Yaskil Avdi* (Jerusalem, 1982), vol. 7, p. 164; R. Hanokh Henokh Maier, *Yad Hanokh* (Brooklyn, 2000), p. 221. While not citing the Zohar, R. Joseph Rozin writes, with reference to *Mishneh Torah, Avodah Zarah* 12:6, that Maimonides' stress on four strands of hair has a kabbalistic source. See *Tzafenat Paneah* (Warsaw, 1902), *ad loc.*: הטעם משום דמבואר בספרי קבלה דיש לפיאה דא"ק [דאדם קדמון] ד' שערות. (There is little question that the correct version of this halakhah is actually "forty strands.")

382. He also cites the saying in his *Commentary* to *Avot* 2:13. An almost identical quote, in the name of חכמים ז"ל, is found in Maimonides' letter to Obadiah the Proselyte, *Iggerot ha-Rambam*, vol. 1, p. 240.

383. See *Kol Sifrei Maharatz Chajes* (Jerusalem, 1958), vol. 2, p. 527, and his gloss to *Shabbat* 105b.

384. *Yad Eleazar* (Vienna, 1870), no. 32. He called attention to Zohar, vol. 2, pp. 182a–b.

385. Vol. 1, p. 27b (and see Margaliot's note for parallels in *Tikkunei Zohar* and *Zohar Hadash*), vol. 3, pp. 179a, 234b.

ple as part of their effort to show that Maimonides indeed knew the Zohar.[386]

Maimonides' *ta'amei ha-mitzvot*, as elaborated upon in the *Guide*, were, of course, the *bête noire* of most kabbalists.[387] In fact, R. Hayyim Eleazar Shapira found them so infuriating, and so out of character with the Maimonides of the *Mishneh Torah*, that he concluded that this section of the *Guide* was forged![388] Yet there were also kabbalists who had a different perspective, and who felt a need to identify Maimonides' *ta'amei ha-mitzvot* with Kabbalah, and in particular the Zohar.

For example, in *Guide* 3:45, Maimonides offers a utilitarian reason to explain the incense offered in the Temple: It was designed to improve the smell which otherwise "would have been like that of a slaughterhouse." This annoyed R. Bahya ben Asher, a consistent opponent of Maimonides' *ta'amei ha-mitzvot*, who declared: "Heaven forbid that we should connect the great foundation found in the secret of the incense . . . with such a weak reason."[389] Yet there are oral traditions that R. Israel ben Shabbetai Hapstein, the Maggid of Kozienice, and R. Menahem Mendel of Kotzk claimed that Maimonides' rationale is actually identical with the kabbalistic reason.[390] While Maimonides saw the value of the incense in that it

---

386. See, e.g., I. Palache, *Avot ha-Rosh*, vol. 1, p. 111b, *id.*, *Yafeh Talmud* (Izmir, 1876), p. 71b. As for Maimonides' source, Rabinovitch, *Yad Peshutah, Deot* 2:3 and *Iyyunim be-Mishnato shel ha-Rambam* (Jerusalem, 1999), pp. 20–21, makes the excellent point that when Maimonides quotes the passage in his *Commentary* to *Avot* he does so in Arabic, even though his practice when quoting rabbinic texts is to cite them in the original Hebrew or Aramaic. Based on this, Rabinovitch argues that Maimonides is actually paraphrasing a text in *Shabbat* 105b. This would mean that the various Zoharic passages as well as the late *Midrash le-Olam*, in Adolph Jellinek, ed., *Beit ha-Midrash* (Jerusalem, 1965), vol. 3, p. 117, have their origin in Maimonides. The only problem that remains is that R. Solomon ben Simeon Duran cites the phrase as appearing in (his version of) tractate *Nedarim*. See *She'elot u-Teshuvot ha-Rashbash*, no. 370. For another example where Rabinovitch uses this same approach, see *Yad Peshutah, Deot* 6:4.

387. See, e.g., R. Shem Tov Ibn Shem Tov, *Sefer ha-Emunot* (Ferrara, 1556), p. 7a. One need not be a kabbalist to have this reaction. See R. Joseph B. Soloveitchik, *The Halakhic Mind* (New York, 1988), pp. 92ff.

388. *Divrei Torah* (Jerusalem, 1998), vol. 5, no. 70.

389. Commentary to Ex. 30:1.

390. See Shapiro, *Or ha-Meir*, no. 31; *Siah Sarfei Kodesh* (Lodz, 1931), vol. 5, p. 52a (CR). *Tikunei Zohar*, p. 56b, states: ‏וקטרת לרחקא רוח הטומאה מההוא אתר‎.

removed the ריח רע, for the Maggid and the Kotzker this was simply another way of saying רוח רעה or רוח הטומאה.[391]

Shaul Magid's description of the approach of R. Gershon Henokh Leiner, who in a lengthy essay also identifies Maimonides as adept in Kabbalah,[392] probably can be applied to the Maggid and the Kotzker as well: "The philosophical reasons [of the commandments] given by Maimonides are not in conflict with the Kabbalistic reasons presented in the Zohar and Lurianic Kabbala. . . . Maimonides' reasons are mostly not his 'opinions' (even when Maimonides says they are) or rational positions—as is conventionally thought—but part of a pre-Sinaitic Sod tradition to which Maimonides had at least limited access."[393] With such an outlook, it should not be surprising that even Maimonides' famous statement that "The Sages figuratively named this Good which is in store for the righteous, Banquet,"[394]—a formulation which aroused Rabad's great wrath—is itself found to have a "source" in the Zohar: הצדיקים שזכו נזונין עד שישיגו השגה שלמה ואין אכילה ושתיה אלא זו וזו היא הסעודה והאכילה.[395] Needless to say, only a "true believer" will be reluctant to conclude that, in reality, it is the Zohar that has incorporated Maimonides' formulation.[396]

391. See R. Yaakov Hayyim Sofer, *Torat Yaakov* (Jerusalem, 2001), pp. 222ff.

392. See his introduction to R. Jacob Leiner, *Beit Yaakov* (New York, 1948). For discussion of this essay, see Shaul Magid, *Hasidism on the Margin* (Madison, 2003), ch. 2.

393. *Hasidism on the Margin*, p. 65. Interestingly, G. Leiner, *Beit Yaakov*, p. 6a, notes that R. David Ibn Zimra, in his kabbalistic work *Metzudat David*, records the reasons Maimonides offers and often explains them kabbalistically. This shows that Ibn Zimra should also be added to those who viewed Maimonides through a kabbalistic lens.

394. *Teshuvah* 8:4.

395. Zohar, vol. 1, p. 135b (*Midrash ha-Ne'elam*). See Leiner, *Ma'amar Zohar ha-Rakia*, p. 142.

396. Here are two other examples where the Zohar used Maimonidean formulations: *Yom Tov* 6:18, where Maimonides cites Mal. 2:3 with reference to those who refuse to feed the less fortunate. No pre-Maimonidean source makes this connection, yet it is found in Zohar, vol. 3, p. 104a. In *Shehitah* 1:3, Maimonides writes: דגים וחגבים אינן צריכין שחיטה אלא אסיפתן היא המתרת אותן. No pre-Maimonidean source uses this precise formulation, yet it appears in Zohar, vol. 3, pp. 42a, 278b (and see also the similar text in *Tikunei Zohar*, p. 59b).

MAIMONIDEAN HALAKHAH
AND SUPERSTITION

"Superstition sets the whole world in
flames; philosophy quenches them."[1]

It has been amply demonstrated that Maimonides showed great originality in his Code. My late teacher, Isadore Twersky, wrote extensively on this subject in his book on the *Mishneh Torah* and in various articles. Of course, originality can be defined in many different ways. Even if one were to assume that the *Mishneh Torah* is simply a collection of rabbinic halakhot, the determination of which halakhot to include is itself a matter requiring a decision by the author. However, with Maimonides there is much more than this. Even discounting those laws in the *Mishneh Torah* that appear, at least at first glance, to have no basis in earlier rabbinic literature, his originality is seen in the way he reworks various talmudic halakhot, emphasizing some aspects at the expense of others, and offering reasons of his own devising.

I feel that it is necessary to make this point because, although this originality of thought should be obvious to all who study the *Mishneh Torah*, often it seems that this is not the case. Some eminent scholars, men who were thoroughly conversant with the *Mishneh Torah* and rabbinic literature, have expressed the opinion that, basically, there is *no* originality in Maimonides' Code. They obviously grant the fact that, when Maimonides chooses to record an opinion, he is using his own decision-making process. However, they strongly assert that every statement found in the *Mishneh Torah* has a source in earlier rabbinic literature; in cases where it is not explicitly cited there, but had to be derived by Maimonides, he adds the phrase "it appears to me."[2] What about the biblical verses Maimonides quotes as proof texts? Here, too,

---

1. Voltaire, *Dictionnaire philosophique*, vol. 13 (Paris, 1816), p. 215, s.v. *superstition*, section 3.
2. See above, pp. 80ff..

there are those who believe that there is a rabbinic source for every such example.[3] It is, of course, true that Maimonides quotes rabbinic *derashot* whose original texts no longer survive.[4] Yet, the vast majority of scholars acknowledge that the practice of Maimonides to sometimes supply his own verses is indeed an original feature of the *Mishneh Torah*, one recognized long ago.[5]

Once we acknowledge the astonishing originality of Maimonides, we can begin to appreciate some of the greatest creativity found in the *Mishneh Torah*. I refer to the way he deals with superstitions that found their way into the halakhah. With regard to aggadah, the commentator has a great deal of room to maneuver and can certainly reject aggadic elements that do not appeal to him. For this, there is a tradition dating back at least until geonic times.[6] However, the rejection of halakhot is an entirely different matter. Furthermore, the examples we will be examining are such that only rarely could Maimonides interpret the halakhah in a rational manner, always a preferred method of his.[7] Rather, these are cases in which the halakhah was clear and Maimonides was forced to consciously reject it.

---

3. See Kasher, *Ha-Rambam*, pp. 27–28; Binyamin Ze'ev Benedikt, *Asupat Ma'amarim* (Jerusalem, 1994), pp. 173ff., 179ff., 184ff.

4. See Michael Guttmann, "Otzarot Genuzim," *Ha-Tzofeh le-Hokhmat Yisrael* 6 (1922), pp. 273–288, *id.*, "Midrashim she-Ne'evdu," in *Festskrift I Anledning Af Professor David Simonsens 70-Aarige Fodselsdag* (Copenhagen, 1923), pp. 45ff. (Hebrew section).

5. See above, p. 79 n. 324.

6. See Marc Saperstein, *Decoding the Rabbis* (Cambridge, 1980), ch. 1; Chaim Eisen, "Maharal's *Be'er ha-Golah* and His Revolution in Aggadic Scholarship—in Their Context and on His Terms," *Hakirah* 4 (Winter 2007), pp. 137–194.

7. See *Teshuvot ha-Rambam*, no. 252: בהיות שכונתי בכל החבור הזה להקריב הדינין אל השכל או אל דרך הרוב. Although the expression אל השכל can include a number of meanings, providing a rational understanding of the law is presumably one of them, even though this is not the immediate context of the responsum. See Twersky, *Introduction*, p. 473; R. Simhah Zissel Broida, *Kitvei ha-Saba ve-Talmidav mi-Kelm* (Bnei Brak, 1992), vol. 1, p. 100; Yisrael Yaakov Dienstag, "Le-Yahas Maran el Mishnat ha-Rambam," in Yitzhak Rafael, ed., *Rabbi Yosef Karo* (Jerusalem, 1969), pp. 163–164; Yehezkel Shraga Lichtenstein, "Shitat ha-Rambam be-Inyan Tefilah, Heftzei Kedushah, u-Vikur be-Veit ha-Kevarot," *HUCA* 72 (2001), p. 15 (Hebrew section). (The anonymous thirteenth-century *Apologia* argues that the *Mishneh Torah* is a tool for inculcating rationalism. See A. S. Halkin, "Sanegoryah al Sefer Mishneh Torah," *Tarbiz* 25 [1956], pp. 419–421.) Cf. the interpretation of this responsum in Jacob Levinger, *Darkhei ha-Mahashavah*, pp. 22–24, and Faur's rejection, *Iyyunim*, p. 57 n. 75. See also *Teshuvot ha-Rambam*, no. 154, where Maimonides uses the phrase קרוב אל השכל and it has nothing to do with understanding the law in a rational manner.

That Maimonides realized he was rejecting a flawed halakhah is of great importance, for this was not necessarily the case when he dealt with aggadic matters. For example, in his *Commentary on the Mishnah, Negaim* 9:1, Maimonides explains that the springs of Tiberias are hot because they pass over a sulfur source. This is a rationalization of the talmudic statement that the Tiberian springs are hot because they pass over the entrance to *gehinnom* (*Shabbat* 39a).[8] Yet Maimonides would not have regarded his explanation as a rejection of the talmudic view, but as a clarification of the talmudic passage's true meaning.

Another example is found in *Tefillin* 4:26: "Whoever wears tefillin regularly (וכל הרגיל בתפילין) will be blessed with longevity, as it is said, *The Lord is upon them; they shall live* (Is. 38:16)." This is a quote from *Menahot* 44a–b, but Maimonides has made a subtle change. While *Menahot* has "he who puts on tefillin (כל המניח תפילין)," Maimonides adds the word "regularly," meaning one who wears tefillin throughout the day.[9] Here, too, Maimonides was not consciously changing the meaning of the talmudic text; he was clarifying what he believed it meant. In doing so, he read the text as directed to the elite who wore tefillin continually, rather than to any individual who simply happened to put them on.

A further example along these lines is *Rosh ha-Shanah* 16b, where, among the "four things [that] cancel the doom of a man," the Talmud lists changing one's name. While it does not explain why this is so, presumably there is some magical element involved, perhaps even the idea of fooling the angel of death. Yet, in recording this passage, Maimonides writes: "Among the paths of repentance is for the penitent to . . . change his name, as if to say 'I am a different person and not the same one who sinned'" (*Teshuvah* 2:4).

The following example shows how Maimonides blunted an anthropomorphic element when recording a talmudic passage; but again, he certainly regarded his understanding as revealing

---

8. See R. Joseph Zekhariah Stern, *Tahalukhot ha-Aggadah* (Warsaw, 1902), p. 12b. Even when Maimonides is able to rationalize only part of a rabbinic statement, he does not refrain from doing so. See, e.g., *Commentary on the Mishnah, Avot* 5:4, regarding the ten miracles in the Temple.

9. See R. Meir Mazuz, "Mi-Segulot Leshono shel ha-Rambam," *Or Torah* (Tevet 5747), p. 264.

the text's true meaning. *Shabbat* 105b states: "Anyone who sheds tears for a worthy man, the Holy One, blessed be He, counts them and lays them up in His treasure house (סופרן ומניחן בבית גנזיו)." Maimonides records this passage as: "Anyone who sheds tears for a worthy man, the Holy One, blessed be He, has a reward in store for him (שכרו שמור אצל הקב"ה על כך כך)" (*Evel* 12:2).[10]

When examining how Maimonides treats laws associated with superstition, we must remember that other codifiers also omit some of these laws. Thus, even if Maimonides had believed in the various superstitions, it is unlikely that he would have codified all of the related halakhot mentioned in the Talmud. Even where the Talmud uses the word אסור, some of these examples would have been regarded by him as halakhot which are not generally binding or as merely good advice, as they are by other codifiers and perhaps even by their talmudic authors.[11] To give two examples to illustrate this point, the Talmud states: "One may not (אסור לאדם) betroth a woman before he sees her. . . . One may not (אסור לאדם) give his daughter in betrothal when a minor" (*Kiddushin* 41a). Yet Maimonides writes as follows, carefully omitting the word אסור: "It is improper (אין ראוי לו) for a man to

---

10. See Dov Rappel, *Ha-Rambam ki-Mehanekh* (Jerualem, 1998), p. 156. Let me offer two more examples, the first of which actually concerns a matter of halakhah. The Talmud states that members of the Sanhedrin must know seventy languages (*Sanhedrin* 17a, *Menahot* 65a). In Maimonides' codification, he writes that they must know "most" of the languages (*Sanhedrin* 2:6, and see R. Reuven Margaliot, *Margaliyot ha-Yam* [Jerusalem, 1977], vol. 1, p. 38a). Maimonides did not believe that he was departing from the talmudic passage. Rather, he was simply recording what the Talmud meant when it hyperbolically used the words "seventy languages." (That Maimonides did not take talmudic numbers literally is also seen in other examples. See, e.g., Mishnah *Sanhedrin* 6:1, which states: אפילו ארבע וחמש פעמים. Maimonides, *Mishneh Torah, Sanhedrin* 13:1, records this as: אפילו כמה פעמים. See also Margaliot, *Margaliyot ha-Yam*, vol. 1, p. 86a.) Similarly, the Talmud states that "a scholar on whose garment a stain is found deserves death" (*Shabbat* 114a). Maimonides records this passage as follows: "It is forbidden for a scholar to have a stain on his garment" (*Deot* 5:9).

11. See R. Hayyim Joseph David Azulai, *Ayin Zokher* (Jerusalem, 1962), 1:113; R. Joseph Zekhariah Stern, *Zekher Yehosef* (Jerusalem, 1968), *Orah Hayyim* no. 24; R. Solomon Zvi Schueck, *She'elot u-Teshuvot Rashban* (Munkacs, 1900), *Orah Hayyim* no. 46; R. Yaakov Hayyim Sofer, *Menuhat Shalom* (Jerusalem, 2003), vol. 12, no. 41.

betroth unto himself a minor female, nor should he betroth (ולא יקדש)
a woman until he has first seen her" (*Ishut* 3:19).[12]

There can be no question that Maimonides distinguished between
halakhah and prudent behavior, and exercised great freedom in rejecting talmudic advice, particularly with regard to medical matters.[13] Still,
the sheer number of halakhot that Maimonides ignored, many of
which are recorded in the other codes, is sufficient to establish his
great originality in the exclusion of superstitious elements from
halakhic codification.[14] It is clear from the way Maimonides formu-
lates his Letter on Astrology that he could not have taken these exclu-
sions lightly. By rejecting astrology—indeed, declaring it a forbidden
practice—he cast out a belief held dear by the overwhelming majority of Jews, both scholars and the masses.[15] Yet, although his view

---

12. See also *Ishut* 10:16 and *Kesef Mishneh, ad loc.*; R. Solomon Duran, *Hut ha-
Meshulash* (Lemberg, 1891;=*She'elot u-Teshuvot ha-Tashbetz*, vol. 4), 1:19. Unlike Maimonides, the *Tur* and *Shulhan Arukh* (*Even ha-Ezer* 35:1) keep the word אסור when codifying the Talmud's first law.

13. Regarding this, see the examples brought by Eliezer Levinger, "Ha-Rambam ve-
Tor Rofe u-Fosek," *Ha-Refuah* 7 (1935), pp. 150–162. See also R. Meir Lebush Malbim,
Artzot ha-Hayyim (Jerusalem, 1960), 4:4: (שהוא הרמב"ם בדברי שלם פרק ואראך אתי נא בוא
פ"ד מה' דעות) שדבר שם בהנהגת הבריאות, ורובו ככולו סותר לדברי הש"ס.

14. A number of writers have discussed individual examples of Maimonides' omission and reformulation of superstitious halakhot. Yet, surprisingly enough, there has
never been a comprehensive examination with the intent of pointing to every superstitious halakhah with which Maimonides was confronted. Needless to say, I do not pretend
that I have been successful in locating every example. Furthermore, I have omitted some
items that others have listed because I do not find them convincing. For example, some
scholars, such as R. Joseph Saul Nathanson, *Shoel u-Meshiv* (Jerusalem, 1973), second
series, vol. 4, no. 87, have pointed to *Edut* 9:9 as deviating from the talmudic description
of insanity (*Hagigah* 3b) because the latter includes superstitious elements. Yet this is not
compelling for, as we shall see, Maimonides was not averse to removing superstitious elements of a halakhah while keeping the basic halakhah intact. Most probably, Maimonides'
formulation here is due to other considerations. See, e.g., *Beit Yosef, Even ha-Ezer* 121:6.

15. The most comprehensive analysis of Maimonides' view of astrology is found in
Y. Tzvi Langerman, "Maimonides' Repudiation of Astrology," *Maimonidean Studies* 2
(1991), pp. 123–158. See also Ralph Lerner, "Maimonides' Letter on Astrology," *History
of Religions* 8 (1968), pp. 143–158; Gad Freudenthal, "Maimonides' Stance on Astrology
in Context: Cosmology, Physics, Medicine, and Providence," in Fred Rosner and Samuel
S. Kottek, eds., *Moses Maimonides: Physician, Scientist, and Philosopher.* (Northvale, 1993), pp.
77–90; Hayyim (Howard) Kreisel, "Gishato shel ha-Rambam le-Astrologyah," *Proceedings
of the Eleventh World Congress of Jewish Studies* (1994) vol. 2, div. c, pp. 25–32; Dov Schwartz,

would offend many, Maimonides knew that this matter was not a positive halakhic requirement,[16] and therefore his rejection of it would not create any questions as to the binding nature of Torah or rabbinic law—antinomianism—an important concern of his.[17]

He did, however, have to consider the threat his anti-astrological view posed to the acceptance of rabbinic authority in general, for the sages of the Talmud clearly accepted the veracity of astrology. Did this mean that the authority of the Talmud was not sacrosanct? Maimonides closes off this line of thought with the judicious phrasing he employs in his rejection of astrology. After writing at length on the uselessness of this pseudo-science and its rejection by the wise philosophers of Greece and Persia, he continues:

> I know that you may search and find sayings of some individual sages in the Talmud and Midrashim whose words appear to maintain that at the moment of a man's birth, the stars will cause such and such to happen to him. Do not regard this as a difficulty, for . . . it is not proper to abandon matters of reason that have already been verified by proofs, shake loose of them, and depend on the words of a single one of the sages from whom possibly the matter was hidden. Or there may be an allusion in those words; or they may have been said with a view to the times and the business before him. . . . A man should never cast his reason behind him, for the eyes are set in front, not in back.[18]

In view of the fact that the sages of rabbinic times seemed to differ, Maimonides prepared a three-pronged defense of his opinion. He

---

Astrologyah u-Magyah be-Hagut ha-Yehudit Bimei ha-Beinayim (Ramat Gan, 1999), ch. 3; Dror Fixler, "Astronomyah ve-Astrologyah be-Mishnat ha-Rambam," *Tehumin* 19 (1999), pp. 439–444; Sarah Pessin, "Maimonides' Opposition to Astrology: Critical Survey and Neoplatonic Response," *Al-Masaq* 13 (2001), pp. 25–41; Sarah Stroumsa, "'Ravings': Maimonides' Concept of Pseudo-Science," *Aleph* 1 (2001), pp. 141–163; Avraham Melamed, *Al Kitfei Anakim* (Ramat Gan, 2003), pp. 121ff.; Michael Katzman, "Maimonides' Rejection of Astrology," *Milin Havivin* 2 (2006), pp. 105–120.

16. Even for one who accepted astrology, there was no compelling reason to regard the practices recommended by the Talmud on the basis of astrological considerations (see, e.g., *Shabbat* 129b) as being in the realm of halakhah rather than good advice.

17. See Twersky, *Introduction*, pp. 391–397.

18. "Letter on Astrology," trans. Ralph Lerner, in *id.* and Muhsin Mahdi, eds., *Medieval Political Philosophy* (Toronto, 1963), pp. 234–235 (=*Iggerot ha-Rambam*, vol. 2, p. 488).

first grants the possibility that a view in support of astrology was expressed by a sage who was not aware of the truth. Once Maimonides is prepared to admit that an individual sage could so err,[19] he is able to reject any view that he regards as unreasonable due to his scientific or philosophical outlook.

Maimonides' second defense is that the objectionable passage is not meant to be taken literally. As Maimonides is even prepared to understand some biblical narratives in a non-literal fashion, this view is not at all surprising, and once again opens up a variety of interpretive possibilities. It is only to be expected that Maimonides should seek to bring a talmudic view into line with what he viewed as the truth, and he mentions this in *Guide* 3:14 with regard to talmudic views concerning astronomy: "For whenever it is possible to interpret the words of an individual in such a manner that they conform to a being whose existence has been demonstrated, this is the conduct that is most fitting and most suitable for an equitable man of excellent nature."

His third defense, which does not necessarily contradict the second, is probably the most intriguing. He argues that perhaps the sage's words are, in fact, meant to be taken literally, but were only "said with a view to the times and the business before him." To rephrase this, the sage did not believe what he was saying, but prudence dictated that he say it anyway. This is what Maimonides refers to in *Guide* 3:28 as a

---

19. See also *Guide* 3:14, which refers to errors committed by more than one sage: "Do not ask me to show that everything they [the Sages] said concerning astronomical matters conforms to the way things really are. For at that time mathematics were imperfect. They did not speak about this as transmitters of dicta of the prophets, but rather because in those times they were men of knowledge in these fields or because they had heard these dicta from the men of knowledge who lived in those times." See, similarly, *Guide* 2:8, and Menachem Kellner's detailed discussion in his *Maimonides on the "Decline of the Generations" and the Nature of Rabbinic Authority* (Albany, 1996), ch. 4. For R. Abraham Maimonides' similar view, see his essay on aggadah in *Milhamot ha-Shem*, pp. 83–88. Also relevant is that in the Introduction to the *Guide*, Maimonides claims that there are contradictions in Midrash and Aggadah that are due to errors. "That is why the Sages have said, 'No questions should be asked about difficulties in the Aggadah.'" Maimonides also cites this saying in *Teshuvot*, no. 458, and it appears in geonic literature as well. However, no earlier source has yet been identifed. See Leiter, *Tziyun le-Nefesh Hayah*, no. 79.

"necessary belief." That is, a belief that, while not actually true, must be adopted by the masses to enable some important goal to be achieved.

In Maimonides' view it is impossible to assume that a significant number of sages, in particular the wisest among them, accepted the veracity of astrology.[20] His citation of the Greek philosophers in order to prove a point regarding the Talmud and Midrash presents no problem. In his opinion, the Greek philosophers and the rabbinic sages, with only a few exceptions, agreed on matters of universal truth.

I believe that the principles revealed by the Letter on Astrology apply to all of the rabbinic superstitions encountered by Maimonides; that is, although these superstitions are recorded in the Talmud, they are to be placed in one of the three categories of explanation mentioned above. With this approach, Maimonides is able to reject talmudic halakhot based on superstition; and he is able to justify his far-reaching statements such as that conversation with demons is an impossibility[21]—an impossibility which is nevertheless attested to in the Talmud.

Before going any further it is necessary to discuss a fundamental issue, one which confronts any reader dealing with the material I will be examining. I refer to the question of what constitutes superstition, particularly what Maimonides included in this category, for it is his conception—and his alone—that concerns me. (The word "superstition," as distinct from the concept, is not part of Maimonides' lexicon, and I realize that many would prefer the term "popular belief.")

In his Letter on Astrology, Maimonides writes that it is not proper to accept something as true unless it falls into one of the following three categories:

1) It can be proven, such as concepts in arithmetic, geometry, and astronomy.
2) It can be perceived through the senses.

---

20. See in this regard *Commentary on the Mishnah, Avodah Zarah* 4:7.
21. See *ibid.*

3) It is received as tradition from the prophets or the righteous ones of previous generations.[22]

The various superstitions I will be examining were regarded by Maimonides as falling into none of these three categories. Yet the fact remains that there is a great deal of arbitrariness in Maimonides' approach. Beliefs that he chooses to consider true cannot really be explained by their inclusion in one of these three categories, but should be regarded as a reflection of his own philosophical biases.

I say this because the three categories he sets forth are in no way controversial, and could easily be accepted by many medieval Jewish scholars who believed in the superstitions Maimonides rejects. For example, advocates of astrology could claim that the veracity of their science was proven and was not, as Maimonides argued, based on a false conception of causation. Even more important for our purposes, they could claim, with obvious justice, that the truth of astrology was attested to in the Talmud and Midrash, thus placing it squarely into Maimonides' third category.

Similarly, the believers in demons, who in medieval times included virtually all Jewish thinkers, could argue that demons were perceived through the senses, putting this belief into Maimonides' second category. Although these believers may never have seen or conversed with demons themselves, enough of their predecessors and contemporaries had done so to make this argument valid.[23] Also, as Maimonides' opponents never tired of pointing out, the existence of demons is attested to throughout rabbinic literature—if not in the Torah itself—thus satisfying Maimonides' third condition.[24]

---

22. In *Milot ha-Higayon* Maimonides suggested four categories: sense perception, primary intelligibles, conventions, and traditions. See Lerner, "Maimonides' Letter on Astrology," p. 145.

23. To give one example of many, Nahmanides, who was far from gullible, writes as follows (*Kitvei Ramban*, ed. Chavel, [Jerusalem, 1991], vol. 1, p. 381): שמעתי בבירור שמנהג אלמניי"ו לעסוק בדברי השדים ומשביעים אותם, ומשלחים אותם ומשתמשים בהם בכמה ענינים.

24. See, e.g., R. Hasdai Crescas, *Or ha-Shem* (Jerusalem, 1990), 4:6, who writes, with reference to demons: ולפי שמציאותם מבואר בתורה ובדברי רז"ל עם שנתפרסם ונמשך באומות ונתאמת אצל החוש. See also R. Joseph ben Shem Tov's similar comment in his translation of Crescas' *Bittul Ikarei ha-Notzrim*, ed. Lasker (Ramat Gan, 1990), p. 93: פשט הכתובים, ורוב דברי החכמים מקיימים מציאותם בלא ספק, והיא סברא מפורסמת מאד. R. Abraham Shalom,

I think it is therefore clear that when Maimonides rejects this or that superstition, he is actually imposing his own philosophical biases on the categories, even as he believes they represent an objective standard. Maimonides may truly believe that astrology is nonsense, that demons are not observable, and that neither of these things are attested to in authentic rabbinic teaching; yet these are points about which learned medievals disagreed. Thus, I think the best definition that can be given as to what Maimonides regards as superstition is any belief or practice which *in his opinion* resulted from ignorance, fear of the unknown, trust in magic, or a false conception of causation.[25]

A central goal of this chapter is to try and understand why there are some cases where Maimonides omits a law based on superstition,

---

Neveh Shalom (Venice, 1575), p. 29a, writes (borrowing some of Crescas' words): אלו המאמרים ודומיהם רבו בדברי רבותינו ז"ל וזה נמשך אחר דעתם במציאות השדים ואם הפילוסופי' יכחישו זה אולם מציאותם מפורסם בתור' ובדברי רבותינו ז"ל עם שנתפרסם ונמשך באומ' ונתאמת אצל החוש. For appeals to rabbinic literature in order to counter Maimonides' general repudiation of superstition, in addition to the sources cited in the succeeding notes, see Nahmanides' commentary to Deut. 18:9; R. Solomon ben Adret, *She'elot u-Teshuvot ha-Rashba* (Bnei Brak, 1982), vol. 1, no. 413 (=*Teshuvot ha-Rashba*, ed. Dimitrovsky [Jerusalem, 1990], vol. 1, *Minhat Kenaot*, ch. 21; an annotated translation appears in Sarah Laidlaw Tilevitz, "Jews, Christians and Lion Pendants: Philosophical and Theological Aspects of Folk Cures as Reflected in Medieval Christian and Jewish Sources" [unpublished doctoral dissertation, Jewish Theological Seminary of America, 1993], pp. 190–242); R. Nissim Gerondi, *Derashot ha-Ran*, ed. Feldman (Jerusalem, 1977), pp. 59–60, 219–220; R. Aviad Sar Shalom Basilea, *Emunat Hakhamim* (Mantua, 1730), p. 19a; R. Isaac Haver, *Magen ve-Tzinah* (Bnei Brak, 1985), pp. 34a–b.

25. A good example of Maimonides' arbitrariness can be seen with regard to the issue of abiogenesis (spontaneous generation), the existence of which is the basis of certain halakhot in the Talmud, halakhot which are also recorded in the *Mishneh Torah*; see *Shabbat* 11:2–3, *Ma'akhalot Asurot* 2:13–14, 23, *She'ar Avot ha-Tum'ah* 4:11 (see also *Commentary on the Mishnah, Shabbat* 14:1). In his *Commentary* to *Hullin* 9:6, Maimonides accepts the scientific possibility of abiogenesis, even though he admits that he does not understand how it can be explained. He does not reject it because he states that many people claimed to have observed the process. This suffices to place it into Maimonides' second category. See also his *Commentary* to *Bekhorot* 8:2, *Niddah* 3:2, and especially *Sefer ha-Mitzvot*, neg. com. 179, where he is most adamant, claiming that only the masses, who are ignorant of natural science, deny abiogenesis. See also *Sefer ha-Mitzvot*, neg. com. 177–178, for halakhot related to this "fact." Yet many people also claimed to have seen demons, magic, etc., and Maimonides rejects these phenomena. Clearly, when Maimonides has convinced himself that something belongs to the realm of the impossible, the testimony of witnesses is not enough to transfer it to a privileged place in his second category.

and others where he quotes the law with a different rationale than that offered by the Talmud. It is certainly incorrect to say that Maimonides would quote superstitious halakhot even if he did not accept the superstition, because he was simply recording a talmudic halakhah.[26] This view ignores the obvious, namely, that Maimonides *does* leave out numerous halakhot based on superstition.

Many of the talmudic halakhot based on superstition concern demons, and Maimonides' denial of their existence can therefore be seen in his halakhic codification. It is true that Maimonides never explicitly denies that demons exist;[27] but the implication of many of

---

26. Malbim, *Artzot ha-Hayyim*, 4:4, writes: . . . ולפמ"ש היה לו לרמב"ם להשמיט דין זה. However, at the beginning of his אין מן התימה כי הרמב"ם העתיק דין הנמצא בגמרא כדרכו comment, Malbim does mention some examples of superstitious halakhot which Maimonides omits from his Code. Apparently, Malbim distinguished between talmudic אזהרה, which Maimonides omits, and talmudic דין, which, in his opinion, Maimonides includes.

27. In *Commentary on the Mishnah, Avodah Zarah* 4:7, Maimonides regards as nonsense the notion that one could talk to a demon. This, however, is not an explicit rejection of the existence of demons. R. Shem Tov ben Isaac Shaprut (see Lester A. Segal, "Late-Fourteenth Century Perception of Classical Jewish Lore," in Jacob Neusner, *et al.*, eds., *From Ancient Israel to Modern Judaism*, [Atlanta, 1989], vol. 2, p. 221); R. Joseph ben Shem Tov in his translation of Crescas' *Bittul Ikarei ha-Notzrim*, p. 93; Kafih, *Ketavim*, vol. 2, pp. 600–601, *id., Sefer Nashim* (2), p. 349; R. Moses Malka, *Mikveh ha-Mayim* (Jerusalem, 1981), vol. 3, p. 168, all point to *Guide* 3:46 as a denial of demons. However, a close reading of the chapter does not reveal this to be the case. Maimonides is only speaking about the various practices of the Sabians in their attempt to communicate with demons, not about demons *per se*. In addition, the passage he quotes from the *Sifrei* speaks of the heathens worshipping imaginary things such as their בבואה, which Maimonides understands to mean "shadow." Regarding this passage from *Sifrei*, see also Michael Schwartz, "Ha-Rambam ve-ha-Bavuah," *Daat* 42 (1999), pp. 3–4. (Regarding "shadow worship," see also his *Commentary* to *Hullin* 2:9.) All this has nothing to do with whether or not demons are imaginary. In *Guide* 3:29 Maimonides does refer negatively to demons, yet he does not explicitly reject their existence; see also *Guide* 1:63. In the Al-Harizi translation of *Guide* 1:51 one finds the following: ויביא מופת על בטול השדים. In other words, Al-Harizi has Maimonides saying that Aristotle has proven the non-existence of demons. However, Al Harizi misread *juz* (atom) as *jinn* (demon), and this in turn led to mistranslations in medieval Latin and Castilian versions of the *Guide*; see J. Perles, "Die in einer Münchener Handschrift aufgefundene erste lateinische Übersetzung des Maimonidischen 'Führers,'" *MGWJ* 24 (1875), pp. 69–70; Hayyim Leshem, *Shabbat u-Moadei Yisrael* (Tel Aviv, 1969), vol. 3, p. 371. Samuel Ibn Tibbon also erred in this regard, but later corrected his translation. See Tzvi Langermann, "Makor Hadash le-Targumo shel Shmuel Ibn Tibbon le-Moreh Nevukhim ve-Hearotav Alav," *Peamim* 72 (Summer 1997), pp. 54–55.

his statements leads to this necessary conclusion, a conclusion that was well understood by the Vilna Gaon when he condemned Maimonides for this denial.[28] Of course, awareness of Maimonides' rejection of demons was common knowledge for a long time before this,[29] and is even alluded to by Samuel Ibn Tibbon[30] and R. Abraham Maimonides.[31] Yet many rabbinic authorities were oblivious to this. For example, R. Samuel Sapurto is quick to respond to those who attacked Maimonides, based on the Al-Harizi translation of the *Guide*, for denying the existence of demons. After noting the inaccuracy of this translation, he stresses that nowhere in Maimonides' writings does he negate the reality of demons.[32] Among other scholars, R. David ben Samuel ha-Kokhavi,[33] R. Joseph Colon,[34] R. Moses Ibn Habib,[35]

28. *Beur ha-Gra, Yoreh Deah* 179:13. (Interestingly, he apparently believed that Maimonides accepted the existence of the evil eye. See *Beur ha-Gra, Hoshen Mishpat* 267:18 n. 29.) R. Joseph Saul Nathanson, *Shoel u-Meshiv*, second series, vol. 4, no. 87, calls attention to Maimonides' failure to explicitly reject the existence of demons, while at the same time omitting demon-related halakhot from his Code. Nathanson explains that although Maimonides did not believe in demons, nevertheless: יראתו קודמת לחכמתו, ולא רצה לומר שאינו מאמין בזה. That is, in rejecting something widely accepted by his co-religionists, Maimonides realized that subtlety was called for.

29. See e.g., the attack on Maimonides in the poems of R. Solomon ben Meshullam da Piera, published by Hayyim Brody, *Yediot ha-Makhon le-Heker ha-Shirah ha-Ivrit* 4 (1938), p. 33: לנו עדים על השדים יוסף שידא בן תמליון. See also *ibid.*, p. 55, where he refers in particular to halakhot that are concerned with demons: ויש לנו עדים בענין השדים וכתות הזדים הלכות מזמים. (Daniel Jeremy Silver, *Maimonidean Criticism and the Maimonidean Controversy* [Leiden, 1965], p. 193, renders this passage as follows: "We have witnesses in the matter of evil spirits, The class of destroying angels actually brought into being certain laws." The second part of this translation is entirely incorrect, for וכתות הזדים הלכות מזמים refers to Maimonides and other philosophers whose denial of demons leads them to contradict halakhot.) See also R. Isaac Abarbanel's commentary to Deut. 18:9; R. Joseph ben Shem Tov's comment in his translation of Crescas' *Bittul Ikarei ha-Notzrim*, p. 93; Basilea, *Emunat Hakhamim*, p. 15b; R. Joseph Ergas, *Shomer Emunim* (Jerusalem, 1965), p. 11; R. Joseph Solomon Delmedigo, *Elim* (Amsterdam, 1628), p. 83; R. Manasseh ben Israel, *Nishmat Hayyim* (Lvov, 1832), 3:12.

30. See *Perush me-ha-Milot Zarot* (found at the end of the standard edition of the *Guide*), s.v. *emet*.

31. See *Milhamot ha-Shem*, p. 55. See also R. Abraham's essay on aggadah (*ibid.*, p. 94), where he states that all talmudic stories dealing with demons did not actually occur but were the product of dreams.

32. *Ginzei Nistarot* 4 (1878), p. 62.

33. *Sefer ha-Batim*, ed. Hershler (Jerusalem, 1983), vol. 2, p. 278.

34. *Hiddushei u-Ferushei ha-Maharik*, ed. Pines (Jerusalem, 1984), p. 168.

35. *Tosefet Yom ha-Kippurim* (Pietrokov, 1912), *Yoma* 77b.

R. Solomon of Chelm,[36] R. Joshua Falk,[37] R. Yedidyah Samuel Tarikah,[38] R. Ze'ev Turbovitz,[39] R. Ze'ev Biednowitz,[40] and R. Isaac Nissim[41] are unambiguous in their contention that Maimonides *did* believe in demons, or as they are often referred to in the Talmud, *ruah ra'ah*.[42] From the implication of their statements, there is no doubt that this was also the view of R. Abraham ben David,[43] *Hagahot Maimoniyot*,[44] Rabbenu Manoah,[45] R. Isaac ben Joseph of Corbeil,[46] R. Nissim Gerondi,[47] R. Joseph Karo,[48] R. Joel Sirkes,[49] R. Abraham di Boton,[50] R. Vidal of Tolosa,[51] R. Shem Tov Ibn Gaon,[52] R. Abraham ben Hananyah,[53] R. Meir of Lublin,[54] R. Abraham Meir Berlin,[55] R.

---

36. *Mirkevet ha-Mishnah, Shevitat Asor* 3:2.

37. *Derishah, Orah Hayyim* 181:4, *Yoreh Deah* 116:7.

38. *Ben Yedid* (Salonika, 1806), *Tefillah* 7:8.

39. *Ziv Mishnah* (Warsaw, 1904), *Shevitat Asor* 3:2. After explaining Maimonides' view, he writes: ומכאן תשובה לאותן שהוציאו לעז על רבינו שאינו מאמין בשדים ור"ר הנאמרים בש"ס.

40. *Divrei Ze'ev* (New York, 1944), vol. 21, p. 24 (CR).

41. *Yein ha-Tov* (Jerusalem, 1979), pp. 13–14.

42. R. David Meir Frish, *Yad Meir* (Lemberg, 1881), first series, no. 19, creates an artificial distinction between *ruah ra'ah* and *shibta* (another type of demon). According to him, Maimonides denies the existence of *ruah ra'ah* but accepts *shibta*.

43. See his *hassagah* to *Tefillin* 4:19 (recorded in *Kesef Mishneh*).

44. Commentary to *Gerushin* 2:13.

45. Commentary to *Shevitat Asor* 3:2 (included in the Frankel edition of the *Mishneh Torah*).

46. *Sefer Mitzvot Katan* (Satmar, 1935), no. 171.

47. Commentary to Alfasi, *Gittin*, p. 32b (commenting on *Gittin* 66a).

48. See *Beit Yosef, Even ha-Ezer* 17:10, where he suggests that perhaps Maimonides believed that people were no longer able to properly distinguish the characteristics of a demon: דהאידנא לא בקיאינן בבבואה דבבואה. See also *Kesef Mishneh, Tefillah* 7:8, *Tefillin* 6:12 (and Kafih's comment, *ad loc.*), *Berakhot* 6:16, *Gerushin* 2:13, 13:23, for other examples where Karo does not recognize the Maimonidean pattern of omitting demon-related halakhot.

49. *Bayit Hadash, Even ha-Ezer* 17:10.

50 *Lehem Mishneh, Gerushin* 2:13, 13:23, *Gezelah ve-Avedah* 3:9. See also *Lehem Mishneh, Avodah Zarah* 11:9, where he seems to be saying that Maimonides believed in the power of divination.

51. See *Maggid Mishneh, Gerushin* 13:23, where he is oblivious to the Maimonidean pattern of omitting demon-related halakhot. He can only say: ורבינו לא הזכיר מדין זה כלום ולא נתבאר לי למה.

52. *Migdal Oz, Tefillah* 7:8.

53. *Beit Avraham* (Jerusalem, 1984), 17:5 (p. 7).

54. *She'elot u-Teshuvot Maharam Lublin* (New York, 1976), no. 116 (end; CR).

55. *Atzei Arazim* (Fuerth, 1790), pp. 80b–81a.

Samuel ben Uri Shraga Phoebus,[56] R. Solomon Cohen,[57] R. Judah Aszod,[58] R. Samuel Yevin,[59] R. Hayyim Zvi Mannheimer,[60] R. Yehiel Mikhel Berkman,[61] and R. Jehiel Mikhel Epstein.[62] The fact that these rabbinic authorities were oblivious to the obvious implication of so many of Maimonides' statements shows how unfathomable it was to their minds that Maimonides, the talmudist *par excellence*, could reject the truth of so many explicit talmudic passages.[63]

Another view has Maimonides adopting a position similar to that expressed by R. Solomon Luria,[64] which was anticipated in a more limited manner by the Tosafists.[65] According to this view, Maimonides does not deny that in talmudic days *ruah ra'ah* was a clear danger; he just felt that in post-talmudic days it had ceased to exist.[66] This expla-

---

56. *Beit Shmuel, Even ha-Ezer* 17:26.

57. Commentary to *Gerushin* 2:13 (p. 475 in the Frankel edition). See also *Beit Shmuel, Even ha-Ezer* 141:28.

58. See *Yehudah Ya'aleh* (Lemberg, 1873), *Orah Hayyim* no. 9, where he wonders why Maimonides omitted the halakhah from *Megillah* 3a, referred to below, p. 124.

59. *Imrei Shmuel* in R. Elijah of Vilna, *Ma'aseh Rav* (Jerusalem, 1990), no. 95.

60. *Ein ha-Bedolah* (Brooklyn, 1981), no. 11.

61. *Lev Yam* (Vilna, 1898), no. 15.

62. *Arukh ha-Shulhan, Orah Hayyim* 4:1–2, *Even ha-Ezer* 17:63, 141:99.

63. We find something similar with regard to Maimonides' rejection of astrology. See, e.g., Shalom, *Neveh Shalom*, 8:5, p. 128b, who claims that according to Maimonides, other than השלם בעיון ומעשה, all people are under the control of the stars.

64. *Yam Shel Shlomo* (New York, 1953), *Hullin*, ch. 8, nos. 12, 31. See also R. Israel Lipschuetz, *Tiferet Yisrael, Sanhedrin* 7:7, section *Boaz*, n. 3.

65. *Hullin* 107b s.v. *hatam*. The Tosafists are sometimes mistakenly understood to have advocated the same position as Luria, namely, that there is no longer any *ruah ra'ah* in existence. However, this is incorrect, for the Tosafists explicitly state that their view is only applicable to the specific type of *ruah ra'ah* then under discussion: לפי שאין אותה רוח רעה מצויה בינינו. A similar formulation is found in Tosafot *Yoma* 77b s.v. *mi-shum*: לפי שאין אותה רוח רעה שורה באלו המלכיות. Neither citation says anything about other forms of *ruah ra'ah*, and the second citation leaves open the possibility that even this type of *ruah ra'ah* may be found in other places. Furthermore, as we shall see, the permission to wash one's hands on Yom Kippur morning, which is not disputed by the Tosafists, is based on the acceptance of *ruah ra'ah*.

66. See Malbim, *Artzot ha-Hayyim*, 4:4; R. Alexander Sendor Schor, *Tevuot Shor* (Lemberg, 1885), *Shabbat* 82a (p. 271a); R. Aryeh Lebush Balkhuver, *Shem Aryeh* (Jerusalem, 1870), *Yoreh Deah* no. 27; R. Mordekhai Brisk, *She'elot u-Teshuvot Maharam Brisk*, (Brooklyn, 1990), vol. 1, no. 10; R. Eliezer David Greenwald, *Keren le-David* (Brooklyn, 1973), *Orah Hayyim* no. 1; R. Shabbetai Kehat Gross, *Masa Benei Kehat* (Jerusalem, 1982), p. 39; R. Yaakov Kamenetsky, *Emet le-Yaakov* (New York, 1998), p. 264 (to Ex. 7:22);

nation removes much of the radicalism from Maimonides' position, for there are no longer any philosophical differences between Maimonides and the Talmud. Their differing statements simply reflect their divergent circumstances. There is thus no difference between Maimonides' view regarding demons and the commonly accepted notion that one can no longer rely on the medical advice in the Talmud, not because the Sages erred, but because the nature of the world has changed. It is even reported in the name of R. Menahem Mendel of Kotzk that since Maimonides knew that God accepted his rulings, he therefore "decided" that demons were not in existence in order to ensure that this would, in fact, be the case![67]

A different approach is taken by R. Hayyim Eleazar Shapira.[68] According to him, Maimonides was well aware of the existence of demons, yet his actions were along the lines of an *averah lishmah*. In other words, by using his great influence he was able, through his denial of demons and all sorts of magical phenomena, to keep large segments of the Jewish population from involving themselves with the supernatural and thus violating Torah prohibitions. Since they regarded it as false, it was easy for them to separate themselves from it.[69]

Yosef, *Yabia Omer*, vol. 1, pp. 183, 189. R. Yekutiel Aryeh Kamelhar, *Ahavat ha-Kadmonim* (Bilgoraj, 1938), p. 14 (second pagination), adopts the Tosafist position, claiming that demons were simply not found where Maimonides lived. He responds as follows to those who asserted that Maimonides denied that demons *ever* existed: וחלילה לתלות בוקי סריקי בהרמב"ם ז"ל (CR). See also *Lehem Mishneh, Shevitat Asor* 3:2. Most interestingly, even Kafih, Commentary to *Tefillah* 4:2, offers the Tosafist approach: ועוד י"ל דס"ל לרבנו שכבר כלו כל הרוחות הללו וכעין דברי התוס'. This is one of a number of examples of Kafih citing, without objection, a view that he knows does not reflect Maimonides' true attitude, and is related to the fact that Kafih himself would sometimes write in an esoteric fashion. See Dov Schwartz, "Hearot al Perushei Shir ha-Shirim le-Rav Shemariah ha-Ikriti," in Zohar Amar and Hananel Sari, eds., *Sefer Zikaron le-Rav Yosef ben David Kafih* (Ramat Gan, 2001), p. 333; Eliyahu Nagar, "Ma'avak ha-Rambam be-Avodah Zarah u-va-Emunot ha-Tefelot," *Mesorah le-Yosef* 3 (2004), p. 165 n. 244.

67. *Siah Sarfei Kodesh*, vol. 5, p. 52a (CR); R. Menahem Mendel of Kotzk, *Emet ve-Emunah* (Jerusalem, 1972), p. 100; Yehezkel Brandsdorfer, *Leket me-Otzar ha-Hasidut* (Jerusalem, 1976), p. 22.

68. *Divrei Torah*, vol. 6, no. 54. See also the similar view of R. Zvi Yehudah Kook, *Sihot ha-Rav Tzvi Yehudah: Bereishit*, ed. Aviner (Jerusalem, 1993), pp. 295–297, 310–312.

69. R. Masud Hai Rakah had a similar approach. See *Ma'aseh Rakah, Avodah Zarah* 11:16 (called to my attention by Ephraim Meth). See also R. Yekutiel Yehudah Halber-

This approach is actually similar to Maimonides' own notion of "necessary beliefs" which, as we have seen, is found in both *Guide* 3:28 and the Letter on Astrology. Shapira explains that he was led to this view by his inability to accept the fact that Maimonides would reject out-of-hand a belief which appears throughout the Talmud. That numerous other scholars, who also shared Shapira's great respect for Maimonides' talmudic learning, did not feel so bound is most illustrative of Shapira's restricted view of what constitutes authentic Jewish doctrine.[70]

A more sophisticated approach is found in the comments of a modern scholar, José Faur.[71] He sees no philosophical considerations that can be said to have influenced Maimonides to deny the reality of demons, since he states that, with the exception of Avicenna, all important Arab philosophers accepted their existence.[72] The same is true regarding the Greek philosophers, including Aristotle. That there is no necessary contradiction between affirming the existence of demons and being a Jewish philosopher is also seen in the fact that R. Hasdai Crescas accepted their existence.[73] According to Faur,

---

stam, *Divrei Yatziv* (n.p., 1998), *Yoreh Deah* no. 31 (CR), and R. Yitzhak Sternhell, *Kokhvei Yitzhak* (Brooklyn, 1969), vol. 1, p. 83 (CR).

70. See also *Divrei Torah*, vol. 5, no. 70, where such an attitude leads him to deny the authenticity of certain sections of the *Guide*. For discussion of some aspects of Shapira's ideology, see Allan L. Nadler, "The War on Modernity of R. Hayyim Elazar Shapira of Munkacz," *Modern Judaism* 14 (1994), pp. 233–264.

71. *Iyyunim*, pp. 1–2. See also his *Homo Mysticus* (Syracuse, 1999), p. 127. However, in his "Anti-Maimonidean Demons," *Review of Rabbinic Judaism* 6 (2003), pp. 3–52, Faur takes for granted that Maimonides indeed rejected the belief in demons.

72. Faur is not correct in this as Averroes also denied the existence of demons. See Moritz Steinschneider, *Die Hebraischen Übersetzungen des Mittelalters und die Juden als Dolmetscher* (Graz, 1956), p. 155.

73. *Or ha-Shem* 4:6. R. Joseph Albo apparently also believed in demons; see *Sefer ha-Ikarim* 3:8. Yet the fact remains that virtually all other important post-Maimonidean Jewish philosophers *did* reject the existence of demons. Furthermore, their opponents recognized that it was their philosophical inclinations which led them to this position. See Levi ben Abraham, *Livyat Hen: Eikhut ha-Nevuah ve-Sodot ha-Torah*, ed. Kreisel (Beer Sheva, 2007), pp. 764ff.; Alexander Altmann, "Gersonides' Commentary on Averroes' Epitome of *Parva Naturalia*, II.3: Annotated Critical Edition," *PAAJR* 46–47 (1978–1979), p. 10 n. 15; R. Nissim of Marseilles, *Ma'aseh Nissim*, ed. Kreisel (Jerusalem, 2000), p. 377; R. Meir Aldabi, *Shevilei Emunah* (Jerusalem, 1990), pp. 394–395; R. Abraham Bibago, *Derekh Emunah* (Constantinople, 1522), p. 39c; R. Joseph ben Shem Tov's comment in Crescas'

Maimonides' omission of demons from his Code is due to the fact that they have no connection to halakhah. That this point is mistaken should be obvious to all after we have examined the evidence.

Faur also claims that Maimonides' belief in demons is revealed in *Guide* 1:7, where he quotes a "Midrash" which states: "During the entire period of a hundred and thirty years when Adam was under rebuke, he begot spirits."[74] Maimonides thereupon adds that the meaning of "spirits" is demons. However, when one examines what Maimonides writes earlier in this chapter, there is no doubt that what he has in mind is people who have not properly developed their intellects.[75] In addition, Faur admits that demons (*shedim*) are identical with what is known in talmudic literature as *ruah ra'ah*, and it can be easily shown that Maimonides indeed denied the existence of *ruah ra'ah*.

Finally, even if one were to assume that Faur is correct that demons are not mentioned in the *Mishneh Torah* because they have no connection with halakhah, what is one to do with the examples from the *Commentary on the Mishnah* in which, explaining a sickness, Maimonides substitutes a medical reason for the talmudic rationale of it being the work of a demon? Here, Maimonides is acting in his role

---

Bittu Ikarei ha-Notzrim, p. 93; Ibn Shem Tov, *Sefer ha-Emunot* 5:1; R. Menahem Zioni, *Tzefunei Tziyoni* (Brooklyn, 1985), p. 25. With regard to pre-Maimonideans, R. Abraham Ibn Ezra, whose love for astrology is well known, agreed with Maimonides when it came to demons. See his commentary to Lev. 17:7, Ps. 106:37. See also Schwartz, *Astrologyah*, pp. 196ff., who discusses an influential medieval work, falsely attributed to Ibn Ezra, which presents a different picture of the latter's view of demons. (For Ibn Ezras rejection of the efficacy of magic, see his commentary to Lev. 19:31. For R. Moses Taku's report of how demons caused Ibn Ezra's death, see *Ketav Tamim*, published in *Otzar Nehmad* 3 [1863], p. 97.) For Kafih's claim that Judah Halevi also denied the existence of demons, see his edition of the *Kuzari* (Jerusalem, 1997), p. 93 n. 19.

74. See *Eruvin* 18b which is very similar to Maimonides' quote (and see R. Zvi Hirsch Chajes' gloss, *ad loc.*). See also the related passages in *Bereshit Rabbah* 20:28, 24:6.

75. See Narboni, Efodi, Shem Tov, and Abarbanel to *Guide* 1:7; R. Solomon ben Adret, *She'elot u-Teshuvot ha-Rashba*, vol. 1, no. 414 (end); Chajes, *Kol Sifrei Maharatz Chajes*, vol. 1, p. 455; Kasher, *Torah Shelemah*, vol. 2, p. 351 n. 33; Saul Lieberman's note in his edition of Maimonides, *Hilkhot ha-Yerushalmi*, p. 15 n. 124. See also R. Solomon Duran, *Milhemet Mitzvah* (Jerusalem, 1970), p. 34b, who writes (without reference to Maimonides' view): לא שיהיו שידין ממש אלא בני אדם הדומין לשידין במעשיהם כלשון בני אדם שאומרים על אדם רע זה שד הוא וכל אדם שמשחית במעשיו ג"כ נקרא שטן. See also R. David Kimhi, *Perushei Rabbi David Kimhi al ha-Torah*, ed. Kamelhar (Jerusalem, 1970), Gen. 5:3; Shalom Rosenberg, *Good and Evil in Jewish Thought* (Tel Aviv, 1990), p. 63.

as commentator, not halakhist, and he still removes the superstitious passages in question.[76]

Following are all of the examples I have found in which Maimonides was forced to confront superstition in talmudic halakhah.

Berakhot 3a: "Our Rabbis taught: There are three reasons why one must not go into a ruin: because of suspicion [that a woman may be waiting for him there], because of falling debris, and because of demons." This halakhah is codified in two places, *Tefillah* 5:6[77] and *Rotzeah u-Shemirat ha-Nefesh* 12:6. In the first example, Maimonides simply cites the halakhah without giving any reasons; in the second, he makes it clear that the reason is because of the danger of falling debris. Maimonides is obviously unconcerned with demons. The fact that the issue of suspicion is not mentioned, even though this has nothing to do with superstition, further illustrates that Maimonides did not regard the reasons offered by the Talmud as binding.[78]

---

76. See *Commentary on the Mishnah, Shabbat* 2:5, *Eruvin* 4:1. In these sources Maimonides interprets *ruah ra'ah* in a naturalistic fashion, despite the fact that the Talmud regards it as a demon. (Needless to say, this is also how *ruah ra'ah* is to be understood the six times it is mentioned by Maimonides in the *Mishneh Torah: Shabbat* 27:12, 13, *Ta'aniyot* 1:6, *Gerushin* 2:14, *Shehitah* 2:12, *Biat ha-Mikdash* 8:16.) In his *Commentary* to *Gittin* 7:1, Maimonides explains, contrary to *Gittin* 67b, that *kordiakos* is not a demon but rather a sickness (see also Meiri, *ad loc.*). In fact, he could have pointed out that the Jerusalem Talmud, in its discussion of *kordiakos* (*Gittin* 7:1, *Terumot* 1:1), makes no mention of demons. (For a modern medical analysis of *kordiakos*, see Yehudah Levi, "Mahu 'Kordiakos,'" *Assia* 6 [1989], pp. 59–60. See also the earlier discussion in Fred Rosner, *Medicine in the Bible and the Talmud* [New York, 1977], pp. 61–65.) Without going too far afield, I should note that there are times when Maimonides explains a passage in accordance with its plain meaning, which has no superstitious elements, yet other commentators read the same passage in a superstitious manner. See, e.g., Rashi, *Nazir* 65b s.v. *u-ve-mar'eh*, and compare this to Maimonides' *Commentary* to *Zavim* 2:2 and *Mehuserei Kapparah* 2:2. In this instance, we need not attempt to explain Maimonides' opinion, with which the Tosafists agree (*Nazir* 65b s.v. *be-shiv'ah*). Rather, we must explain why Rashi felt the need to bring demons into what appears to be a straightforward halakhah. For one attempted solution, see *Likutim* to *Nazir* 9:4 (printed in the Vilna edition of the Mishnah).

77. See *Kesef Mishneh* and *Lehem Mishneh, ad loc.*

78. See Levinger, *Darkhei ha-Mahashavah*, pp. 112–114. Meiri discusses both danger and suspicion, but omits any mention of demons. Whereas Maimonides uses the word אסור in codifying the law, Meiri regards the talmudic passage as merely reflecting מדות החכמים ומטכסיסיהם. (Although a separate study is needed to analyze how Meiri deals with superstition, and how he relates to Maimonides in this respect, I thought it would be helpful to make brief mention of Meiri's view with regard to the examples cited. See also

Berakhot 4b–5a:

> R. Joshua ben Levi says: "Though a man has recited the *shema* in the synagogue, it is a religious act to recite it again upon his bed." . . . R. Nahman, however, says: "If he is a scholar, then it is not necessary." Abaye says: "Even a scholar should recite one verse of supplication." . . . R. Isaac says: "If one recites the *shema* upon his bed, it is as though he held a two-edged sword in his hand [Rashi: to kill the demons]." . . . R. Isaac says further: "If one recites the *shema* upon his bed, the demons keep away from him."

The Jerusalem Talmud states: "R. Huna in the name of R. Joseph: 'On what basis must one recite the *shema* in his house in the evening? So that he may chase away the demons'" (*Berakhot* 1:1). We thus see that the recitation of the *shema* upon the bed was connected with protection from demons. Apparently, a scholar is always protected by his studying; therefore, R. Nahman rules that he is not required to recite this *shema*. Maimonides codifies the law as follows: "He then reads the first section of the *shema* and sleeps. If he is overcome by drowsiness he reads even if it be only one verse [of the *shema*] or verses of a supplicatory character and sleeps" (*Tefillah* 7:2). Maimonides has omitted R. Nahman's view that a scholar need not recite the final *shema*. That is, because he rejects the Talmud's demon-related reason for the law, Maimonides does not place the scholar in a special category. This, then, leads him to adopt the view of Abaye, originally stated with regard to scholars, and formulate it as a generally applicable rule.[79]

Gregg Stern, "Menahem ha-Meiri and the Second Controversy over Philosophy" [unpublished doctoral dissertation, Harvard University, 1995], pp. 82ff.). Ivor Jacobs kindly sent me an unpublished essay by his late father, Louis Jacobs, entitled "Demythologising the Rabbinic Aggadah: Menahem Meiri."

79. See Levinger, *Darkhei ha-Mahashavah*, pp. 151–152. Meiri has a very original interpretation: להבריח את המזיקים, וביארו אצלי המזיקים הידועים והם הדעות הכוזבים, והזקיקוהו בעתות הפנאי ליחד את השם שלא יטעה באמונות השניות וכשיקרא על הכונה הראויה תהא מטתו בטוחה מהם. See also Meiri, *Hibbur ha-Teshuvah*, ed. Sofer (Jerusalem, 1976), p. 574. In *Hilkhot ha-Yerushalmi*, p. 20, Maimonides also records the reason להבריח את המזיקין. As the late Prof. Yaakov Levinger pointed out to me, not knowing the criteria by which this work was composed, it is possible that Maimonides could have included a passage the basis of which he did not agree with. See below, p. 140 n. 173. Lieberman's attempt to understand this passage in a Maimonidean vein is very far-fetched, as was noted by Levinger, *Darkhei ha-Mahashavah*, p. 152 n. 185. For R. Abraham Maimonides' view of the final *shema*, see *Sefer ha-Maspik*, pp. 244–245.

Berakhot 18a: "R. Hiyya and R. Jonathan were once walking about in a cemetery, and the blue fringe of R. Jonathan was trailing on the ground. Said R. Hiyya to him: 'Lift it up, so that they [the dead] should not say: "Tomorrow they are coming to join us and now they are insulting us!"'" Since, in Maimonides' view, dead people do not observe the actions of humans, he omits this law. Furthermore, as Maimonides could well point out, the Talmud never indicates that this is a generally applicable law rather than simply a conversation between two *amoraim*.

There is a similar halakhah on the same page of Talmud. "A man should not walk in a cemetery with *tefillin* on his head or a scroll of the Law in his arm, and recite the *shema*, and if he does so, he comes under the heading of *He that mocketh the poor* [80] *blasphemeth his Maker* (Prov. 17:5)." Maimonides records this halakhah since it is not based upon superstition. That is, the verse from Proverbs is directed at the living, and, unlike the previous example, there is no assumption that the dead realize they are being mocked.[81]

Berakhot 43b: "Our Rabbis taught: Six things are unbecoming for a scholar. . . . Some add that he should not take long strides." Following this Baraita, the Talmud examines each of the examples listed. The reason given for the last example is "because a Master has said: 'Long strides diminish a man's eyesight by a five-hundredth part.' What is the remedy? He can restore it with [drinking] the sanctification wine of Sabbath eve." A similar passage is found in *Shabbat* 113b, in which, however, it is stated flatly that *no one* is to take long strides, the reason being that one's eyesight will be diminished.

Maimonides writes as follows: "A scholar . . . should not run in a public place after the fashion of the mad. . . . Even from the way a

---

80. לועג לרש, i.e., the dead, who are "poor" in precepts.

81. See *Keriat Shema* 3:2, *Tefillin* 4:23, *Sefer Torah* 10:6, *Evel* 14:13. It is significant that Maimonides never actually mentions the phrase לועג לרש; see R. Yitzhak Arieli, *Einayim la-Mishpat* (Jerusalem, 1947), *Berakhot, ad loc.*, and Kafih, *Ketavim*, p. 622. See also R. Yehudah Parnes, "Shitat ha-Rambam be-Loeg la-Rash," *Yevul ha-Yovelot* (New York, 1986), pp. 248–251. For a different understanding of Maimonides' approach here, see Lichtenstein, "Shitat ha-Rambam," pp. 8ff. *Shulhan Arukh, Orah Hayyim* 23:1 and *Yoreh Deah* 367:4, following the *Tur*, merges the halakhah regarding *tzitzit* with the explanation of לועג לרש. The same approach is followed by Meiri.

person walks it is apparent whether he is wise and sensible or foolish and imprudent" (*Deot* 5:8). Maimonides records the opinion of the Rabbis as quoted in *Berakhot*, while discarding the Talmud's superstitious reason and substituting a rational one, namely, the need to prevent a scholar from being dishonored. He no doubt believed that the Rabbis shared his reason, and that the superstitious reason was a later, inauthentic, explanation. Because of this, Maimonides also neglects to record the passage from *Shabbat* according to which all people should refrain from taking long strides. In this passage it is clear that the only reason to refrain from doing so is to prevent one from losing one's eyesight. There is no way to separate this advice/prohibition from the superstition since the author of this statement himself explains his reasoning. Not seeing any rational reason why laymen should avoid taking great strides, Maimonides omits any mention of the passage in *Shabbat*.[82]

Similarly, in *Berakhot* 43b it is stated that a scholar should not go out alone at night so as not to arouse suspicion, unless he has an appointment (Rashi: to study). Maimonides records this, including the reason, in *Deot* 5:9. The reason given in *Berakhot* is totally rational and is only directed towards the scholar.[83] However, in *Pesahim* 112b one finds a parallel passage which is directed towards all people. According to it, one should not go out at night, "that is, on the nights of either Wednesday or the Sabbath, because Igrath the daughter of Mahalath [the queen of demons] and 180,000 destroying angels go forth, and each has permission to wreak destruction independently." Needless to say, this passage finds no echo in the *Mishneh Torah*.

Berakhot 51a: The following laws are stated: Do not take your shirt from the hand of your attendant when dressing in the morning. Do

---

82. A passage similar to the *Shabbat* text appears in *Ta'anit* 10b. Here, too, all people are cautioned against taking great strides. However, unlike in *Shabbat*, this caution appears in a Baraita without any explanation. The superstitious reason is a later explanation of the Baraita. Thus, had Maimonides wished, he could have relied upon the non-superstitious *Ta'anit* Baraita to preclude laymen from taking great strides. Meiri omits any mention of the passages in *Berakhot*, *Shabbat*, and *Ta'anit*, thus signifying his rejection of the "walking" superstition.

83. In *Hullin* 91a it is also stated that a scholar should not go out alone at night, and although no explicit rationale is offered, the context seems to makes clear that it is due to demons. See Rashi *ad loc.*, s.v *mi-de-ka'amar*, Tosafot, *ad loc.*, s.v. *mi-kan*. However, Meiri rationalizes this passage as follows: שהקנאה מצויה לבריות עליו וההיזק מחזר ורודף אחריו.

not let water be poured over your hands by one who has not already washed his own hands. Do not return a cup of asparagus brew to anyone save the one who has handed it to you. Do not stand in front of women when they are returning from the presence of a dead person. The reasons given for these laws have to do with demons and the Angel of Death. Maimonides omits them all.[84]

Berakhot 51b: "R. Assi also said: 'One should not say Grace over the cup of punishment.' What is the cup of punishment? R. Nahman ben Isaac said: 'a second cup.' It has been taught similarly: He who drinks an even number should not say grace." Here we have the problem of *zugot* (pairs),[85] and as Rashi explains, one involved with *zugot* can be harmed by demons. The issue of *zugot* is also discussed at length in *Pesahim* 109b-110b, and here, too, it is related to harm caused by demons. Maimonides does not include anything about *zugot* in his Code, a fact very easily explained by his rejection of this superstition.

Earlier I put forth the view that, even though Maimonides rejects talmudic halakhot which are based on superstition, he believed that the wisest sages also rejected them. This is an assumption for which Maimonides generally would not have been able to find an explicit source. However, this is not the case with regard to *zugot*, for the Talmud records: "In the West [Eretz Israel] they were not particular about *zugot*" (*Pesahim* 110b).[86] Maimonides could certainly have regarded this passage as confirmation of his view regarding the innocuous nature of *zugot*, as well as proof that there were sages who opposed this superstition.[87]

---

84. Meiri also does not deal with any of them.

85. Regarding *zugot*, see D. Joël, *Der Aberglaube und die Stellung des Judenthums zu demselben* (Breslau, 1881), vol. 1, pp. 60ff.

86. Following this, the Talmud adds: "This is the position in general: When one is particular [about *zugot*], they [the demons] are particular about him, while when one is not particular, they are not particular about him. Nevertheless, one should take heed." Although this particular passage could be used to justify disregard of *zugot*, since it acknowledges the existence of demons, it is obvious that Maimonides could not have found any support in it. Meiri's view of *zugot* is discussed later in this chapter.

87. For a related example, from which we see that the Sages held different views about these types of matters, see *Rosh ha-Shanah* 16a-b, where the practice of blowing the shofar during *musaf* is explained as being "in order to confuse the Satan." Yet in *Rosh ha-Shanah* 32b and the Jerusalem Talmud, *Rosh ha-Shanah* 4:8, two separate "realistic" explanations, both relating to the reaction of gentiles, are offered as the origin of this practice.

Although it has often been regarded as axiomatic that Maimonides' omission of *zugot* is a prime example of the way he deals with superstitious halakhot, this must be called into question by the publication of a work authored by Maimonides' son, R. Abraham, in which he records an oral teaching of his father.[88] According to him, Maimonides did not regard *zugot* as superstition. Rather, the prohibition of *zugot* is directed against—and intended to keep Jews far away from—dualist ceremonies in which religious rites are carried out twice. By prohibiting *zugot*, the Sages attempted to neutralize the idolatrous practice, an approach similar to that which Maimonides ascribes to the Torah itself with regard to a number of biblical commandments. The demon-related reason given for the prohibition of *zugot* is merely designed to ensure the obedience of the masses, for whom fear of demons is a practical concern. Thus, it is a "necessary belief" of the sort Maimonides describes in *Guide* 3:28.

However, if we are to accept the accuracy of R. Abraham's transmission of this seemingly unprecedented view,[89] we are confronted with a problem: namely, why did Maimonides not record the law of *zugot* in the *Mishneh Torah*? One cannot reply that since the fear of dualism was no longer present, Maimonides chose to omit the law, for this would contradict what he writes in *Mamrim* 2:2–3 about the proper procedure for the abolishment of rabbinic prohibitions (and I assume that *zugot* would fall into this category). Presumably, Maimonides would call attention to the requirement in *Mamrim* 2:2 and 2:6 that for such a prohibition to be valid, it must be accepted throughout all Israel; and, as we have seen, the Talmud writes that "In the West [Eretz Israel] they were not particular about *zugot*" (*Pesahim* 110b). Thus, if Maimonides were to assume that many people never accepted the prohibition of *zugot*, in accordance with *Mamrim* 2:2 and 2:6 the law would have no validity and this fact, rather than superstition, would explain his omission of it in the *Mishneh Torah*.

---

88. *Sefer ha-Maspik*, p. 222. For the proper translation, see Paul B. Fenton in *JQR* 82 (1991), p. 206; Kafih, *Ketavim*, vol. 3, pp. 1405–1406.

89. Among post-Maimonidean scholars, R. Bahya ben Asher and R. Hezekiah ben Abraham also connected the prohibition of *zugot* with the desire of the Sages to keep Jews far away from dualistic notions. See *Kitvei Rabbenu Bahya*, ed. Chavel (Jerusalem, 1970), p. 487; *Malkiel* (Warsaw, 1876), pp. 13ff. (In his commentary to Gen. 1:4, R. Bahya offers a different reason for the prohibition.)

Berakhot 54b: "Rav Judah said: 'Three persons require guarding, namely, a sick person, a bridegroom, and a bride.' In a Baraita it was taught: A sick person, a midwife, a bridegroom and a bride; some add, a mourner, and some add further, scholars at night." Rashi explains that these people must be guarded from evil spirits. Presumably, Maimonides understood this passage in the same manner, and this explains why he omitted it from the *Mishneh Torah*.[90]

Berakhot 55b: The ritual of improvement of a dream (*hatavat halom*) is omitted from the *Mishneh Torah*.[91]

Shabbat 12b and *Sotah* 33a: "Did not Rav Judah say, 'One should never petition for his needs in Aramaic . . . [for] the Ministering Angels do not heed him, for they do not understand Aramaic?'" The notion that angels play any sort of role in ensuring that one's prayers reach God is regarded as superstitious, and Maimonides therefore omits this halakhah.[92]

Shabbat 109a states that in order to remove the *ruah ra'ah*, one must wash one's hands three times; this leads many halakhic authorities to rule that in the morning, before praying, this same procedure

---

90. Meiri also omits any mention of this passage.

91. Meiri discusses *hatavat halom* and, as Jacobs, "Demythologising," notes, even refers to the formula as an incantation (לחש). Elsewhere, Maimonides does record halakhot that have to do with dreams. For example, *Talmud Torah* 7:11 states that if one dreams that he has been excommunicated, he must have the ban officially voided. This must be viewed in line with Maimonides' understanding that a dream is "not a new product of one's soul or a new idea from the outside, but is rather brought up from the imaginative faculty," *EJ*, vol. 6, col. 210. Therefore, actions taken in response to dreams are all inner-directed, and a *ta'anit halom* is described by Maimonides as a method to encourage introspection and repentance. See *Ta'aniyot* 1:12.

92. See, however, his *Commentary* to *Sotah* 7:1 where, without mentioning the talmudic reason, he writes: "An individual should make every effort to only pray to God in Hebrew." In the *Mishneh Torah*, Maimonides does not even offer this as a recommendation. Cf. Meiri to *Shabbat* 12b where, unlike Maimonides, he quotes the law but substitutes his own reason: לעולם אל ישאל אדם צרכיו בלשון ארמי שמתוך שאין הלשון שגור בפי הבריות אין הכונה מצויה בדבריו עד שתהא תפלתו מקובלת. See also Meiri's commentary to *Sotah* 33a, *Hibbur ha-Teshuvah*, pp. 509ff.; and R. Aaron ha-Kohen of Lunel's similar explanation in *Orhot Hayyim* (Jerusalem, 1956), *Keriat Shema*, no. 19. In his commentary to *Shabbat* 12b, Meiri also adds another interesting rationalization: כתבו הגאונים בתפלת הציבור שהוא בכל לשון מטעם זה שהציבור שכינה עמהם ר"ל שכונתם מצויה הרבה עמהם. See Meiri to *Berakhot* 6a, where the phrase שכינה עמהם is understood in the same fashion, and see also *Perush Rabbenu ha-Meiri: Avot*, ed. Havlin (Jerusalem, 1994), Introduction, pp. 45–47.

must be followed.[93] However, in *Tefillah* 4:2, Maimonides merely states that one must wash one's hands before praying, without mentioning anything about the number of times.[94] Here we can identify the basic law, unencumbered by superstition, which is that one must wash one's hands before prayer, either because of cleanliness or a fear that they might have become ritually impure. The notion of washing three times to remove the *ruah ra'ah* is an unacceptable insertion that can be omitted without affecting the basic law.[95]

Shabbat 128b: The Mishnah states: "We may deliver a woman on the Sabbath, summon a midwife for her from place to place, desecrate the Sabbath on her account, and tie up the navel string. R. Jose said: 'One may cut it too and all the requirements of circumcision may be done on the Sabbath.'" In discussing this law, the Talmud (129b) quotes R. Jose as also saying that "we hide the afterbirth, so that the infant may be kept warm." In recording these halakhot in *Shabbat* 2:11, Maimonides leaves out R. Jose's statement about the afterbirth. Presumably, he regarded this as a superstitious practice.[96]

Shabbat 151b: "R. Hanina said: 'One may not sleep in a house alone, and whoever sleeps in a house alone is seized by Lilith [a female demon].'" The reason given for not sleeping alone seems to be inseparable from R. Hanina's first statement; because of this, Maimonides omits it from the *Mishneh Torah*.[97]

---

93. See, e.g., *Shulhan Arukh, Orah Hayyim* 4:2, 23. Many authorities rule that one must wash one's hands immediately upon awaking, and before walking four cubits. This is derived from a passage in the Zohar, vol, 1, p. 10b, referring only to the especially pious: הכי הוו עבדי חסידי קדמאי נטלא דמייא הוו יהבי קמייהו. There is also a version of the Zohar that adds that one who violates this is deserving of death, a formulation adopted by some later authorities; see Azulai, *Birkei Yosef, Orah Hayyim* 1:1.

94. See also *Tefillah* 7:4 and Epstein, *Arukh ha-Shulhan, Orah Hayyim* 4:1–2.

95. Regarding Meiri's view, see below, p. 131 n. 136. For detailed discussions of the morning washing, see Martin L. Gordon, "*Netilat Yadayim shel Shaharit*: Ritual of Crisis or Dedication," *Gesher* 8 (1981), pp. 36–73; R. Yosef Shevah, *Imrot Yosef* (Jerusalem, 1994), section 1.

96. Concerning hiding the afterbirth, Meiri writes: והיה זה רפואה אצלם כדי שיחם הולד. See also Saul Lieberman, *Yerushalmi ki-Feshuto* (Jerusalem, 1935), p. 204; Raphael Patai, "Ha-Leidah ba-Minhag ha-Amami," *Talpiot* 6 (1955), pp. 698ff.

97. Meiri has an interesting formulation which blunts the superstitious element of the passage: אסור לישן בבית יחידי וכן בכל שהוא מביא עצמו לידי נסיון של פחד אסור והכל לפי טבעו.

Pesaḥim 10b: "If a loaf is in a snake's mouth, does he need a snake-charmer (חבר) to take it out or does he not need [one]?" This question remains unanswered. Maimonides writes: "If a snake with bread in its mouth enters a hole, one need not bring a snake-charmer (חבר) to get it out" (*Hametz u-Matzah* 2:13). R. Hayyim Eleazar Shapira questions why, if Maimonides denies the validity of charms,[98] he uses the language "one need not bring a snake-charmer"?[99] Shapira could have also noted that this passage contradicts Maimonides' view that it is *forbidden* to use make use of charms (*Avodah Zarah* 11:10, *Sefer ha-Mitzvot*, neg. com. 35; I am assuming that there is no difference between using magic and hiring someone else to do so on your behalf.[100])

The answer to both of these questions would seem to be that there is nothing magical about the snake-charmer in *Hametz u-Matzah*, and this is also how Maimonides understands the text in *Pesaḥim*.[101] In other words, the snake-charmer simply uses his *skill* to tame the snake. However, when Maimonides defines חובר in *Avodah Zarah* 11:10, he is referring to a magician whose incantations have no effect, that is, one who casts a spell on a snake to prevent it from causing harm to humans. Nevertheless, even in this latter case we see Maimonides' removal of superstition; for the Talmud, *Sanhedrin* 65a, accepts the possibility that one's charms will be able to control the snake.

Pesaḥim 111a–111b: Various rules are given about who can pass between whom, how one is to relieve oneself, drinking borrowed water, and passing over spilt water. They are all connected to demonic forces, and Maimonides therefore ignores them.

Pesaḥim 112a: "If food and drink [are kept] under the bed, even if they are covered in iron vessels, an evil spirit rests upon them." In codifying this passage, Maimonides writes: "One should not put a dish of food (תבשיל) under his seat even during a meal, lest something

---

98. See *Avodah Zarah* 11:10.

99. *Minhat Eleazar* (Brooklyn, 1991), vol. 3, no. 16.

100. See *Avodah Zarah* 11:10: וכן אדם שאמר עליו החובר אותם הקולות והוא יושב לפניו ומדמה שיש לו בזה הנאה מכין אותו מכת מרדות מפני שנשתתף בסכלות החובר.

101. See R. Yehudah Herzl Henkin, *Bnei Vanim* (Jerusalem, 1992), vol. 2, p. 236.

harmful fall into it without his noticing it" (*Rotzeah u-Shemirat ha-Nefesh* 12:5). In this example, Maimonides has followed the talmudic prescription regarding leaving food under the bed, but has offered his own reason for it. This is why he omits the talmudic clarification that if food is covered in an iron vessel, it still cannot be left there. An evil spirit can surely penetrate an iron vessel, but, as Maimonides would point out, such a vessel is enough to keep something harmful from falling in. In defense of his ruling, Maimonides would be able to point to the Jerusalem Talmud, *Terumot* 8:3, which also states that one must not put food under a bed, but does not give any reason for this. This means that the law *per se* has nothing to do with evil spirits, and Maimonides therefore feels comfortable rejecting the explanation for the law given in *Pesahim* 112a and offering his own rationale.[102]

Directly following the law against placing food under a bed, the following passage appears: "A man must not drink water either on the nights of the fourth days [Wednesdays] or on the nights of Sabbath, and if he does drink, his blood is on his own head, because of the danger. What is the danger? An evil spirit."[103] Maimonides excludes this law from his Code. What must be determined is why Maimonides viewed the first law, discussed in the previous paragraph, as different than this law. That is, why did he record the first law, substituting his

---

102. Maimonides clearly used the Jerusalem Talmud for his formulation, since unlike the text in *Pesahim*, the Jerusalem Talmud uses the word תבשיל and Maimonides uses this word as well. See Levinger, *Darkhei ha-Mahashavah*, pp. 111f. Rabad, in his comment to *Rotzeah* 12:5, notes that the law is found in the Jerusalem Talmud, and explains that its reason is due to *ruah ra'ah*. The purpose of Rabad's comment is not clear. Perhaps he wishes to point out that Maimonides' health-related reason is baseless, because even the Jerusalem Talmud, which does not give a reason, should be understood as being concerned with *ruah ra'ah*. It is also possible, as R. Abraham Danzig argues, that Rabad's version of *Pesahim* 112a did not include the passage about placing food under the bed. See *Hokhmat Adam* (Jerusalem, 1966), *Binat Adam* 68:63. Even if he did have this passage, perhaps the phrase "an evil spirit rests upon them" was missing. I say this because Rabad writes: ומפרשים משום רוח רעה. If he had our version of the text in *Pesahim* 112a, why didn't he mention that this reason is stated there?

103. See, similarly, *Pesahim* 112b: "Do not go out alone at night, for it was taught: One should not go out alone at night, that is, on the nights of either Wednesday or the Sabbath, because Igrath the daughter of Mahalath and 180,000 destroying angels go forth, and each has permisssion to wreak destruction independently."

own reason, rather than omitting it entirely, as he did with the law that one must not drink water on Wednesday or Saturday nights?

In answer to this problem, it seems clear that the first law is one that can be explained rationally, as a health measure, and as such there was no reason for it to be rejected. Maimonides was undoubtedly convinced that the law had the imprimatur of the more philosophically-minded sages, and the talmudic rationale was merely a suggestion by one *amora* trying to explain the law, but from whom the truth was hidden. That the reason offered by this *amora* is not an essential element of the law is further illustrated by the fact that it is not to be found in the Jerusalem Talmud. This is not the case with regard to the second law we have been discussing. There is simply no rational way to explain why one should not drink water on certain nights.[104]

Pesahim 112b: "Three things did R. Jose son of R. Judah charge Rabbi: . . . Do not stand naked in front of a lamp . . . for it was taught: He who stands naked in front of a lamp will be an epileptic and he who cohabits by the light of a lamp will have epileptic children. . . . Our Rabbis taught: If one cohabits in a bed where an infant is sleeping, that infant will be an epileptic." From this passage, Maimonides only records that intercourse is forbidden by light of a lamp (*Issurei Biah* 21:10). However, relying on another talmudic passage,[105] he explains that such activity must be avoided because it is "shameless," not because there is a danger of epilepsy.[106]

Yoma 77b: "It is forbidden to wash part of the body [on Yom Kippur]. . . . The School of R. Manasseh taught: R. Simeon ben Gamaliel said: 'A woman may wash one of her hands in water to give bread to an infant without any fear. . . .' Why that? Abaye said: 'Because of *shibta* [some sort of *ruah ra'ah*].'" The first law, that it is forbidden to wash part of the body on Yom Kippur, is understood by Maimonides to also include the standard morning washing before prayer (*Tefillah* 7:8). We have already seen that he does not refer to washing one's hands three times before morning prayers, which is a

---

104. Meiri omits mention of both of these laws.
105. See *Niddah* 17a.
106. Meiri omits mention of the entire passage in *Pesahim*.

clear indication that he does not believe that the reason for this washing is to remove the *ruah ra'ah*. It is merely a general hygiene measure or due to a concern that one's hands might have become ritually impure, and both of these considerations are overridden by the sanctity of Yom Kippur. It is true that if one's hands are dirty, one is permitted to wash them on Yom Kippur; but this is a separate law, unrelated to the standard morning washing which is not concerned with soiled hands.[107] For those authorities who view the morning washing as necessary to remove the *ruah ra'ah*, Yom Kippur does not nullify this washing, since hands which are contaminated with *ruah ra'ah* are regarded as no different than soiled hands.[108]

Maimonides codifies R. Simeon ben Gamaliel's law as follows: "A woman may rinse one hand in water in order to give her child a slice of bread" (*Shevitat Asor* 3:2). *Lehem Mishneh* asks the obvious question: Why does Maimonides record this law if it is entirely based upon the notion of *shibta*, and Maimonides ignores this demonic element elsewhere in his Code? The answer to this is presumably that Maimonides regarded R. Simeon ben Gamaliel's law as a health measure. Indeed, given the example he cites directly before this law, there seems to be no escaping this conclusion.[109] Maimonides therefore must have believed that Abaye's explanation did not provide the law's true rationale.[110]

---

107. Regarding Maimonides' view in this regard, *Hagahot Maimoniyot, ad loc.*, writes: ההיא פליגא על כל רבותינו. R. Nissim Gerondi, Commentary to Alfasi, *Yoma* 2a (commenting on *Yoma* 77b), writes simply: ואינו נכון. R. Abraham Maimonides, *Sefer ha-Maspik*, pp. 70–71, also disagrees with his father.

108. See Tosafot, *Yoma* 77b s.v. *mishum, Hullin* 107b s.v. *hatam*; R. Nissim Gerondi, Commentary to Alfasi, *Yoma* 1b (commenting on *Yoma* 77b). Even those authorities (e.g., *Tur, Orah Hayyim* 613:2) who do not mention *ruah ra'ah* would presumably agree that it is sufficient cause to permit washing. However, having set forth the principle that in the morning סתם ידים מלוכלכות, there is no necessity to further justify the washing. Alternatively, מלוכלכות could also include *ruah ra'ah*.

109. מי שהיה מלוכלך בצואה או טיט רוחץ מקום הטנופת כדרכו ואינו חושש.

110. See Rabinovitch, *Yad Peshutah, ad loc.* There is no contradiction between this law and *Mishneh Torah, Berakhot* 6:18 (based on *Hullin* 107b), where Maimonides writes that one who feeds another need not wash his hands. The law in *Berakhot* is only concerned with ritual washing, and this has no relevance to whether or not one's hands are dirty (see *Mishneh Torah, Berakhot* 6:1). Regarding Meiri's understanding of *Yoma* 77b, see below, p. 131 n. 136.

Megillah 3a: "Did not R. Joshua ben Levi say: 'It is forbidden for a man to greet another by night, for fear that he is a demon?'" This is omitted from the *Mishneh Torah*.[111]

Megillah 28a: "R. Johanan said: 'It is forbidden for a man to gaze on the face of a wicked man.'" Presumably, Maimonides believed this law was based on some superstition, and this explains why it is omitted from the *Mishneh Torah*.[112]

Ta'anit 16a: "Why do they go to the cemetery [to pray for rain in a drought]? R. Levi ben Lahma and R. Hama ben Hanina differ as to the reason. The one maintains that it signifies: We are before Thee as dead, while according to the other it is in order that the departed ones should pray for mercy in our behalf." Since, as already noted, Maimonides does not accept the belief that the dead are aware of what occurs on earth, it is understandable that he omits the second reason offered by the Talmud (*Ta'aniyot* 4:18).[113] Maimonides could find support for his approach in the Jerusalem Talmud, *Ta'anit* 2:1, which, in its discussion of going to the cemetery in time of drought, only records the first view.[114]

Ta'anit 4:6 (26b)[115]: "With the beginning of Av we should limit our rejoicing." To this, the Talmud adds: "Said R. Papa: 'Therefore a Jew

---

111. In his commentary to *Megillah*, Meiri is also silent on this point. However, in his commentary to *Sanhedrin* 44a (the parallel passage), he writes the following: עובדי האלילים זובחי לשעירים ולשדים וכיוצא באלו מאותם האמונות הקדומות ראוי לנו שלא להתחבר עמהם כל כך בדברי חבה ואהבים. וכל שאנו צריכים ליתן להם שלום אין ראוי להזכיר להם אחד משמעותיו של הקב"ה, והאיך נזכירהו יתברך מציאותו למי שכופר או מכחיש יכלתו ומסלק השגחתו. I don't know what the connection of this is to the talmudic passage, as it doesn't appear to be an explanation.

112. Meiri understands this passage to be in the nature of good advice, which was only followed by some scholars.

113. However, I do not know how to explain the fact that Maimonides does not record the Talmud's first reason exactly. Instead, he offers a variation of it. Whereas the Talmud's reason for going to the cemetery is directed towards God ("We are before thee as dead"), Maimonides' reason is directed towards the people: "Unless you return from your [sinful] ways, you are like these deceased ones."

114. If the Babylonian Talmud's second reason, given in the name of R. Hama ben Hanina, means that the dead are being *asked* to intercede with God, as opposed to them taking this step on their own accord, it may violate the fifth of Maimonides' Thirteen Principles. See my *Limits*, p. 78 n. 1.

115. A few pages prior to this, on *Ta'anit* 22b, there is also a halakhah concerning *ruah ra'ah*. However, since there is an alternate reading of this text, "*hayah ra'ah*," and it is

who has a lawsuit with a heathen in the month of Av should try to avoid it, because his luck is bad, but if he has a lawsuit in the month of Adar he should prosecute it, because in that month his luck is good'" (Ta'anit 29b). In recording the law (Ta'aniyot 5:6), Maimonides includes the mishnaic passage that one should limit rejoicing in Av. However, he omits the talmudic addition that one should avoid a lawsuit in Av and prosecute one in Adar, because this is based on the notion of "luck" (mazal), which is part of the astrological system Maimonides rejects.[116]

Moed Katan 18a: "Three things were said in reference to nails: One who buries them is righteous; one who burns them is pious; and one who throws them away is a villain.[117] What is the reason? Lest a pregnant woman should step over them and miscarry." Nothing about the necessity of proper disposal of nails is found in the Mishneh Torah.[118]

Hagigah 16a: "Anyone who looks at three things, his eyes become dim: at the rainbow, at the Prince (nasi), and at the priests." From the continuation of the talmudic discussion, it would seem that one is always forbidden to look at a rainbow or a prince, and therefore the Talmud clarifies that with regard to the priests, one is only forbidden to look at them during their priestly blessing in the Temple. In the Jerusalem Talmud, Megillah 4:8, the reason given for not looking at the priests during their blessing is that this may cause one to be distracted. It is this reason that Maimonides records in Tefillah 14:7. Contrary

---

impossible to know which version Maimonides had, I have omitted any discussion of it. R. Isaac Alfasi had "ruah ra'ah" in his version, as did Meiri, who interprets it as follows: יחיד שנרדף . . . מפני רוח רעה שבעתתו ובורח מצד שהוא מדמה שאדם רודפו.

116. Although Maimonides writes that one should limit rejoicing in Av, for reasons that are unclear he omits the parallel passage (Ta'anit 29a) that one should increase rejoicing in Adar. For attempts to solve this problem, including solutions not in accord with Maimonides' philosophical outlook, see R. Moses Sofer, She'elot u-Teshuvot Hatam Sofer, Orah Hayyim no. 160; R. Hayyim Eleazar Shapira, Nimukei Orah Hayyim (Jerusalem, 1968), no. 686; Levinger, Darkhei ha-Mahashavah, p. 118. Meiri, too, omits all mention of avoiding and prosecuting a lawsuit; however, his view of astrology is not as uncompromising as that of Maimonides. See Schwartz, Astrologyah, pp. 224ff.; Binyamin Ze'ev Benedikt, Merkaz ha-Torah be-Provence (Jerusalem, 1985), p. 253.

117. In Niddah 17a, R. Simeon ben Yohai is quoted as saying that one who throws his nails away in a public thoroughfare forfeits his life, and his blood is upon his head.

118. Meiri also omits any mention of the disposal of nails.

to Salo Baron, this is not an example of Maimonides accepting "only a part of a talmudic statement which he considered rationally sustainable," and omitting the rest.[119] As has just been noted, the text in *Hagigah*, unlike the Jerusalem Talmud, is only referring to Temple times, and for this reason Maimonides' omission of "dimming of eyesight" in favor of the Jerusalem Talmud's reason is not significant.[120] However, as Baron notes, it is significant that he neglects to mention anything about gazing at a rainbow or a prince.[121]

Gittin 66a: The Mishnah states: "If a man had been thrown into a pit and cried out that whoever heard his voice should write a *get* for his wife, the *get* should be written and presented to her." Regarding this, the Talmud discusses the possibility that the man in the pit may actually be a demon. It concludes by saying that the Mishnah concerns a case where one sees the man's "shadow of a shadow"[122] (which demons do not have). In recording this law in *Gerushin* 2:13, Maimonides omits any reference to demons or the need to see a "shadow of a shadow," which is actually a significant halakhic detail.[123] A very similar case is found in *Yevamot* 122a, where a mishnaic halakhah is clarified based on the idea that a demon does not have a "shadow of a shadow," and once again Maimonides leaves out this detail.[124] As I have already noted, Maimonides could argue that the amoraic elaboration of these *Mishnayot* did not reflect the view of the

---

119. *A Social and Religious History of the Jews* (Philadelphia, 1958), vol. 6, p. 178.

120. This fact was also ignored by Isidore Epstein, "Maimonides' Conception of the Law and the Ethical Trend of His Halachah," in *id.*, ed., *Moses Maimonides* (London, 1935), p. 72.

121. Meiri also adopts the Jerusalem Talmud's explanation, and says nothing about looking at a rainbow or a prince. See his commentary to *Megillah* 24b. (For a radically different interpretation of the talmudic passage, which perhaps could be used to explain Maimonides' formulation, see Adolf Jellinek's note in R. Judah Aryeh Modena, *Shulhan Arukh*, trans. Solomon Rubin [Vienna, 1867], pp. 129–130.)

122. Presumably, this refers to the penumbra.

123. Meiri also omits any mention, but he does add the following: אם הוא בבורות העמוקים צריך שיכונו את הקול אם הוא קול גמור או ערבוב של איזה דמיון.

124. *Gerushin* 13:23. Strangely enough, in this case Meiri does record the talmudic clarification. This last halakhah is complicated by the fact that Maimonides leaves out another element unrelated to demons. See Levinger, *Darkhei ha-Mahashavah*, pp. 124–126, who attempts to solve this problem.

tanna who did not believe in demons. Still, Maimonides' view is very significant since his ruling—that the woman is to be regarded as divorced—appears to contradict the talmudic halakhah that lacking sight of a "shadow of a shadow" she is still married, with all the halakhic ramifications this status entails.[125]

Gittin 70a: "The Rabbis taught: On coming from a privy, a man should not have sexual intercourse until he has waited long enough to walk half a *mil*, because the demon of the privy is with him for that time." This law is omitted from the *Mishneh Torah*.[126]

Baba Kamma 21a: "R. Sehorah stated that R. Huna quoting Rav had said: 'He who occupies his neighbor's premises without having any agreement with him is under no legal obligation to pay him rent, for Scripture says, *Through emptiness even the gate gets smitten* (Is. 24:12).'" From the continuation of the passage we see that the verse refers to a demon who haunts uninhabited premises. The person who dwells in the building without the owner's knowledge is actually giving the latter benefit by keeping the demon out. Yet this is not the only reason offered for the halakhah in *Bava Kamma* 21a. In fact, an earlier passage on this page also quotes Rav without giving any reason. Thus, the halakhah can be understood apart from the superstitious reason, and Maimonides codifies it in *Gezelah ve-Avedah* 3:9.[127]

Bava Metzia 29b-30a: The Mishnah states: "If one finds a cloth . . . he must spread it out for its own benefit [to be aired], but not for his honor [e.g., to use as a tablecloth]." The Talmud adds: "If he was visited by guests, he may not spread it over a bed or a frame, whether in his interests or in its own . . . because he may thereby destroy it, either through an [evil] eye or through thieves." In recording this halakhah, Maimonides writes: "If one finds a woolen garment . . . he may spread it on a couch for its own benefit alone, but not both for its benefit and his own. If he has visitors, he may not spread it out in their presence even for its own benefit, lest it be stolen" (*Gezelah ve-Avedah* 13:11). Not believing in the power of the evil eye (see next

---

125. For the view that Maimonides' ruling does not contradict the talmudic halakhah, see R. Joel Sirkes, *Bayit Hadash, Even ha-Ezer* 17:10.

126. Meiri also omits it.

127. Meiri omits any mention of the superstitious reason.

example), Maimonides omits this reason from his codification. However, since the halakhah is not dependent on the evil eye, as the Talmud also offers a rational reason for it, it is recorded in the *Mishneh Torah* without any of its halakhic elements altered.[128]

Bava Batra 2b: The Talmud discusses the separation that joint owners erect in a courtyard between their fields. In establishing that there is real damage when one man looks over into another's vegetable garden, the Talmud quotes the following law: "R. Abba said in the name of R. Huna, who said it in the name of Rav: 'It is forbidden for a man to stand about in his neighbor's field when the corn in it is in the ear.'" As Rashi explains, this is to prevent the evil eye from having any negative impact.[129] Maimonides states that the required height of the wall needed to separate one man's garden from another is ten *tefahim*.[130] While ten *tefahim* is sufficient to suitably delineate where one property ends and the other begins, Maimonides is clearly not taking into account any negative impact that the evil eye might have on the neighbor's garden, the prevention of which, according to *Bava Batra* 2b, would require a wall at least four *amot* high. It is with this in mind that Rabad characterizes Maimonides' ruling as an "error."

The sages of Lunel asked Maimonides to justify his view, and in his response he explains that the notion of the "evil eye" is only *divrei hasidut*—not halakhah.[131] It is significant that he does not simply reject the talmudic decision as being based on superstition. Rather, through a new interpretation he shows that his view is actually supported by the talmudic discussion.[132] As we have already seen, Maimonides is willing to reject a talmudic halakhah outright when it is based on

---

128. Whereas the Talmud writes: אי משום עינא אי משום גנבי, Meiri, in his commentary to *Pesahim* 26b, combines the two reasons: שמא אחד מהם יהא נותן עיניו עליה ויגנבנה. In his commentary to *Bava Metzia* 29b, the same language appears, minus the word נובנה–ויג. (Meiri believed in the evil eye; see below, p. 129 n. 131.) See also *Yad Peshutah, ad loc.*, who suggests explaining Maimonides in this fashion.

129. See *Bava Metzia* 107b where Rav also stresses the importance of the "evil eye": "*And the Lord shall take away from thee all sickness* (Deut. 7:15). Said Rav: 'By this, the [evil] eye is meant. This is in accordance with his opinion [expressed elsewhere] . . . ninety nine [have died] through an evil eye, and one through natural causes.'"

130. *Shekhenim* 2:16.

131. *Teshuvot ha-Rambam*, no. 395.

132. See the complete analysis in Benedikt, *Ha-Rambam*, pp. 9–18.

superstition. However, it is always preferable to him to show that the talmudic sources agree with his own outlook.

In explaining his view to the sages of Lunel, Maimonides also makes a distinction between this law and *Shekhenim* 2:14, where he writes that one can compel another to build a wall in the middle of a jointly owned courtyard "so that one will not see the other when he uses his portion, inasmuch as the injury caused to one by the sight of the other is a real injury." In this latter example, we are confronted with real damage, that is, the loss of privacy suffered by the person being observed.[133] With regard to the first case—since Maimonides does not believe that one can damage another's field with his eye—it is not clear what he means by *divrei hasidut*. Maimonides never introduces this element concerning other superstitions, such as *ruah ra'ah*.

Maimonides' point might be that because one's neighbor might believe in the power of the evil eye, it is good neighborliness, that is, *divrei hasidut*, to abstain from looking into his garden. In my opinion, a better explanation is that since, according to the *Commentary on the Mishnah*,[134] the "evil eye" means a desire for money and material possessions, when Maimonides writes of *divrei hasidut*, he is referring to the extra measures one takes to avoid this moral flaw.[135]

Sanhedrin 47a: "Whence is it inferred that a wicked man may not be buried beside a righteous one? From the verse, *And it came to pass*

133. Regarding the issue of *hezek re'iyah*, see *Entzyklopedia Talmudit* (Jerusalem, 1957), vol. 8, pp. 659–702.

134. *Avot* 2:8, 10. See also the rejection of this view by R. Simeon ben Zemah Duran, *Magen Avot*, ed. Zeini (Jerusalem, 2000), to *Avot* 2:16 (p. 146).

135. Maimonides justifies his position talmudically, without even mentioning that he denies the concept of the evil eye. Therefore, R. Joseph Karo, who takes the evil eye very seriously, was able to adopt this opinion; see *Hoshen Mishpat* 158:3. (Incidentally, the logic behind this halakhah is contradicted by *Hoshen Mishpat* 378:5.) Needless to say, Maimonides does not base the prohibition to count Jews (*Yoma* 22b) upon the notion of the evil eye (see *Temidin u-Musafim* 4:4), a reason given by other authorities (e.g., Rashi, Ex. 30:12). *Maggid Mishneh*, *Shekhenim* 2:16, admits that Maimonides' view makes sense; it is just that the Talmud seems to disagree. Nahmanides is more forthright and rejects Maimonides' view out of hand: ואינו נכון ולא דעת כל רבותינו ז"ל; see his commentary to *Bava Batra* 4a. Meiri accepts the notion of the evil eye; see his commentary to *Bava Batra* 2b, where he also discusses Maimonides' view. It is noteworthy that Meiri is unaware of Maimonides' responsum to the sages of Lunel, and furthermore, attempts to justify Maimonides' opinion as if the latter accepted the concept of the evil eye. (As far as I can tell, Meiri never cites Maimonides' responsa to the sages of Lunel.)

as they were burying a man that behold they spied a band and they cast the man into the sepulchre of Elisha, and as soon as the man touched the bones of Elisha, he revived and stood up on his feet (II Kings 13:21)." In other words, the touch of the body of a righteous one can bring someone back from the dead. Not believing this to be true, Maimonides omits this halakhah, presumably understanding the biblical verse to be dealing with someone who only appeared to be dead.[136]

Sanhedrin 65a: "Our Rabbis taught: [*There shall not be found among you* . . .] a charmer (Deut. 18:10–11). This applies to one who charms large objects [Rashi: cattle and beasts], and to one who charms small ones [Rashi: insects and reptiles], even snakes and scorpions. Abaye said: 'Therefore even to imprison wasps or scorpions [by charms], though the intention is to prevent them from doing harm, is forbidden.'" Although the talmudic opinions assume that these charms have real power, when Maimonides codifies the law, he writes: "Who is a charmer? A person who chants incantations . . . and imagines in his foolish perception that his words have an effect" (*Avodah Zarah* 11:10).[137] Because the charms have no effect, it is obvious that he cannot codify Abaye's statement.

Sanhedrin 65b: "*One that consults the dead* (Deut. 18:11): This means one who starves himself and spends the night in a cemetery, so that an unclean spirit may rest upon him." Rashi, reflecting the common understanding, explains "unclean spirit" to be that of a demon. In recording the law, Maimonides interprets "unclean spirit" in a different fashion: "Who is one who consults the dead? A person who starves himself and goes to sleep in a cemetery so that a deceased person will come to him in a dream and reply to his questions" (*Avodah Zarah* 11:13).[138] In this example, I think it is clear that Maimonides did not believe that he was rationalizing the talmudic passage. Rather, he regarded his understanding as the original intent of the text. Of course, according to Maimonides, there is no more chance for a deceased person to come to you in a dream than a demon, but if a talmudic passage can possibly be interpreted in a non-demonological way, that is the direction Maimonides will go.[139]

---

136. Cf. *Guide* 1:42.
137. See also *Guide* 1:61, 3:37. For Meiri's view, see below, p. 147 n. 195.
138. See also *Commentary on the Mishnah, Sanhedrin* 7:7.
139. Meiri follows Maimonides in his explanation of the passage.

Sanhedrin 101a: There is no reference in the *Mishneh Torah* concerning the permissibility of consulting demons and the spirits of oil or eggs.[140]

Sanhedrin 101a: ולוחשין לחישת נחשים ועקרבים בשבת. Rashi interprets this to mean "snakes and serpents may be charmed to render them harmless on the Sabbath." However, Maimonides interprets the passage as follows: "When a person has been bitten by a scorpion or a snake, it is permitted to recite incantations over the bite, even on the Sabbath." In line with his philosophical outlook, Maimonides adds the following comment: "Even though [the incantations] are of no avail, since the victim's life is in danger, permission was granted lest he become overly disturbed" (*Avodah Zarah* 11:11).

Makkot 6b: "Rava said: 'If they both saw the admonitor, or he saw them both, they can be conjoined in the testimony as a whole.' Rava further said, in reference to the requisite admonition, that if it was uttered even by the victim himself, or even if it came from some [invisible] demon [it is sufficient]." Maimonides codifies the second law as follows: "Once warning was given him . . . even if he heard the

---

140. Meiri,. *ad loc.*, has a very interesting formulation: ואלו שמאמינים במציאות השדים ופעולותיהם אסור להם לשאול בהם אף בחול. (See R. David Ibn Zimra's comment on this passage in *She'elot u-Teshuvot ha-Radbaz*, no. 848 [end].) From this passage, and the numerous examples referred to in the notes to this chapter (see also his commentary to *Shabbat* 29b, *Eruvin* 41b, *Avodah Zarah* 27b, *Perush Rabbenu ha-Meiri: Avot*, p. 242), we see that Meiri rejects the existence of demons and rationalizes *ruah ra'ah*. However, elsewhere we find that he seems to accept the existence of demons, *ruah ra'ah*, and *shibta*; see his commentary to *Shabbat* 109a, *Yoma* 77b, *Sanhedrin* 67b, *Hibbur ha-Teshuvah*, pp. 480–481, *Hiddushei ha-Meiri: Pesahim*, ed. Blau (New York, 1978), p. 379. *Ruah ra'ah* is generally understood to be simply another way of saying demon, and Meiri himself, in his commentary to *Rosh ha-shanah* 28a, quotes without objection Rashi's identification of the two (see Rashi, *ibid.*, s.v. *ha-tokea*). In his commentary to Proverbs 14:15, he does not deny the reality of demons, but simply says that their existence has not been proven. I am therefore not sure how to explain Meiri's view in this matter. While discussing Meiri, it is worth noting that his teacher, R. Reuven ben Hayyim, in his discussion of *Shabbat* 2:5, also rationalizes *ruah ra'ah*. See his *Sefer ha-Tamid*, published by Jacob Moses Toledano in *Otzar ha-Hayyim* 7 (1931)], p. 3 (second numbering). As Moshe Halbertal, *Bein Torah le-Hokhmah* (Jerusalem, 2000), p. 143, has pointed out, R. Abraham of Montpelier, Meiri's contemporary, rejected the existence of demons. This is seen from his comment on a talmudic passage which describes the characteristics of demons: יש מרבותינו אנשים שהיו מאמינים שהיו מציאות השדים (*Perush Rabbi Avraham Min ha-Har: Hagigah*, ed. Blau [New York, 1975], p. 203).

admonition but did not see the admonitor . . ." (*Sanhedrin* 12:2).
Maimonides does not interpret Rava's second law restrictively. That is,
he does not view it as applicable only to demons. Rather, it is intended to set forth a principle of admonition, for which the demon—
which is understood to be invisible[141]—is merely an illustrative example.[142] With this in mind, Maimonides feels free to accept the principle while rejecting the example given. The two are not inseparable.[143]

Avodah Zarah 4b: "No one should recite the Prayer of the
Additional Service on the first day of the New Year during the first
three hours of the day in private, lest, since judgment is then proceed-
ing, his deeds may be scrutinized and the prayer rejected." Because
Maimonides does not share this conception of God and his dealings
with man, he omits this law from the *Mishneh Torah*.[144]

Avodah Zarah 12b (almost identical law in *Pesahim* 112a):

> Our Rabbis taught: One should not drink water [*Pesahim*: from rivers or
> pools] in the night; if he does drink, his blood is on his head, for it is
> dangerous. What danger is there? The danger of Shabriri.[145] But if he
> be thirsty, how can he put things right? If there is another person with
> him, he should wake him and say: "I am thirsty for water." If not, let
> him knock with the lid on the jug and say to himself: "Thou [giving his
> name] the son of [naming his mother], thy mother hath warned thee to
> guard thyself against Shabriri, briri, riri, iri, ri, which prevail in blind
> vessels."

In codifying this law, Maimonides writes: "One may not . . . drink
at night from rivers or ponds, lest he swallow a leech while unable to
see" (*Rotzeah u-Shemirat ha-Nefesh* 11:6).[146] Once again, we see
Maimonides recording the talmudic halakhah, yet offering an alterna-

---

141. See Radbaz and *Kesef Mishneh, ad loc.* Radbaz writes: ורבינו השמיט דבר זה לסיבה
ידועה אצלו.

142. For another such example, Maimonides could have pointed to *Rosh ha-Shanah*
28a, where כפאו שד is used in the same sense as שוטה.

143. Meiri interprets the law in a similar fashion, and he even regards Rava's reference to demons as never having been meant literally: כל שהותרה בפני עדים אפילו מפי השד
ר"ל דרך משל ששמע קול המתרה ולא ראהו.

144. Meiri also omits mention of this law.

145. The demon appointed over the affliction of blindness.

146. See also *Berakhot* 11:4.

tive reason. However, in this case Maimonides was on sure ground, for on the very same page in *Avodah Zarah* we find the reason cited by Maimonides—fear of swallowing leeches—offered to explain why one must not drink from rivers or pools in a way that does not allow examination of the water (for example, by drinking with one's mouth submerged). Since the fear of swallowing leeches applies to all cases in which one cannot see what one is drinking, not only to the specific case mentioned in the Talmud, Maimonides feels comfortable substituting this reason for the superstitious Shabriri. In Maimonides' opinion, the reason he records represents the true—that is, the philosophically acceptable—rabbinic outlook.[147]

Hullin 105a-b: "The first washing [before a meal] may be performed either over a vessel or over the ground; the last washing must be performed over a vessel. Others read: The last washing may not be performed over the ground. . . . Abaye said: 'At first I thought the reason why the last washing may not be performed over the ground was that it made a mess, but now my Master has told me, it is because an evil spirit rests upon it.'" Maimonides quotes this law in *Berakhot* 6:16,[148] and we must therefore assume that he did not view the reason given by Abaye in the name of his Master as authoritative.[149]

Niddah 17a: "R. Simeon ben Yohai stated: 'There are five things which [cause the man] who does them to forfeit his life and his blood is upon his own head: Eating peeled garlic, a peeled onion or a peeled egg. . . .'" The Talmud explains that this is because an evil spirit rests upon them. Maimonides omits all mention of this.[150]

Niddah 24b: "R. Judah citing Samuel ruled: If an abortion had the likeness of Lilith, its mother is unclean by reason of the birth; for it is a child, but it has wings." Clearly, "Lilith," a female demon, is only

---

147. Meiri writes: ולא ישתה אדם מים בלילה אף של כלים אלא אם מוזגם בכוס ובודקם לאור הנר. He thus agrees with Maimonides as to the danger of drinking water at night, and that there is no need for an incantation against Shabriri. However, in *Hiddushei ha-Meiri: Pesahim*, p. 380, he rationalizes the incantation against Shabriri as follows: ומתמעט פחד דמיונו במיעוט המלה.

148. The standard printed version reads: "The last washing must be performed over a vessel." However, the best manuscripts have: "The last washing may not be performed over the ground."

149. Meiri also records the law.

150. Meiri also does not mention this.

cited to aid in describing the fetus, and does not substantially affect the law. Therefore, Maimonides is able to excise it. In *Issurei Biah* 10:10, he writes: "If an abortion is shaped like a human being, but has wings of flesh, the mother is likewise deemed unclean through childbirth."[151]

Another possible example of Maimonides' deletion of superstition is found in *Tefillah* 9:11:

> Why did the Sages institute this [practice]? Because the majority of people come to recite the evening service on Friday night. It is possible that someone will come late, remain alone in the synagogue, and thus be endangered. Accordingly, the leader of the congregation repeats his prayers in order that the entire congregation will remain, [allowing] the one who came late to conclude his prayers and leave together with them.

Lehem Mishneh gives the source for Maimonides' ruling as *Shabbat* 24b, and says that the reason given there as to why one who remains behind is endangered is because of demons. Thus, according to *Lehem Mishneh*, it is Maimonides who has omitted this element. However, our text of *Shabbat* reads simply "on account of danger," without demons being mentioned. Since it cannot be determined whether Maimonides had the text recorded by *Lehem Mishneh*, we must regard this example as questionable.[152]

Another example worth noting is found in *Nedarim* 39b.[153] Although this passage is aggadic, it is significant; for here, too, we find Maimonides subtly removing the superstitious element in the same way he does when dealing with halakhic passages. The text in *Nedarim* reads: "R. Abba son of R. Hanina said: 'He who visits the sick takes

---

151. Meiri writes: השיליא [צ"ל המפלת] בריה שיש לה כנפים של בשר <u>והוא שקראוהו דמות</u> <u>לילית</u>. Whereas the Talmud refers to the abortion as actually having the likeness of Lilith (דמות לילית), Meiri, who rejects the existence of Lilith, inserts the word שקראוהו.

152. In truth, it is most unlikely that Maimonides had the text recorded by *Lehem Mishneh*. Rashi, *Shabbat* 24b s.v. *mishum*, explains that the talmudic phrase "on account of danger" refers to the danger of demons, and this comment was probably inserted into the text of the Talmud used by *Lehem Mishneh*. See Weinberg, *Seridei Esh*, vol. 4, pp. 116–118, regarding this common phenomenon.

153. See R. Yaakov Hayyim Sofer, *Zera Hayyim* (Jerusalem, 1988), p. 22.

away a sixtieth of his pain . . . [providing that] he [the visitor] is of his affinity.'" Maimonides writes: "He who visits the sick *is as though* he would take away part of his sickness and lighten his pain" (*Evel* 14:4).

Whereas the Talmud seems to say that one who visits the sick literally removes some of his pain, Maimonides presents the passage in a more rational manner. Also significant is that Maimonides leaves out the phrase requiring that the visitor be "of his affinity" (בן גילו). It is likely that Maimonides interpreted this in the same way as R. Asher ben Jehiel[154] and R. Nissim Gerondi,[155] who take בן גילו to mean one who is born under the same planetary influence. If so, Maimonides' omission is clearly understood.[156]

---

154. *Nedarim, ad loc.*

155. *Nedarim, ad loc.*, s.v. *u-ve-ven gilo*.

156. Meiri also rationalizes the passage: ובבני גילו ר"ל שבקורם ערב עליו שמצד הנאתו מהם חליו מיקל.

It would require another study to examine the way Maimonides incorporates aggadic elements into the *Mishneh Torah*. Such a study would, I believe, reveal the same characteristics we find with regard to halakhah; that is, both the complete rejection of some talmudic statements as well as a reworking of others. At times, Maimonides' parting with talmudic views is obvious, e.g., *Mezuzah* 5:4, where he denies that the mezuzah provides protection; see Kafih's commentary, *ad loc.*; R. Wolf Boskowitz, *Seder Mishneh* (Jerusalem, 1966), *ad loc.* (esp. p. 197); Isaac Hirsch Weiss, "Toledot ha-Rambam," *Beit Talmud* 1 (1881), p. 230 n. 31. Sometimes, it is so subtle that the casual reader will not even notice. See, for example, his Introduction to the *Commentary to the Mishnah*, p. 2, and his Introduction to the *Mishneh Torah*, where he says that before Moses' death, the latter wrote a Torah for each of the twelve tribes. This is based on *Devarim Rabbah* 9:9, where, however, it adds that Moses wrote them all in *one day*. See also *Hanukkah* 3:2, where Maimonides closely follows the Talmud's explanation for the institution of Hanukkah (*Shabbat* 21b), but leaves out the crucial words נעשה בו נס. (In the late nineteenth century, there was a great debate between *maskilim* and traditionalists as to whether Maimonides believed in the Hanukkah miracle; see Geulah Bat Yehudah, "Rabbi Shmuel Alexandrov," *Sinai* 100 [1987], pp. 202–207, and the sources cited by Jacob I. Dienstag, "Art, Science and Technology in Maimonidean Thought," *TUMJ* 6 [1995–1996], pp. 152–155.) While on the subject of miracles, it should also be noted that there are times when Maimonides accepts a miracle in the *Commentary on the Mishnah* but ignores it in the *Mishneh Torah*, presumably implying its rejection. See, e.g., his *Commentary* to *Yoma* 6:6, which repeats the talmudic account of the scapegoat ceremony (*Yoma* 67a), but which is missing in his reconstruction of events in *Teshuvah* 1:2 and *Avodat Yom ha-Kippurim* 3:7. Of course, even when the Talmud mentions a miracle that Maimonides omits, this does not necessarily mean that he viewed himself as rejecting the talmudic view. Rather, as noted previously, it is possible that he regarded his understanding of the "miracle" to be the proper interpretation of the talmudic passage. A clear proof for this is seen in his *Commentary to Berakhot*

There is another relevant passage which, strictly speaking, does not concern superstition; however, it is worth quoting since it shows again how Maimonides offered his own rationale when recording a halakhah. Maimonides writes: "The duty of lighting the lamp [upon the beginning of the Sabbath] devolves upon women more than upon men, because the former are usually at home and household tasks are their usual concern" (*Shabbat* 5:3). That women are supposed to light the Sabbath candle is stated in the Jerusalem Talmud, *Shabbat* 2:6 (and midrashic parallels[157]). The reason given there is that because a woman put out the "candle of the world" (i.e., caused Adam's death), she therefore now lights the candle. R. Jacob ben Asher is the first to point out that Maimonides' reason differs from that offered by the Rabbis.[158] Kafih, in his commentary on this halakhah, explains that Maimonides could not record the rabbinic explanation because he regards the story of Adam, Eve, and the snake as an allegory.[159] Thus, Adam's death cannot be attributed to the historical Eve.

1:9, where he rationalizes the talmudic story of R. Eleazar ben Azariah's miraculous aging (*Berakhot* 28a), but describes his view as being in accordance with the Talmud's account. (For R. Moses Sofer's attempt—completely at odds with Maimonides' philosophical outlook—to reconcile Maimonides' statement with the Talmud's miracle story, see *Torat Moshe* [Vienna, 1908], *Hayyei Sarah*, p. 13a, s.v. *ve-zaken*.) There are also times when we find that he takes a different approach. See, e.g., *Sotah* 3:17, where Maimonides records the miracle that the paramour of the *sotah* would also die. This miracle is not mentioned in the Torah and, although it is discussed in the Mishnah (*Sotah* 5:1, and see Maimonides' *Commentary, ad loc.*), it was not necessary for Maimonides to record it, as he could have interpreted it in a non-literal fashion.

157. See *Bereishit Rabbah*, ed. Theodor and Albeck (Jerusalem, 1996), 17:8 (p. 160).

158. *Tur, Orah Hayyim* 263. Remarkably, after quoting the rabbinic explanation, Rashi, *Shabbat* 32a, s.v. *hareni*, also offers the same common-sense explanation as Maimonides.

159. Kafih cites *Guide* 2:30 in support of this contention. While Maimonides—mindful of the religious feelings of the masses—is careful not to state explicitly that the story is an allegory, there is no doubt that this is what he had in mind. See Narboni and Efodi, *ad loc.*, Abarbanel, Commentary to *Guide* 1:7, *id.*, Commentary to Genesis, ch. 2 (s.v. *ve-omer she-ha-parashah*); Gersonides, Commentary to Genesis, ed. Brenner and Freiman (Ma'aleh Adumim, 1993), p. 115; Sara Klein-Braslavy, "The Creation of the World and Maimonides' Interpretation of Gen. i-v," in Shlomo Pines and Yirmyahu Yovel, eds., *Maimonides and Philosophy* (Dordrecht, 1986), pp. 71ff., *id.*, *Perush ha-Rambam la-Sippurim al Adam be-Farashat Bereshit* (Jerusalem, 1987), *id.*, *Perush ha-Rambam le-Sipur Beriat ha-Olam* (Jerusalem, 1987), ch. 11; Abraham Nuriel, *Galui ve-Samui be-Philosophyah ha-*

For a prominent example of Maimonides' rationalism as it affected his halakhic rulings, many scholars have pointed to a responsum in
which Maimonides denies that there is any prohibition in marrying a
katlanit (a woman who has been widowed twice).[160] Since Mordechai
A. Friedman[161] and Avraham Grossman have discussed this,[162] there is
no need for me to elaborate on Maimonides' view. However, I do
believe that too much emphasis has been placed on this example. To
be sure, Maimonides' ruling fits in well with his rationalistic bent, but
this does not mean that we are confronted here with Maimonidean
originality. It certainly does not mean that "for all intents and purposes Maimonides 'exorcised the demon' and abolished the talmudic prohibition of marrying a 'killer wife.'"[163] We must not forget that
Maimonides claims that his view was supported by a number of earlier scholars, including R. Isaac Alfasi and R. Joseph Ibn Migash—
men who did not share his view regarding superstition. This suffices
to show that what we have here is not a Maimonidean "cleansing" of
halakhah, but simply a well-attested view that did not regard the *katlanit* prohibition as absolutely binding.[164]

In actuality, this issue presents great difficulties with regard to
Maimonides' view, for the simple reason that he does not entirely
reject the prohibition of *katlanit*. What he says is that a pious one
should not officiate at the betrothal of a *katlanit*, since it is "reprehensible" for her to marry, but if she does find a man willing to betroth

---

Yehudit Bimei ha-Beinayim (Jerusalem, 2000), pp. 152–153; Charles Manekin, *On Maimonides* (Belmont, CA, 2005), p. 81.

160. *Teshuvot ha-Rambam*, no. 218. See also *ibid.*, no. 15. For Meiri's view, see his commentary to *Yevamot* 64b, *Ketubot* 43b. Although he limits the law's applicability, Meiri
believes that a true *katlanit* is forbidden to marry.

161. "Tamar, a Symbol of Life: The 'Killer Wife' Superstition in Jewish Tradition,"
AJS Review 15 (Spring, 1990), pp. 50–54.

162. "Temurot be-Ma'amadah shel ha-Ishah ha-Yehudiyah bi-Sefarad," in Fleischer,
et. al., eds., *Me'ah She'arim*, pp. 102ff.

163. Friedman, "Tamar," p. 54.

164. See R. David of Navaradok, *Galya Masekhet* (Vilna, 1844), *Even ha-Ezer* no. 11,
who discusses at length the talmudic sources for this view. Because of contradictions
between Maimonides' testimony concerning Alfasi and Ibn Migash and the writings of
these two, Grossman offers a forced reading of Maimonides which is very hard to reconcile with his words. See "Temurot be-Ma'amadah," pp. 108–109. Kafih, Commentary to
Issurei Biah 21:31, assumes that Ibn Migash did not write the responsum attributed to him.

her, and the betrothal is observed by two witnesses, then the *beit din* allows the wedding to go forward.

We have already seen that Maimonides, though rejecting the existence of the evil eye, nevertheless regards the talmudic admonitions concerning it as belonging to the realm of *divrei hasidut*. In that case, it is unclear what Maimonides means by *divrei hasidut;* so, too, it is not apparent why he regards the marriage of a *katlanit* to be "reprehensible." After all, in his opinion, the whole notion of *katlanit* belongs to the category of "soothsaying, divination, conjecture, and fantasies, from which at some time bodies of weak constitution might be affected."[165] It is also puzzling that, in his responsum, Maimonides never actually states that a pious man should avoid marrying a *katlanit*, only that he not officiate at the betrothal. If the marriage is indeed "reprehensible," why the difference between these two cases? Finally, how is one to reconcile the almost offhand way that Maimonides deals with the issue of *katlanit* in his responsum with the serious manner in which it is treated in the *Mishneh Torah* (*Issurei Biah* 21:31), where he states without qualification that a *katlanit* should not marry?[166]

---

165. Translation in Friedman, "Tamar," p. 50.

166. In *Issurei Biah* 21:31, Maimonides also writes that if one marries a *katlanit*, he is not compelled to divorce her, demonstrating that there is no real prohibition against such a marriage in the first place. For those who view the issue of *katlanit* as law, it is clear that divorce is required; see R. Asher ben Jehiel, *Ketubot*, 4:3; R. Yom Tov Ishbili (Ritva), *Yevamot* 64b; R. Jacob ben Asher, *Tur, Even ha-Ezer* 9:1. Maimonides' view in the *Mishneh Torah* cannot be considered radical, and it is because of this that many post-Maimonidean halakhists agreed with him, including R. Isaac bar Sheshet, *She'elot u-Teshuvot Rivash*, nos. 241–242, and R. Joseph Karo, *Shulhan Arukh, Even ha-Ezer* 9:1 (see also *Beit Yosef, Even ha-Ezer* 9:1, where Karo is unaware of Maimonides' responsum which he himself quotes in *Kesef Mishneh, Issurei Biah* 21:31). Even those who did not completely agree with Maimonides' views, as expressed both in the *Mishneh Torah* and in his responsum, were still willing to use them as supporting arguments in their own decisions, or offer talmudic support in their behalf; see, e.g., R. Solomon ben Adret, *She'elot u-Teshuvot ha-Rashba*, vol. 3, no. 364: חזרתי על כל צדדי ולא מצאתי מקום שיסמך הרב ז"ל בזה זולתי שאני מדמה אולי סמך על מה ששנו . . . . See, similarly, *She'elot u-Teshuvot ha-Rashba ha-Meyuhasot le-ha-Ramban* (Jerusalem, 1989), no. 121 (see, however, *She'elot u-Teshuvot ha-Rashba*, vol. 7, no. 311, where he seems to agree with Maimonides). See also Sofer, *She'elot u-Teshuvot Hatam Sofer, Even ha-Ezer*, vol. 1, no. 24, vol. 6, no. 70; Shapira, *Minhat Eleazar*, vol. 2, no. 76. As is to be expected, numerous attempts were made to bring Maimonides' opinions more into line with those of other codifiers. See, e.g., R. Eleazer Fleckeles, *Teshuvah me-Ahavah*, vol. 1, no. 92, who suggests that Maimonides' formulation in the *Mishneh Torah* is only stated

R. Zadok ha-Kohen of Lublin argues that because the masses of Maimonides' time attached great significance to the *katlanit* prohibition, he felt that he had to record it, as opposed to other superstitions, that were not as widespread, which could be easily omitted.[167] Yet apart from the dubious historical assumption that all the other superstitious halakhot had fallen into abeyance, can it really be said that Maimonides' Code was guided by the sentiments of the masses? While one might be able to identify a few examples of this,[168] on the whole, the work attempts to disabuse the masses of their mistaken beliefs.

Although we have looked at a number of examples where Maimonides removed superstitious elements from his codification of halakhah, there still remain some problematic cases where it appears that Maimonides did allow superstition to enter the *Mishneh Torah*. A glaring example is *Shabbat* 19:13-14, where, basing himself on tannaitic passages recorded in tractate *Shabbat*,[169] Maimonides writes:

> One may go out on the Sabbath into a public domain . . . wearing a locust egg, a fox tooth, a nail from the gallows of an impaled convict, or any other article suspended on the body for medical reasons, provided that physicians say that it is medically effective. A woman may go out wearing a preserving stone[170] or its counterweight which has been weighed accurately for medical use. Not only a woman already pregnant

---

with regard to a woman whose two previous husbands had died. However, had she been widowed three times, even Maimonides would require her to be divorced if she remarried again. This approach was anticipated by R. Jacob Weil, *She'elot u-Teshuvot Mahari Weil* (Jerusalem, 1988), no. 183, who states that if all three husbands died from the same cause, "possibly" Maimonides would require the fourth husband to divorce her. Sofer, *She'elot u-Teshuvot Hatam Sofer*, vol. 6, no. 70; R. Israel Eisenstein, *Amudei Esh* (Lemberg, 1880), p. 96a; and R. Shalom Taubes, *She'elat Shalom* (Lemberg, 1885), vol. 2, no. 119, properly reject any such reading of Maimonides.

167. *Tiferet Tzvi* (Bilgoraj, 1909), p. 34b.

168. See, e.g., *Avodah Zarah* 3:11, *Tefillah* 7:5, *Mezuzah* 5:4, discussed later in this chapter.

169. Mishnah *Shabbat* 6:2, 10, *Shabbat* 61a, 66b.

170. אבן תקומה. Regarding this stone and its alleged properties, see Julius Preuss, *Biblisch-talmudische Medizin* (Berlin, 1911), pp. 446–447; Yaakov Yisrael Stoll's appendix to his edition of R. Judah he-Hasid, *Amarot Tehorot Hitzoniyot u-Fenimiyot* (Jerusalem, 2006), pp. 313–320.

may wear such a stone, but any other woman also may do so as a preventive of miscarriage in the event of pregnancy. One may also wear a tested amulet, that is, an amulet which has already cured three patients, or was made by someone who had previously cured three patients with other amulets. If one goes out into a public domain wearing an untested amulet, he is exempt,[171] because he is deemed to have worn it as apparel when transferring it from one domain to the other.

There is a great deal of difficulty with this formulation of Maimonides. To begin with, he appears to ascribe healing power to locust eggs, fox teeth, amulets, and other such things, which is surprising, since his view of these matters is well known.[172] Furthermore, the factor that determines whether one may go out with an amulet on the Sabbath is whether it is a "tested," or "expert," amulet. Thus, it seems that his acceptance of the superstitious even enters into the halakhic sphere.[173]

I have no doubt that this law must be understood in the same fashion as *Avodah Zarah* 11:11, where Maimonides permits one to recite a charm on behalf of another who has been bitten by a snake. Maimonides does not believe that this can cure the victim, but permits the recitation since "it will prevent his mind from being disconcerted."[174] Similarly, in the above passage Maimonides does not accept the

---

171. That is, he is exempt from punishment, but it is still forbidden.

172. See *Commentary on the Mishnah*, *Yoma* 8:4, *Mishneh Torah*, *Avodah Zarah* 11:16, *Guide* 1:61; and Aviezer Ravitzky, *Iyunim Maimoniyim* (Jerusalem, 2006), ch. 6. Shem Tov, Commentary to *Guide* 1:61, notes that the efficacy of amulets is attested to in the Mishnah, and adds: לבטל זה השבוש רצה הרב להאריך. R. Abraham Maimonides, *Milhamot Hashem*, p. 84, states explicitly that the preserving stone does not work.

173. See also his *Commentary* to *Shabbat* 6:2. Weiss, "Toledot," p. 229 n. 27, points out that Maimonides' addition of the phrase "provided that physicians say that it is medically effective" suffices to ensure that this situation will only rarely occur. However, this does not explain why Maimonides—if he did not believe in the power of amulets—recorded the law in the first place. See also Levinger, *Darkhei ha-Mahashavah*, pp. 129–130, who places this passage in the context of other talmudic laws that appear in the *Mishneh Torah*, even though they do not fit in with Maimonides' worldview. One such example he notes is *Temidin u-Musafin* 8:3: חטים שירדו בעבים. Although Levinger's approach is probably correct with regard to this example and some of the others he cites, I don't believe that it can be applied to *Shabbat* 19:13–14.

174. Kafih, Commentary to *Avodah Zarah* 11:11, claims that when Maimonides permits the recitation of a charm, he is referring to a situation in which the reciter knows that his words are meaningless, and his purpose is merely to calm the one who was bit-

healing power of amulets, locust eggs, etc.; but he does recognize that they have psychological value. With regard to the Sabbath, if an amulet is widely believed to be of value, that is, believed to have cured three times, the rabbis declared that one who wears it as an ornament, as opposed to carrying it, is not in violation of the halakhah.[175] In Maimonides' opinion, as far as the Sabbath law is concerned, popular perception, supported by medical opinion, of the efficacy of amulets, locust eggs, etc., suffices to turn them into an ornament. It is not relevant that, in reality, the belief that amulets can cure is a mistaken conception.[176]

Related to this are Maimonides' comments in *Guide* 3:37. Here, he explains that the Sages permitted one to wear a fox tooth and similar healing devices that were connected to the idolatrous practices of the nations,[177] not because they truly worked, but because in the days of

---

ten. However, when the reciter believes in the power of the charm, then it is forbidden. As far as I can tell, Kafih's interpretation has not been offered by any other commentator. R. Joseph David Sinzheim, *Yad David* (Jerusalem, 2002), *Sanhedrin* 101a, suggests that Maimonides' permission to recite an incantation refers to someone doing it on behalf of the person who was bitten; but the victim may not do it himself. There is nothing in Maimonides' words to lead one to this conclusion.

175. As Rashi puts it, *Shabbat* 60a, s.v. *she-eino*: בקמיע מומחה שרי דתכשיט הוא לחולה באחד ממלבושיו. See also Ibn Zimra, *She'elot u-Teshuvot ha-Radbaz*, nos. 1436, 1526; Nathanson, *Shoel u-Meshiv*, fourth series, vol. 3, no. 86.

176. Meiri notes that although the amulet itself is not a remedy, the psychological (placebo) effect of the amulet could effect a cure. See his commentary to *Shabbat* 53a: שמצד שהיו ההמון באותו זמן, *Shabbat* 67a: שאדם אפשר שטבעו מתחזק מתוך בטחונו על הקמיע בטוח באותם העניינים היה טבעם מתחזק ונמצא מצד ההרגל עזר טבעי. Meiri's approach explains why, in *Avodah Zarah* 11:11, Maimonides permits one to recite a charm even though calming a person's nerves is not sufficient justification to violate a biblical commandment. To do that, one must be confronted with a case of real *pikuah nefesh*. Thus, even though Maimonides only speaks of the psychological effect that reciting a charm has upon the one bitten, it is clear that he permits this recitation precisely because he believes that the charm's psychological impact can affect the person's physical well-being and save his life. (This interpretation of the talmudic passage is actually offered by R. Perahyah ben Nissim, an Egyptian scholar from the generation after Maimonides. See his commentary to *Shabbat*, ed. Shoshana and Hirschfeld [Jerusalem, 1988], p. 279: והתירו לחישה זו שלא תיטרף דעת הנישוך וימות מחמת פחדו.) We must not forget that in his responsum dealing with *katlanit*, Maimonides discusses "soothsaying, divination, conjecture, and fantasies, from which at some time bodies of weak constitution might be affected." We thus see that he was fully aware that psychological factors could have a bodily effect; see Alter Hilvitz, *Li-Leshonot ha-Rambam* (Jerusalem, 1950), p. 264; Levinger, *Darkhei ha-Mahashavah*, p. 131.

177. See Mishnah *Shabbat* 6:10.

the Sages these were commonly believed to have real healing power.[178] The fact that Maimonides himself records this mishnaic ruling implies that even in his day people and doctors had faith in these folk remedies.[179] Contrary to Levinger's understanding,[180] one need not connect Maimonides' comments in the *Guide* with the permission to wear these devices on the Sabbath. Rather, his only concern in the *Guide* is to explain why the Sages permitted one to make use of these semi-idolatrous, fraudulent practices for healing.

It is not clear, as Levinger would have it, that Maimonides would permit one to go out with a fox tooth on the Sabbath even if people became convinced that it had no value, for then it would apparently cease to be an ornament. Despite the fact that the Mishnah permits this action, according to Maimonides, this permission is contingent upon the fox tooth being regarded as having therapeutic value.[181] If there is a general consensus among physicians that the fox tooth has no value, one would not be permitted to wear it on the Sabbath, although in accordance with the Mishnah's ruling, it would not be regarded as *darkhei emori*. It is true that Maimonides refuses to admit the possibility that, with scientific advances, the laws of *terefot* can be updated.[182] However, unlike the case of *terefot*, the question of whether the fox tooth is regarded as an ornament is dependent on public perception, which *does* change with time.[183]

---

178. See *Teshuvot ha-Rashba*, vol. 1, pp. 284–288, where R. Solomon ben Adret notes an apparent internal contradiction in *Guide* 3:37, and the response to this in R. Judah Moscato, *Kol Yehudah* 4:23 (printed in the standard Hebrew editions of the *Kuzari*). See also Schwartz, *Astrologyah*, ch. 3.

179. See also *Commentary on the Mishnah, Shabbat* 6:9–10.

180. *Darkhei ha-Mahashavah*, p. 137.

181. See Maimonides' comment appended to the law: "One may go out on the Sabbath into a public domain . . . wearing a locust egg, a fox tooth, a nail from the gallows of an impaled convict, or any other article suspended on the body for medical reasons, *provided that physicians say that it is medically effective.*" Popular perception not based on expert opinion does not confer upon something the status of ornament. By the same token, only expert opinion would be able to determine when an amulet is to be regarded as "tested."

182. *Shehitah* 10:12–13.

183. This may explain why Maimonides does not codify Mishnah *Shabbat* 6:9: "Boys may go out with garlands." For an entirely different reading, according to which Maimonides accepted the power of at least some amulets, see J. David Bleich,

There is another example in which Maimonides appears to codify superstition. *Berakhot* 60b reads:

> On entering a privy one should say: "Be honored, holy honorable ones, servants of the Most High. Give honor to the God of Israel. Wait for me until I enter and do my needs, and return to you." Abaye said: "A man should not speak thus, lest they should leave him and go. What he should say is 'Guard me, guard me, help me, help me, support me, support me, wait for me, wait for me, until I enter and come out, as this is the way of humans.'"

As Rashi points out—and there appears to be no other way to understand the passage—this law is directed towards the angels who are said to accompany one. They were especially necessary in this situation, since the privy was regarded as a place inhabited by demons (because of the privy's lack of cleanliness, it was not expected that the angels would actually accompany a person inside). One would have expected Maimonides to either omit this law or record it in a vastly different form, but this is not what he does.

In *Tefillah* 7:5 he states: "Whenever one enters the privy, before entering, he says: 'Be honored, holy honorable ones, servants of the Most High. Guard me, guard me. Wait for me until I enter and come out, as this is the way of humans.'" Maimonides has combined the view of the anonymous *amora* and that of Abaye, and in so doing has lent his support to the talmudic notion of two angels that accompany one in his daily routine.[184] It is not clear to me why Maimonides chose

---

"Maimonides on the Distinction between Science and Pseudoscience," in Rosner and Kottek, eds., *Moses Maimonides: Physician, Scientist, and Philosopher*, pp. 105–115, and his lengthy note on pp. 253–254. Israel Finkelscherer, *Mose Maimunis Stellung zum Aberglauben und zur Mystik* (Breslau, 1894), p. 91 n. 3, gives an interesting, but mistaken, solution to the problem we have been discussing: "Soll dies nicht mit der ganzen Anschauungsweise Maimunis in Widerspruch stehen, so müssen wir darunter nur eine קמיעא של עיקרין, ein heilbringendes Kräuterbündel verstehen, welches auch sonst schlechtweg als Kamea (T. b. Kidd. 73b, dagegen heisst hier eine geschriebene Kamea פיתקא) bezeichnet wird." To begin with, Finkelscherer has put forth Rashi's understanding of the passage in *Kiddushin*, and we do not know if Maimonides shared this interpretation. Furthermore, even if Finkelscherer is correct in his identification of קמיעא, this says nothing about Maimonides' mention of the fox tooth, locust egg, etc.

184. See *Ta'anit* 11a, *Hagigah* 16a, *Shabbat* 119b.

to include this law. To begin with, since he denies the existence of demons, why ask the angels for protection at the privy? Furthermore, in the *Guide* Maimonides interprets the idea of two angels accompanying one as referring to the good and evil inclinations.[185]

In fact, it is not only in the *Guide* that Maimonides rationalizes angels. In *Mezuzah* 6:13, he writes: "Our ancient teachers said: 'He who has phylacteries on his head and arm, fringes on his garment, and a mezuzah on his door may be presumed not to sin, for he has many monitors—angels that save him from sinning, as it is said: *The angel of the Lord encamps round about them that fear Him and delivers them* (Ps. 34: 8).'" From this passage, we see that Maimonides interprets "angels" to mean the positive spiritual effect engendered by the commandments.[186] Therefore, it is strange that Maimonides would include *Tefillah* 7:5 in the *Mishneh Torah*, as it appears to entirely contradict his

---

185. *Guide* 3:22. For Maimonides' other interpretations of "angels," see Finkelscherer, *Mose Maimunis Stellung*, pp. 29ff.; Alexander Altmann, "Angels and Angelology," *EJ*, vol. 1, col. 975; Kellner, *Maimonides' Confrontation*, ch. 8.

186. R. Zvi Hirsch Chajes, in his commentary to *Ta'anit* 11a, *Hagigah* 16a, and *Shabbat* 119b, calls attention to *Mezuzah* 6:13 in order to explain how Maimonides must have understood the talmudic passages which state that one is accompanied by two angels. This is significant, for it shows that Chajes, although a *maskil*, was unaware of what Maimonides himself wrote in the *Guide*. As we have seen, he understands the two angels to be referring to the good and evil inclinations, and not, as Chajes would have it, the spiritual power of the mitzvot.

While on the topic, it is worth noting that Maimonides also rationalizes Satan, understanding him to be, among other things, the evil inclination; see *Meilah* 8:8, *Guide* 3:22; Twersky, *Introduction*, p. 413 (Twersky's note 140 should be corrected to read *Guide* 3:22); Nuriel, *Galui*, pp. 110–118; Michael Zvi Nehorai, "Ha-Rambam ve-ha-Ralbag—Shetei Gishot be-Hashgahah," *Da'at* 20 (1988), p. 55; Robert Eisen, *The Book of Job in Medieval Jewish Philosophy* (Oxford, 2004), pp. 51ff; Warren Zev Harvey, "Two Jewish Approaches to Evil in History," in Steven T. Katz, ed., *Wrestling with God* (Oxford, 2007), pp. 328–329. See, however, *Guide* 3:26, where Maimonides quotes the same rabbinic text upon which *Meilah* 8:8 is based, but with the term "Satan" included. Having already explained in *Guide* 3:22 what Satan is, he felt no need to remove the term in *Guide* 3:26. Yet, since he had not given such an explanation in the *Mishneh Torah*, he felt it appropriate to remove mention of Satan in *Meilah* 8:8. In his rationalization of Satan, Maimonides was not being original, for the Talmud, *Bava Batra* 16a, identifies Satan with both the Angel of Death and the evil inclination. That not only rationalists adopted the latter identification is evident from Rashi's comments in *Shabbat* 89a s.v. *ba*, *Yoma* 67b s.v. *ha-Satan*, *Sukkah* 38a s.v. *le-igruyei*, *Kiddushin* 30a s.v. *havah*, *ibid.*, 81a s.v. *idamei*, where he, too, explains that Satan is the evil inclination. As can be seen elsewhere, e.g., *Rosh ha-Shanah* 16b s.v. *kedei*, Rashi accepted the existence of Satan, but he did not always regard the talmudic references to him as meant to be taken literally. See also R. Joel Sirkes, *Bayit Hadash, Orah Hayyim* 585:3.

view of angels.[187] Furthermore, even though Maimonides has omitted the talmudic words "help me, help me, support me, support me," what he does quote still contradicts his Fifth Principle, which states that all prayers must be directed towards God.[188]

One must apparently conclude that we have here an example of Maimonides including a law in the *Mishneh Torah* even though he rejected its basis. As to how this differs from all the other instances we have seen where Maimonides omitted elements that did not fit in with his philosophical outlook, this example—of reciting a prayer upon entering the privy—was presumably a very common practice, valued by the average Jew. In such a case, Maimonides was willing to be tolerant and allow people to continue with the practice, since it does not undermine any basic principles of Judaism. This then is similar to *Mezuzah* 5:4, where Maimonides permits one to write the word *Shadai* on the outside of the mezuzah. One who writes holy names and names of angels on the inside loses one's share in the world to come, for he treats the mezuzah as an amulet. However, writing *Shadai* on the outer side of the mezuzah parchment is permitted by Maimonides, as it has no relevance to the mitzvah *per se* and does not violate any halakhic prohibition.[189]

187. See Finkelscherer, *Mose Maimunis Stellung*, p. 38 n. 2. I posed the problem to Professor Warren Zev Harvey, who offered an intriguing suggestion to explain *Tefillah* 7:5. According to him, Maimonides might be referring to the intellects. Entering the privy, one breaks off conjunction with them; upon exiting, one hopes to resume the conjunction. See, similarly, Rabbenu Manoah, *Sefer ha-Menuhah*, ed. Hurvitz (Jerusalem, 1970), *ad loc.*; Rabinovitch, *Yad Peshutah, ad loc.*

188. See my *Limits*, ch. 5. For an implausible solution to this problem, see R. Meir ben Simeon of Narbonne, *Sefer ha-Meorot*, ed. Blau (New York, 1964), p. 180 (called to my attention by Menachem Silber). There are a few other passages in the *Mishneh Torah* which, at first glance, also appear to contradict Maimonides' philosophical outlook. However, most of them can be explained with little difficulty. For example, Levinger, *Darkhei ha-Mahashavah*, p. 130 n. 128, calls attention to *Avodah Zarah* 11:15 as implying an acceptance of magic: המכשף חייב סקילה והוא שעשה מעשה כשפים. However, I believe Kafih, Commentary to *Avodah Zarah* 11:11, has adequately explained the passage: וכוונת רבנו בעשה מעשה הוא מעשה הקיטור או כיוצא בו, לא עשיית דבר על ידי כשוף כי זה לדעת רבנו לא עשה ולא עושה ולא יעשה, כי הכל שקר גמור ומוחלט הבל הבלים, והבל מהובל. See also the interesting suggestion of David Horwitz, "Rashba's Attitude towards Science and its Limits," *TUMJ* 3 (1991–1992), p. 73 n. 26. A less plausible explanation of this passage has been suggested by Bezalel Safran, "Maimonides' Attitude to Magic and to Related Types of Thinking," in *id.*, and Eliyahu Safran, eds., *Porat Yosef: Studies Presented to Rabbi Dr. Joseph Safran* (Hoboken, 1992), p. 103 n. 2.

189. Cf. Nagar, "Ma'avak ha-Rambam," p. 138 n. 120.

Another similar instance of Maimonides' tolerance for the masses' mistaken views is found in *Avodah Zarah* 3:11. Here, Maimonides codifies a talmudic halakhah that one is not permitted to draw the likeness of the angels.[190] He does this even though he believes that angels are incorporeal, meaning that it is impossible to draw such an image.[191] Yet, just as Maimonides states that one need not correct people who mistakenly believe that angels are corporeal,[192] so too he is prepared to codify a halakhah based on this false assumption. I must confess, however, that I cannot explain why in this particular instance—which certainly was not a treasured practice of the masses—Maimonides chose to be so "tolerant."

Now we must ask what impact Maimonides' implacable opposition to superstition had among later halakhists. For the most part, it seems that his influence was negligible. Superstition-related halakhot did not disappear from halakhic writings; on the contrary, as time passed, they greatly increased, so that modern halakhists often deal with superstitions that earlier generations were entirely unaware of. At first glance, it is astounding that the most prominent post-talmudic halakhist should have had so little impact in this area. Yet when one considers the fact that his demand for philosophical and scientific study, as elaborated upon in *Yesodei ha-Torah*, chapters 1–4, was likewise rejected by the halakhists, their repudiation of his halakhic rationalism is only to be expected.

Still, it is incorrect to say that Maimonides had no influence with his rejection of superstition-related halakhot. His son, R. Abraham, and the circle around him certainly carried on Maimonides' rationalist approach to talmudic halakhah. Maimonides' influence in this area is also seen in the recently published commentary of R. Perahyah ben Nissim to *Shabbat*,[193] as well as in certain formulations of R. David ben Samuel ha-Kokhavi in his *Sefer ha-Batim*.[194] However, both R.

---

190. *Avodah Zarah* 43b.

191. See *Yesodei ha-Torah* 2:3, *Teshuvah* 8:2, *Guide* 1:49, 2:6, *Iggerot ha-Rambam*, vol. 1, pp. 323, 327 (Arabic), 346–347, 354 (Hebrew).

192. See *Guide* 1:5, *Iggerot ha-Rambam*, vol. 1, pp. 323 (Arabic), 346–347 (Hebrew).

193. See the Introduction, pp. 7–9.

194. Regarding the wide-ranging Maimonidean influence on Kokhavi, see Halbertal, *Bein Torah le-Hokhmah*, ch. 6.

Perahyah's and R. David's opposition to superstition is not as uncompromising as that of Maimonides. As I have pointed out in this chapter, Meiri is indebted to Maimonides for several of his formulations. Maimonidean influence can also be seen in the many halakhot that Meiri omits. Yet he also shows great originality and diverges from Maimonides on many occasions.[195] I have already indicated that a separate study is needed to clarify Meiri's approach. Such a study would help to determine the role of Maimonides' ground-breaking rationalization of talmudic halakhah in creating an atmosphere of intellectual freedom vis-a-vis these halakhot, a freedom that presumably encouraged Meiri to offer his own rationalizations.

One significant point that should be noted here is Meiri's understanding of the prohibition of *zugot*, an issue which has already been discussed with regard to Maimonides. Meiri, while also rejecting the idea of any demon-related harm resulting from *zugot*, approaches mat-

---

195. In addition to examples already mentioned, see his commentary to *Shabbat* 53a, where Meiri speaks of amulets that can cure animals. In his commentary to *Sanhedrin* 67b, he speaks of people who have the ability לברא בריאות יפות שלא מזווג המין, and people who can do things ממש דרך כשוף. In his commentary to *Sanhedrin* 65b and 68a, he accepts the talmudic view that one can control animals through charms. As for reciting an incantation over a bite, in his commentary to *Sanhedrin* 68a, he follows Maimonides, and only mentions the psychological effect. However, in his commentary to *Sanhedrin* 101a, he puts forth an original halakhic view. In order to appreciate it, one must remember the following: 1. Maimonides allows one to recite a charm over a snake bite because of its psychological effect (*Avodah Zarah* 11:11). 2. Maimonides forbids one to recite a charm in order to prevent a snake from biting (*Avodah Zarah* 11:10). As far as Maimonides is concerned, this is always forbidden, even if one is about to be bitten. Since charms are meaningless, this is obviously not a case of *pikuah nefesh*, which would permit one to violate the biblical prohibition against engaging in sorcery. 3. On the other hand, Rashi, *Sanhedrin* 65a s.v. *asur*, who accepts the magical power of charms, permits their recitation if there is a danger that one is going to be bitten, because this is a case of *pikuah nefesh* (see also Rashi, *Sanhedrin* 101a s.v. *ve-lohshin*). In his commentary to *Sanhedrin* 101a, Meiri combines the opinions of Rashi and Maimonides, and writes that one can recite a charm *before* being bitten. Even though it has no effect, it is permitted שלא תטרף דעתו עליו. As we have seen, this last justification, which is original to Maimonides, is only used by him with regard to *after* one is bitten. A further example of Meiri's halakhic divergence from Maimonides is found in his discussion of astrology; see Schwartz, *Astrologyah*, pp. 224ff.; Benedikt, *Merkaz ha-Torah be-Provence*, pp. 252–253. Regarding the general issue of Maimonides' halakhic influence on Meiri, see R. Dov Berish Zuckerman, *Beit Aharon: Beurei ha-Rambam al pi ha-Meiri* (Jerusalem, 1983).

ters from a different perspective. According to him, the Sages realized that fear of *zugot* was nonsense. Yet, because this fear was so ingrained in the people's psyche, and since the belief in the harmful nature of *zugot* did not violate the prohibition against following gentile practices, the Sages saw no need to uproot the notion; they even lent it support by offering a special reason as to why there is no problem of *zugot* with the four cups of wine on Passover. In Meiri's day, however, no one paid any attention to *zugot*, and it was permissible to disregard it entirely.[196]

While this bears certain similarities to the reason Maimonides offers for sacrifices, there is a crucial distinction. According to Maimonides, the very notion of sacrifices was due to the masses' unsophisticated religious conceptions; nevertheless, the practice was not abolished by the Torah, but directed towards a good end. According to Meiri's view of *zugot*, not only was the practice not abolished, but no attempt was even made to foster a positive end. If there is any basis for Meiri's view of *zugot* in Maimonides' understanding of sacrifices, it is only a very general shared understanding regarding the relationship between halakhah and the opinions of the masses.

However, there seems to be another Maimonidean source which, assuming he was familiar with it, could have had more of an impact on Meiri's formulation. I refer to the Letter on Astrology discussed at the beginning of this chapter. In this Letter, Maimonides explains that one of the reasons why astrology appears in the Talmud and Midrash is that a sage may have been expressing himself "with a view to the times and the business before him." This fits in very well with Meiri's understanding of the Sages' tolerance of popular custom. Furthermore, as we have seen, although Maimonides does not permit one to

---

196. Commentary to *Berakhot* 51b, *Pesahim* 109b (and see the similar explanations regarding other superstitions in his commentary to *Shabbat* 67a, *Sanhedrin* 101a, and *Avodah Zarah* 27b). In *Pesahim* 109b, the Talmud concludes: "When one is particular [about *zugot*], they [the demons] are particular about him, while when one is not particular, they are not particular about him." According to Meiri's rationalization of this passage, the problem is not that demons are a danger for one who is particular about *zugot*; it is that one's psychological state is affected: שהיה טבעם מקבל בענין חזוק או חולשה, וכמו שהעידו בסוגיא זו דקפיד קפדינן ליה, דלא קפיד לא קפדינן ליה. (Strangely enough, in *Hiddushei ha-Meiri: Pesahim*, p. 379, Meiri characterize *zugot* as dangerous on account of demons.)

write holy names and names of angels on the inside of a mezuzah, he does permit one to write *Shadai* on the outer side of the parchment.[197] Here we have an example where, because Maimonides does not see any halakhic prohibition in the practice—a practice popularly believed to ward off demons and other harm[198]—he is willing to allow the masses to continue with their custom. This fits in well with Meiri's understanding of *zugot*.

Another instance of indebtedness to Maimonides is found in the *Shulhan Arukh*,[199] which repeats the view of Maimonides[200] that one may utter an incantation over a snake wound even though it does not cure and is merely a psychological device. What makes this ruling of Karo so significant is that although he took incantations very seriously, and did not hesitate to include numerous superstitions in the *Shulhan Arukh*, in this case he chose to follow Maimonides' formulation. Further research into Karo's approach to superstition would do much to clarify matters in this regard.[201]

Although it is true that, for the most part, Maimonides' view of superstitious halakhot is ignored by later authorities, there are times when it is cited in support of a lenient decision. For example, there are numerous discussions about what the halakhah prescribes if one leaves food under a bed or touches food in the morning without hav-

---

197. *Mezuzah* 5:4.
198. See Joshua Trachtenberg, *Jewish Magic and Superstition* (New York, 1939), p. 146.
199. *Yoreh Deah* 179:6.
200. *Avodah Zarah* 11:11.
201. Without going too far afield, it is worth noting that *Shulhan Arukh, Yoreh Deah* 179, is full of superstitions. Eliav Shochetman could have cited this section to further bolster his claim that the contradictions in the *Shulhan Arukh* show that it was never intended to be a code of practical halakhah, but rather a collection of halakhic rulings left to the discretion of the decisor. See his "Al ha-Setirot ba-Shulhan Arukh ve-al Mahuto shel ha-Hibur u-Matarotav," *Asupot* 3 (1989), pp. 323–329. In 179:5, quoting the *Tur*, Karo accepts the magical power of incantations. In 179:6 he quotes Maimonides' rejection of the value of incantations. In 179:7 he returns to quoting the *Tur's* acceptance of incantations. (Regarding the *Shulhan Arukh* containing mutually exclusive opinions of Maimonides and the *Tur*, see the passage from R. Hayyim Vital published in *Asupot* 3 [1989], pp. 273–274.) Commenting in his *Beit Yosef, Yoreh Deah* 179:7, on the *Tur's* ruling that one can recite a charm to prevent a pursuing snake from biting him, Karo writes

ing washed one's hands to remove the *ruah ra'ah*.[202] According to Maimonides, if nothing fell into the food, or the hands which touched the food were not dirty, there is no problem eating it. However, according to those who view the prohibition as based on the fear of *ruah ra'ah*, matters are more complicated. A good number of halakhists simply declare that when dealing with evil spirits there is no such thing as an *ex post facto* leniency. Yet this approach is not universal, and there are halakhic authorities who do argue for an *ex post facto* leniency, citing Maimonides' view to support this position.[203]

In conclusion, I believe there can be no doubt as to the far-reaching significance of Maimonides' approach to superstition in talmudic halakhah. It was unprecedented and courageous, and there are probably other examples of this approach that I have overlooked. Nevertheless, we have seen that Maimonides' approach is not free from difficulties, and there are times when he appears to deviate from his general pattern. These examples require further study, as does the larger question of Maimonides' influence on later halakhah, which we were only able to touch on in this chapter.

---

that this is obvious since nothing stands in the way of *pikuah nefesh*. It is only because Karo accepts the magical power of incantations that the *Tur's* ruling appears obvious to him. Maimonides, however, disagrees. See above, p. 147 n. 195; *Bayit Hadash, Yoreh Deah* 179:7; *Derishah, Yoreh Deah* 179:3.

202. Regarding these issues, see the many sources cited by Yosef, *Yabia Omer*, vol. 1, *Yoreh Deah* no. 9, vol. 4, *Orah Hayyim* no. 1.

203. See Malbim, *Artzot ha-Hayyim*, 4:4: אחר שלהרמב"ם אין לחוש בזה"ז על סכנה של ר"ר ממילא אע"ג שהטור והש"ע הזהירו ליטול ידיו ג"פ משום ר"ר וראוי לכל בע"נ לזהר בזה . . . מ"מ לענין דיעבד ולאסור המאכל עי"כ כדאי הוא הרמב"ם לסמוך עליו כ"נ ברור. See also Yosef, *Yabia Omer*, vol. 1, p. 189.

A NOTE ON MAIMONIDES AND MUHAMMAD

Maimonides, together with other medieval Jewish writers, referred to Muhammad in a variety of pejorative ways. One of the terms Maimonides uses to refer to him is *pasul*, meaning "unfit" or "flawed."[1] This is a play on the Arabic term *rasul* ("apostle"), by which Muhammad was known. Seeking to keep the play on words, Abraham Halkin coined the fitting translation "prepostle."[2]

The other term Maimonides uses to refer to Muhammad is *meshuga* (madman).[3] As Kafih notes, this expression was very common among Jews in the Muslim world.[4] Prior to Maimonides we find it used by R. Sherira Gaon,[5] R. Abraham Bar Hiyya,[6] and in the anonymous *Sefer Pitron Torah*.[7] Ephraim E. Urbach dates this latter work to the late ninth-early tenth century,[8] which would mean that it is the earliest recorded use of the expression.

Moritz Steinschneider claimed that the term arose from the popular view that Muhammad was possessed by *jinn*, a view that, according to the Koran, God himself refuted on three separate occasions.[9] Jews were influenced by this view and connected Muhammad

---

1. אלפסול; see Sheilat, *Iggerot ha-Rambam,* vol. 1, pp. 93 n. 11 (Arabic) 131 (Hebrew).

2. Halkin and David Hartman, *Crisis and Leadership: Epistles of Maimonides* (Philadelphia, 1985), pp. 107.

3. Sheilat, *Iggerot ha-Rambam,* vol. 1, pp. 86–87, 92–93 (Arabic), 42, 121, 123, 131 (Hebrew). The Arabic version of the *Letter to Yemen* which Sheilat used for his text substitutes a non-offensive term each time *pasul* and *meshuga* are mentioned (he notes the alternate version in his notes). Yet, contrary to Davidson, *Moses Maimonides,* p. 493 n. 33, this "softer" version could not have been what appeared in Maimonides' original text, as it is not found in any of the early Hebrew translations.

4. *Iggerot ha-Rambam,* p. 22 n. 36.

5. *Iggeret Rav Sherira Gaon* (Haifa, 1921), French version (the word has been removed in the Spanish version.)

6. *Sefer ha-Ibbur,* ed. Filipowski (London, 1851), p. 100, *Megilat ha-Megaleh,* ed. Ponzanski (Berlin, 1924), pp. 96–97.

7. Ed. Urbach (Jerusalem, 1978), p. 241.

8. *Ibid.,* p. 32.

9. See Michael W. Dols, *Majnun: The Madman in Medieval Islamic Society* (Oxford, 1992), p. 217.

to *meshuga,* as the term is used in Hos. 9:7: אויל הנביא משגע איש הרוח
("The prophet is a fool, the man of the spirit is mad.")[10] The four-
teenth-century R. Netanel ben Isaiah appears to be the first to explicitly connect the verse in Hosea to Muhammad,[11] but there is no doubt
that he is reflecting a much older tradition. Yet throughout the scholarly literature I have not seen anyone who has called attention to the
fact that the verse in Hosea immediately preceding this one is relevant
to the application of the term *meshuga* to Muhammad. Hosea 9:6
reads: מחמד לכספם קמוש יירשם.[12]

---

10. *Polemische und apologetische Literatur in arabischer Sprache* (Hildeheim, 1966), p. 302.

11. *Maor ha-Afelah,* ed. Kafih (Jerusalem, 1957), p. 121.

12. As far as I know, this fact was first noted in the rabbinic journal *Or Torah,*
Heshvan 5751, p. 141.

BIBLIOGRAPHY*

Works by Maimonides:

Commentary on the Mishnah, ed. Joseph Kafih (Jerusalem, 1965); *Commentary* on *Avot,* ed. Yitzhak Sheilat (Jerusalem, 1994); *Commentary* on *Avodah Zarah,* ed. Dror Fixler (Jerusalem, 2002); *Tikkun Mishnah: Commentary* on *Avodah Zarah, Horayot,* ed. Yitzhak Sheilat (Jerusalem, 2002).

Mishneh Torah, ed. Shabse Frankel (Jerusalem, 1975–2007); ed. Joseph Kafih (with extensive commentary; Jerusalem, 1984–1996); ed. Nachum L. Rabinovitch (with extensive commentary entitled *Yad Peshutah*; Jerusalem, 1984–2006); ed. Yitzhak Sheilat (Ma'aleh Adumim, 2003–2006).

Guide of the Perplexed, ed. and trans. Salomon Munk (Paris 1856–1866); ed. Issachar Joel (Jerusalem, 1931); trans. Shlomo Pines (Chicago, 1963); ed. and trans. Joseph Kafih (Jerusalem, 1977); ed. and trans. Michael Schwartz (Tel Aviv, 2002).

Hilkhot ha-Yerushalmi, ed. Saul Lieberman (New York, 1948).

Iggerot ha-Rambam, ed. Yitzhak Sheilat (Jerusalem, 1987).

Teshuvot ha-Rambam, ed. Joshua Blau (Jerusalem, 1989).

Sefer ha-Mitzvot, ed. Joseph Kafih (Jerusalem, 1971); ed. Chaim Heller (Jerusalem, 1980); ed. Charles B. Chavel (Jerusalem, 1981); ed. Shabse Frankel (Jerusalem, 1995).

---

* Only works that are cited more than once appear. In addition, standard rabbinic texts are omitted.

Other Works:

Adret, Solomon ben, *She'elot u-Teshuvot ha-Rashba* (Jerusalem, 1997–2005).

_____ *Teshuvot ha-Rashba,* ed. Haim Zalman Dimitrovsky (Jerusalem, 1990).

Anushiski, Dov Ber, *Matzav ha-Yashar,* vol. 2 (Vilna, 1886).

Azulai, Hayyim Joseph David, *Birkei Yosef* (Vienna, 1859).

_____ *Hayyim Sha'al* (Livorno, 1795).

_____ *Yosef Ometz* (Jerusalem, 1987).

Barzilay, Isaac, *Shlomo Yehudah Rapoport (1790-1867) and His Contemporaries: Some Aspects of Jewish Scholarship in the Nineteenth Century* (Israel, 1969).

Basilea, Aviad Sar Shalom, *Emunat Hakhamim* (Mantua, 1730).

Benedikt, Binyamin Ze'ev, *Ha-Rambam le-lo Setiyah min ha-Talmud* (Jerusalem, 1985).

_____ *Merkaz ha-Torah be-Provence* (Jerusalem, 1985).

Blidstein, Gerald J., "Where Do We Stand in the Study of Maimonidean Halakhah?" in Isadore Twersky, ed., *Studies in Maimonides* (Cambridge, 1990), pp. 1–30.

_____ *Samhut u-Meri be-Halakhat ha-Rambam* (Tel Aviv, 2002).

Chajes, Zvi Hirsch, Kol Sifrei Maharatz Chajes (Jerusalem, 1958).

Crescas, Hasdai, *Or ha-Shem* (Jerusalem, 1990).

_____ *Bittul Ikarei ha-Notzrim,* trans. Joseph ben Shem Tov, ed. Daniel Lasker (Ramat Gan, 1990).

Davidson, Herbert A., *Moses Maimonides: The Man and His Works* (Oxford, 2005).

Duran, Simeon ben Zemah, *She'elot u-Teshuvot ha-Tashbetz,* ed. Yoel Catane (Jerusalem, 1998).

Duran, Solomon ben Simeon, *She'elot u-Teshuvot ha-Rashbash,* ed. Moshe Sobel (Jerusalem, 1998).

Emden, Jacob, *Mitpahat Sefarim* (Jerusalem, 1995).

Ergas, Joseph, *Shomer Emunim* (Jerusalem, 1965).

Faur, José, *Iyyunim ba-Mishneh Torah le-ha-Rambam* (Jerusalem, 1978).

Finkelscherer, Israel, *Mose Maimunis Stellung zum Aberglauben und zur Mystik* (Breslau, 1894).

Fleckeles, Eleazer, *Teshuvah me-Ahavah* (New York, 1945).

Fleischer, Yehudah, *et al,* eds., *Me'ah She'arim: Studies in Medieval Jewish Spiritual Life in Memory of Isadore Twersky* (Jerusalem, 2001).

Friedman, Mordechai A., "Tamar, a Symbol of Life: The 'Killer Wife' Superstition in Jewish Tradition," *AJS Review* 15 (Spring, 1990), pp. 23–61.

Ginsburg, C. D., *Esrim ve-Arba'ah Sifrei ha-Kodesh* (London, 1908).

Grossman, Avraham, "Temurot be-Ma'amadah shel ha-Ishah ha-Yehudiyah bi-Sefarad," in Yehudah Fleischer, *et al,* eds., *Me'ah She'arim: Studies in Medieval Jewish Spiritual Life in Memory of Isadore Twersky* (Jerusalem, 2001), pp. 87–111.

Guttel, Neriah, "Derekh ha-Melekh ba-Mishnah," in Yosef Eliyahu Movshovitz, ed., *Kovettz ha-Rambam* (Jerusalem, 2005), pp. 79–146.

Habib, Levi ben, *She'elot u-Teshuvot ha-Ralbah* (Vienna, 1565).

Ha-Kohen, Malakhi, *Yad Malakhi* (Bnei Brak, n. d.).

Ha-Kohen, Meir Simhah, *Or Sameah* (New York, 1946).

Ha-Kokhavi, David ben Samuel, *Sefer ha-Batim*, ed. Moshe Hershler (Jerusalem, 1983).

Halbertal, Moshe, *Bein Torah le-Hokhmah* (Jerusalem, 2000).

Havlin, Shlomo Zalman, ed., *Mishneh Torah le-ha-Rambam, Mada ve-Ahavah: Ha-Sefer ha-Mugah* (Jerusalem, 1997).

Hirschenson, Hayyim, *Malki ba-Kodesh* (St. Louis/Seini, 1919-1926).

Hopkins, Simon, ed., *Maimonides's Commentary on Tractate Shabbat* (Jerusalem, 2001).

Ibn Shem Tov, Shem Tov, *Sefer ha-Emunot* (Ferrara, 1556).

Jacobs, Louis, "Demythologising the Rabbinic Aggadah: Menahem Meiri," unpublished essay.

Joel, D. *Der Aberglaube und die Stellung des Judenthums zu demselben* (Breslau, 1881).

Joshua ha-Nagid, *Teshuvot R. Yehoshua ha-Nagid*, ed. Yehudah Ratsaby (Jerusalem, 1989).

Kafih, Aharon, *Yeriot Aharon* (Jerusalem, 2003).

Kafih, Joseph, *Ketavim* (Jerusalem, 1989, 2002).

Kahana, Kalman, "Perush ha-Mishnah shel ha-Rambam bi-Khetav Yado?" *Ha-Ma'ayan* 26 (Tishrei 5746), pp. 55–63, (Tevet 5746), pp. 54–64.

Kalai, Samuel, *Mishpetei Shmuel* (Venice, 1599).

Kanievsky, S. H., *Kiryat Melekh* (Jerusalem, 1983).

Karo, Joseph, *She'elot u-Teshuvot Beit Yosef* (Jerusalem, 1987).

Kasher, Menahem M., *Ha-Rambam ve-ha-Mekhilta de-Rashbi* (Jerusalem, 1980).

_____ *Torah Shelemah* (Jerusalem, 1992).

Kellner, Menachem, *Maimonides' Confrontation with Mysticism* (Oxford, 2006).

Kunitz, Moses, *Ben Yohai* (Vienna, 1815).

Landau, Ezekiel, *Noda bi-Yehudah* (Jerusalem, 1994).

Leiner, Jacob, *Beit Yaakov* (New York, 1948).

Leiner, Yeruham, *Ma'amar Zohar ha-Rakia*, published as an appendix to David Luria, *Kadmut Sefer ha-Zohar* (New York, 1951).

Leiter, Nathan Neta, *Tziyun le-Nefesh Hayah* (Jerusalem, 1964.)

Lerner, Ralph, "Maimonides' Letter on Astrology," *History of Religions* 8 (1968), pp. 143–158.

Levinger, Yaakov, *Darkhei ha-Mahashavah ha-Hilkhatit shel ha-Rambam* (Jerusalem, 1965).

Lichtenstein, Yehezkel Shraga, "Shitat ha-Rambam be-Inyan Tefilah, Heftzei Kedushah, u-Vikur be-Veit ha-Kevarot," *HUCA* 72

(2001), pp. 1–34 (Hebrew section).

Magid, Shaul, *Hasidism on the Margin* (Madison, 2003).

Maimonides, Abraham, *Birkat Avraham* (Lyck, 1859).

_____ *Teshuvot Rabbi Avraham ben ha-Rambam,* ed. Abraham Freimann (Jerusalem, 1937).

_____ *Milhamot ha-Shem,* ed. Reuven Margaliot (Jerusalem, 1959).

_____ *Sefer ha-Maspik le-Ovdei ha-Shem,* ed. Nissim Dana (Ramat Gan, 1989).

Malbim, Meir Lebush, *Artzot ha-Hayyim* (Jerusalem, 1960).

Margaliot, Reuven, *Nefesh Hayah* (Tel Aviv, 1954).

_____ *Margaliyot ha-Yam* (Jerusalem, 1977).

_____ *Peninim u-Margaliyot* (Jerusalem, 2006).

Meiri, Menahem, *Beit ha-Behirah* (Israel, n.d.).

_____ *Hibbur ha-Teshuvah* (Jerusalem, 1976).

_____ *Hiddushei ha-Meiri: Pesahim,* ed. Moses ha-Kohen Blau (New York, 1978; bound with David ben Samuel Kokhavi, *Sefer ha-Batim*).

_____ *Perush Rabbenu ha-Meiri: Avot,* ed. Shlomo Zalman Havlin (Jerusalem, 1994).

Nagar, Eliyahu, "Ma'avak ha-Rambam be-Avodah Zarah u-va-Emunot ha-Tefelot," *Mesorah le-Yosef* 3 (2004), pp. 111–180.

Nathanson, Joseph Saul, *Shoel u-Meshiv* (Jerusalem, 1973).

Neuhausen, Simon A., *Torah Or le-ha-Rambam* (Baltimore, 1941).

Nuriel, Abraham, *Galui ve-Samui be-Philosophyah ha-Yehudit Bimei ha-Beinayim* (Jerusalem, 2000).

Oberlander, Barukh, "Iyyun be-Mahadurot ha-Hadashot shel ha-'Mishneh Torah' le-ha-Rambam," *Or Yisrael* 23 (Nisan 5761), pp. 215–224.

Palache, Hayyim, *Kol ha-Hayyim* (Izmir, 1874).

Palache, Isaac, *Avot ha-Rosh,* vol. 1 (Salonika, 1862).

Perahyah ben Nissim, *Perush Rabbenu Perahyah ben Rabbi Nissim al Masekhet Shabbat,* eds. Avraham Shoshana and Barukh Hayyim Hirschfeld (Jerusalem, 1988).

Rosner, Fred and Samuel S. Kottek, eds., *Moses Maimonides: Physician, Scientist, and Philosopher* (Northvale, 1993).

Rakah, Masud Hai, *Ma'aseh Rakah* (Jerusalem, 1976).

Scholem, Gershom, "Mi-Hoker li-Mekubal (Aggadat ha-Mekubalim al ha-Rambam)," *Tarbiz* 6 (1935), pp. 90–98.

Schwartz, Dov, *Astrologyah u-Magyah be-Hagut ha-Yehudit Bimei ha-Beinayim* (Ramat Gan, 1999).

Shalom, Abraham, *Neveh Shalom* (Venice, 1575).

Shapira, Hayyim Eleazar, *Minhat Eleazar* (Brooklyn, 1991).

_____ *Divrei Torah* (Jerusalem, 1998).

Shapiro, Marc B., *The Limits of Orthodox Theology: Maimonides' Thirteen Principles Reappraised* (Oxford, 2004).

Shapiro, Meir, *Or ha-Meir* (Petrokow, 1926).

Sheshet, Isaac bar, *She'elot u-Teshuvot Rivash* (Jerusalem, 1975).

Siah Sarfei Kodesh, vol. 5 (Lodz, 1931).

Sofer, Moses, *She'elot u-Teshuvot Hatam Sofer* (Jerusalem, 1989).

Sofer, Yaakov Hayyim, *Berit Yaakov* (Jerusalem, 1985).

_____ "Al Sefarim ve-Soferim," *Tzefunot* 19 (1993–1994), pp. 76–81.

Soloveitchik, Hayyim, *Hiddushei Rabbenu Hayyim ha-Levi* (Warsaw, 1936).

Solomon of Chelm, *Mirkevet ha-Mishneh* (Jerusalem, 2000).

Ta-Shma, Israel M., *Keneset Mehkarim,* vol. 2 (Jerusalem, 2004).

Tikkunei Zohar, ed. Reuven Margaliot (Jerusalem, 1978).

Twersky, Isadore, *Introduction to the Code of Maimonides* (New Haven, 1980).

_____ ed. *Studies in Maimonides* (Cambridge, 1990).

Weinberg, Jehiel Jacob, *Seridei Esh* (Jerusalem, 1977).

_____ *Kitvei ha-Gaon Rabbi Yehiel Yaakov Weinberg,* ed. Marc B. Shapiro,
     vol. 1 (Scranton, 1998), vol. 2 (Scranton, 2003).

Weiss, Isaac Hirsch, "Toledot ha-Rambam," *Beit Talmud* 1 (1881), pp. 161–169, 193–200, 225–233, 257–265, 289–296.

Yellin, David, "Shenei Dapim mi-Ketav Yado shel ha-Rambam," *Tarbiz* 1:3 (1930), pp. 93–106.

Yosef, Ovadiah, *Yabia Omer* (Jerusalem, 1986).

Zimra, Ibn David, *She'elot u-Teshuvot ha-Radbaz* (New York, n.d.).

Zohar, ed. Reuven Margaliot (Jerusalem, 1984).

Zohar Hadash, ed. Reuven Margaliot (Jerusalem, 1994).

Index of Maimonidean Passages[*]

[*] For ease of reference, sources are arranged in alphabetical order.

---

[1] This is actually the introduction to the entire order of *Toharot*; it appears before tractate *Kelim*.

[2] This is actually the conclusion of the entire *Commentary on the Mishnah*.

Iggerot ha-Rambam, ed. Sheilat

Teshuvot ha-Rambam, ed. Blau

אגרת תוכחה נגד שד"ל מאת החכם נחמן יצחק פישמאן

שנת תקצ"ח פה לבוב

בעזר החונן לאדם דעת!

מאתי נחמן יצחק הכהן פישמאן אל גבר משכיל[1] שד"ל

זה ימים אחדים, ראיתי כרם חמד חלק ג. וכאשר הרשה לי
הזמן לעיין בו, ותבאנה נגד עיני, שתי אגרות, אחת חתומה בשמך,
ואחת בשם ידידך יש"ר.[2] ראיתי, והשתוממתי, חזיתי, ונבהלתי,
צפיתי, ואחז בשרי פלצות. בשגם אני אמרתי בלבי, טרם ראותי
האגרות האלה, כי אתה הוא האיש הראשון, אשר נודע לי בזמננו זה,
כי לבו שלם עם אלקים ותורתו, וכבוד עם ישראל נוגע עד נפשו, וכל
ימי חייו יתעשת איך לגדור פרצות, ולשובב נתיבות, להקים
מנצורי-ישראל, היכל כלו אומר כבוד, אכן מה אעז? מה אומר? מה
אשים אל לבי עתה, בראותי ממך מכתב דובר סרה על חז"ל, ותשא
מרום עיניך אל קדוש ישראל מאור עינינו הרמב"ם ז"ל, החכם
שבחכמים, הגאון שבגאונים, אשר לו כל חכמי זמננו עתה יעלו נגדו
בכף מאזנים, כהנדוף עשן ינדופו, והבל יהיו גם יחד.

ואתה קמת להוריד כבוד איש גדול ורם, ותבזהו כאחד
הריקים על לא חמס עשה, ופעולתו אמת. יען לא ידעת, ולא שמעת
ולא הבינות כל דבריו, לא בספרו היקר והנחמד היד החזקה ולא
בספרו המורה תועה בדרך. חי נפשי! נשגבו הם מרעיונך ולא באת
עד תכלית כונת האומר. תאלמנה שפתי שקר הדוברות על צדיק עתק
בגאוה ובוז, קרא בנעים זמירותיו דוד מלך ישראל, גם זאת פעלת

---

1. אם השמאל ואימינה, ואם הימין ואשמאילה [הערת הכותב].
2. יצחק שמואל ריג'ייו

שוטנים מאת ד׳,[3] והדוברים רע על חכמי ישראל, ומשיבין את הארי לאחר מותו, וכלב חי נובח בלשונו, על ארי׳ המת והדר גאונו, התורה מתפלשת באפר, ותצעק מרה, על כי קמו בדור הזה שועלים מחבלים כרמים, אשר אינם יודעים רק להגות ולצפצף כפאפיגייא וכל עיונם רק בחכמת הדדקדוק לבד אשר גם בה לא יועילו, ולא יצילו, ודברו דברים שאין בהם ממש, ויפרשו כתובים בהבלים הבלים שונים, אשר כל שומעם תצלנה אזניו, ורק להם מתק לשון ודוברי צחות יתנו לחרפות תורה שבע״פ מתת שמים, להנתיק מוסרות הדת, ולצאת חפשי כפרא, ולעשות מה שלבם חפץ. צאו מתוך הדת, אתם פוסחי סעיפים! כתבו על קרן השור, אין לכם חלק באלקי ישראל, מה שדי כי נעבדנו? ומה תורתו כי נשמע בקולה? ולמה עוד תפרשו רשת הכפירה, ללכוד ילדי ישרון, אשר לא חטאו לכם ולא פשעו? בהדפיסכם אגרות כמו אלה לחלקם ביעקב, ולהפיצם בתוך עמנו לקחת מעל ראשם עטרת כבוד חכמינו ז״ל, אשר יגילו ברעדה, בזכרם שם הגדולים, כי היו להם לאנשי מופת ללכת בתורתם, ולשמור מוצא פיהם.

אף אם אמרתי כי צדקת בהשגתך נגד כבוד אדוננו מאור עינינו הרמב״ם זצלה״ה (אשר באמת שוא וכזב כל תפישותיך, כאשר אחוך הלאה באגרת הזאת) לא היה לך לפרסם הדברים בקהל עם, נגד השמש ונגד עם ד׳. כי פועל חכם לא יעשה דבר אשר יוכל לצאת עוד תקלה וקלקול לכל העם על ידו. וכמאמרם ז״ל: חזקה שאין יוצא מתחת ידי חבר דבר שאינו מתוקן,[4] אף כי בדברים חרופים וגדופים כמו אלה, אשר מוצא שפתי, שמרתי מעבור על דל שפתותי, ומכ״ש להביאם אלי ספר, כאלו היה הרמב״ם ז״ל נער משולל דעת ופרוע המדות ח״ו. ובכל אלה הכי אתה הוא הראשון אשר השגת בדבר זה ומקום הניחו להתגרד בחרסים[5] כאלה? לא! רק מעלה גרה אתה,

3. תהלים קט, כ.
4. עירובין לב ע״א.
5. ראה איוב ב, ח.

דברים אשר נושנו ונאמרו ונשנו זה כמה מאות שנים מהראב"ד ובעלי התוס' ז"ל ינון לנצח אשר כונתם היו לשם שמים (ועיין בפרק ח' מה' תשובה בדברי הראב"ד שם) ואחרי כבר נחה ושקטה כל הארץ והאירה שנית מכבודו, באת כעת שנית לחרוץ עליו בלשון מדברת גדולות מה עשה לך הרמב"ם הקדוש ז"ל?

אם לא חפצת לשמוע בקולו קום חבי אותך בחדריך, התהולל עליו, אכול בשר עוף בחלב ובלא נטילת ידים, או שאר דברים אשר לפי דעתך המה רק ערמת חז"ל וערמת הרמב"ם ז"ל לאסף בני ישרון תחת דגלם, ולשמוע בקולם, ומה לך לצעוק בפרהסיא אשר לא נאבה ולא נשמע לך? אם אין בינינו נביאים, ולא אתנו יודע עד מה, בכל זאת הלא בני נביאים אנחנו לדעת מוצאך ומבואך כל הימים כי אך לעקל ולקלקל עלינו את הדת. ולהרים מאתנו מצנפת הקדש, חכמת חכמינו וחכמת הרמב"ם זללה"ה, הלא כונתיך ערומה מתיצבת, כי אך לעקור תורה שבע"פ יצאת הפעם; לכן הניפות יד ותבחר לשון ערומים, להקטין כבוד הרמב"ם ז"ל ולאמר: כי נחש כרוך, בעקב דבריו. כי ידעת כי הוא עמוד התוך אשר כל בית ישראל נשען עליו, אחריו יפנו כל כתות בני עמינו, ויגדלוהו למעלה ראש, אם ישטה איש, מדברי רבותינו הקדושים, כי יאמר שבחקירתו מצא דבריהם רעועים. הלא נשיב לו אמרים: כלום חכמת יותר מאדוננו החכם השלם האלקי הרמב"ם ז"ל, ובכל אלה הטה אוזן לדברי החכמים, ויט שכמו לסבול כל דבריהם באהבה, ואז ישוב גם האיש, אשר פורה ראש, בלבו, הן צדקו תשובת האומרים כי הרמב"ם ז"ל חכם שבחכמים, לא הטה מדרכיהם ימין ושמאל כאשר העיד על עצמו כמה פעמים באגרותיו. אדרבה שגבם בכל עוז ואיך אתה אני? לכן בחרת כעת לגלות ערותו (והיא ערותך) ברבים, להשימהו לשמצה ולקלון בעיני כל, כי לא האמין בתחיית המתים, למען בתחלה יסירו ממנו ולא ישמעו לדבריו, ואח"כ יכפרו בהלכותיו, עדי יכפרו בחז"ל, ותהי תורת ד' נעדרת, וכל הולך בשרירות לב יאמר:

לא ד' פעל כל זאת, אוי לכם! רבה רעת, ואין קץ לעונותיך!

ומעתה אבא להשיב על דבריך אחת לאחת, ואתה תקבצם על
יד, ויהי' לך לאחרים. מה שכתבת: כי המאמר של החכם גייגער,
היתה לך לששון ולשמחה, רק השתוממת ונבהלת בראות כי החכם
הזה מקיים כי רבנו הקדוש כתב את המשנה, ולא זו בלבד, אלא
שהוא מקיים כי גם קודם רבי שאר תנאים כתבו משניות, ע"כ מה
החרדה הזו אשר חרדת? מה ההשתוממות וההבהלה אשר נפלה עליך?
קול פחדים באזנך, ולא ידעת על מה, ככה גם נפשי תדמה, ולבבי
כמו כן יחשוב, כי אף קודם ר' יהודא הנשיא נכתבו משניות מגילות
מגילות, ומדוע תחרד ותלפת? גם כל ראיותיך אשר הבאת יעלו
בתוהו ויאבדו, לו בכור הבחינה יבחנו. אך מה לי ולהוסיף אם כבר
רעך יש"ר נהפך עליך בדבר זה ויהי עֶרֶךְ – רק מה שאמרת מדוע לא
אמרו מעולם נייתי ספר ונחזה? הוא דבר מבוטל מצד עצמו, כי הלא
לא היו אז המשניות סדורות, להיות כלם בלשון ובסגנון אחד, להביא
ממנו ראיה, כי כל תנא ותנא כתב לו מה שלמד מרבו, במגילה קצרה,
ובאמת היו הרבה פעמים המגילות מְחֻלקות, כמו דבית שמאי היו
להם מגילות ע"פ פסקי והוראות שמאי, ודבית הלל ע"פ פסקי
והוראות הלל. לכן לא היה אפשר להם לומר נייתי ספר ונחזה, כי לא
היה מועיל להם במחלוקתם כי עדיין היה המחלוקת קיים, כי
כל אחד היה מביא מגילות סתריו כפי מכתבו. כי אין לעיין רק בספר
מפורסם, אשר כבר עבר עליו ההסכמה.

ואשר אמרת:

ואמנם אם היה שגם שאר התנאים כתבו משנתם, איך היה
שלא היו ספריהם נמצאים בימי חכמי התלמוד, כדרך
שנמצאים עתה בידינו ספרים כ"י רבים שנכתבו ג' מאות וד'
וה' מאות שנה ויותר? התעלה על הדעת לומר כי לכבודו של
ר' יהודה הנשיא נשרפו או נגנזו כל המשניות אשר נכתבו
לפניו? והלא נשארו המכילתא וספרא וספרי והתוספתא וכל

הברייתות המפוזרות בתלמוד אשר בהם כמה וכמה דברים המתנגדים למה שהעלה רבי במשנתו? עכ"ל.

דבריך אלה יסתרו א"ע, וטח מראות עיניך לראות כי כבר תרצת בעצמך קושיתך, קושיי האחרונה מתרצת הראשונה, כי באמת ספרי וספרא ומכילתא ותוספתא וברייתות, הן הם באמת המשניות אשר היו קודם רבי ונשארו מימות תנאים הראשונים עד זמנינו זה, וכמו שאמרו חז"ל,[6] סתם ספרא ר"מ [צ"ל ר"י], סתם ספרי ר"י [צ"ל ר"ש], וכולהו אליבא דר"ע. וכעין שמצינו הרבה פעמים בש"ס דתנן או דתניא ורש"י ובעלי תוספות אמרו כי לא ידעו מקומם, כמו שבת קו ע"א ברש"י ד"ה מתניתין ר' יהודא ע"ש. והמה מן המשניות שהיו בימי הש"ס, ובימי רש"י כבר נאבדו. כאשר נאבדו הרבה ספרי קודש ולא הגיעו עוד אל חכמי התלמוד, כמו דברי הימים ממלכי ישראל, ונבואות הרבה נביאים.

ואשר שאלת: אם היו כותבים, למה נקרא על פה? עד אן תרבה הבלים כאיש שפתים? וכי מפני שלא כתבוה החכמים היתה נקראת תורה שבע"פ? הלא באמת יען לא כתבוה השם בתורתו, וילמדה למשה בע"פ, נקראת תורה שבע"פ, שלמדה במ' יום על הר סיני, וכעין שהביא הטור, ריש הלכות שחיטה, ברייתא וזבחת כאשר צויתיך, מלמד שנתנה שחיטה ומשה בע"פ, ואף היום שכבר נכתבה מחז"ל יצדק עליה שם בע"פ, כי נתינתה מסיני היתה בע"פ, ומה זה שהרעשת העולם על דבר קטן כזה, אשר דרדקי דבי רב יודעין אותו ושפכת דיו חנם? ועל כל זה מה שסיימת המאמר בזה"ל: "הנה נא ידידי, הארכתי בחקירה הזאת לעוצם חשיבותה בעיני, כי עומדים אנחנו בדור שידיעת יסודות דתינו צריכה והכרחית לנו יותר מאשר היתה בכל הדורות שעברו, ואעפ"כ אנו רחוקים מאוד מידיעת היסודות ההם. והנה כל זמן שלא נדע כי התורה שבע"פ נשמרו החכמים מלכתוב אותה על ספר, למען יוכלו ב"ד שבכל דור ודור

6. סנהדרין פו ע"א.

לתקן ולהחליף כפי צורך המקום והזמן, לא נדע כלל יסוד התורה שבע"פ." מי יראה דבריך אלה, וישם לבו על מה שבתוכם, ולא יסמרו שערות בשרו? כי בדית מלבך טעם, אשר לא ידענו ולא שמענו בלתי היום, לדבר סרה על חז"ל, שלכן הסתירו הדברים ולא כתבום, כדי שיוכלו לשנות בכל פעם כרצונם, א"כ איפו [!] עתה ידעתי מה החרדה הזה אשר חרדת, בראותך דברי החכם גייגער כי נכתבו המשניות קודם, כי אם היו כתובות עוד קודם רבנו הקדוש לא תוכל להכחיש בקבלתה. אכן כאשר הראית לדעת, כי לא היו כתובות, רק נמסרו בע"פ למען יוכלו לשנות בכל פעם כרצונם, א"כ התורה שבע"פ איננה תורת ד' מסיני. אלא בכל דור ודור חדשו בלבם כפי סברתם, והעולה על רוחם. אכן לא אאריך פה בראיות נגדך, אך קח ספר הכוזר [!] וראה במאמר ג סי' סה עד סוף, וכל מה שהשיב לקראים הראשונים תהי' תשובה גם לקראים אחרונים; או עשה זאת איפה והנצל, פרוק משא הדת מעליך ומכל ריעך הדומים לך, משא, אשר הכבידו עליכם חז"ל בערמה ודבר כזב, ואל תהי פתי המאמין לכל דבר.

וכאשר הפנית שכמך מחז"ל, פגעת את שש ועושה צדק[7] אדוננו מורינו ורבינו הרמב"ם זללה"ה, וירקת חלאת פיך על פני משה כי קרן עור פניו. מה לך תנשמת עור עינים לגלות מסוה הודו במקום לא תוכל ראות? אחרי מי יצא פרעש אחד לרדוף, אחרי מלך ישראל, וקורא בהרים אחרי נשר גדול כנפים? היכסה זבוב בכנפיו עריפי שמש שמש מעל עין הארץ? היעלה פח מן הארץ, ולכוד ילכוד אראלי שמים? שם נשמת משה, מסתתרת בסתר כנפי אל, תתענג מזיו כבוד עליון, ואתה לנפש תדרשנה לרדת אליך פלאים, עשות אתך מלחמה? בן אדם! עמוד על רגלך, אשאלך והודיעני, מי שם לך פה לדבר חרפות וגדופים כמו אלה, ועל מי הרימות קול כי היה בעוכרנו, מי הוא העוכר ישראל כבוד אדוננו הרמב"ם זללה"ה או

---

7. ע"פ נוסח הברכה שבסוף ברכת המזון בסעודת הברית: "הרחמן הוא יברך בעל ברית המילה אשר שש לעשות צדק בגילה..."

אתה חדל אישים באין דעת ותבונה? בין נא בעצמך בדבריך אשר אמרת: "והנה הרמב"ם (ומעולם לא אמרת ז"ל) עם כל התפלספותו היה בעוכרינו, כי בתחלה היו דברי חכמים כדרבונות להנהיג את הבהמה (הלא הוא ההמון) אל כל אשר יראו החכמים טוב ומועיל לפי הזמן והמקום, והוא הרמב"ם עשה אותם כמסמרות נטועים לא יזיזו ממקומם" עכ"ל. מה תוכן כונתך בזה המאמר? אן כונת המאמר מוליך אותנו? כי התורה שבע"פ היא רק ערמת חז"ל, לא תורה מקובלת מפי משה, מפי הגבורה, ותצעק חמס על הרמב"ם ז"ל על אשר עשה כמסמרות נטועים בתורת קבלה, והביא אותנו במסורת להיות לעם אחד ולשמוע תורת ד' מפי מקבלים נאמנים. אוי לך שד"ל, מי יתן והחרשת, ולא גלית קלונך ברבים!

ומה שכתבת: "ועצור במילין לא אוכל על אמונה אחת אשר לקח הרמב"ם מאריסטו ומפרשיו, אשר הזיקה לבני עמנו מצדדים הרבה, הלא הוא אמונתו במהות הנפש שהוא כח ההכנה לבד, והדבר הנבדל אחר המות הוא הדבר המגיע בפועל (מורה נבוכים ח"א פרק ע) והיא הדעה שהשיגה הבורא כפי כחה, והשיגה הדעות הנפרדות (הלכות תשובה פ' ח)" ע"כ. באמת כן הוא דעת הרמב"ם ז"ל, אך לא ידעתי מה עון מצאת בהדעה הזאת, שהרעשת העולם בעבורה? הכי להרמב"ם לבדו הדברים האלה, כמהו סוברים רבים לפניו, ועוד רבים לאחריו. ואעתיק לך הנה רק דברי הבעל עקידה משער שישי [בראשית, עמ סז ע"א], וז"ל:

וכמה הפליגו חז"ל (חגיגה דף יב ע"ב) לספר בשבח זאת הנשמה, במ"ש ערבות שבו נשמותיהן של צדיקים, ונשמות ורוחות שעתידין להבראות, אך כשיובן על הפירוש הנכון שפירש הרב המורה פרק ע חלק א אמר ומה נכבד ענין זה למי שיבינהו, כי הנשמות הנשארות אחר המות אינה הנשמה ההווה באדם כשיתהוה, שזאת ההויה בעת התהוותו היא כח ההכנה לבד, והדבר הנבדל אחר המות, הוא הדבר המתקיים בפועל, ולא הנשמה ג"כ ההווה הוא הרוח ההווה,

ולזה מנו להויות נשמות ורוחות. אמנם הנבדלים הם דבר
אחד לבד, וכבר בארנו באריכות שתוף רוח, ובארנו עוד בספר המדע,
מה שנפל באלו השמות מן השתוף ע"כ ראה דבריו דברי
אלהים חיים, מכוונים לכל מה שאמרנוהו הנה, כי הוא נתן
הבדל מפורש בין הנשמות הברואות לבין העתידין
להבראות ואמר כי הברואות והטובות בשלמותן הן הנה
הנשארות אחר המות, ואשר ייחסו חז"ל מושבם במדרגת
גלגל ערבות, שהוא המניע הנבדל הנמצא ראשונה לכל
הנמצאות כמו שהוא ג"כ בהנעתו מסייע בהויות הנשמות
רצוני לתת נפשות ורוחות בגופים, שהם להם ההכנה
הראשונה, כמו שאמרנו. ואמרם ז"ל שהם בו כלומר
שמציאותם תלוי בו כפי אשר הפקד עליו מאת הבורא ית'
שמו, ראה כונת הרב טובה באלו הענינים, שהם עיקר
מציאות האדם, וחלילה לשמוע על זה פירוש אחר עכ"ל.

אלו הדברים דים לדעתי להשבית שאון כל התרגזך על
הרמב"ם ז"ל, ואם יקרו בעיניך דברי הבעל עקידה דורשם מעל ספרו,
ותמצא בהם דברים רבים אשר יתנו מרגוע לנפשך ולא ידעת זולתו.
אמנם בעיקר הדעה הזאת אנא השמיעני, אם יש לך ראיה ברורה
לסתור דברי הרמב"ם ז"ל במהות הנפש. אדרבה אני אומר לך אחרי
ראותי דעות פלסופי זמנינו במהות הנפש, המתחדשים לבקרים,
בלבול מחשבותם, הפסק רעיונותם, כי דעת הרמב"ם ראויה מאוד
להאמר, ולהביאה שנית בכור הבחינה, ואולי תצדק יותר ויותר מכל
מתפלספי זמנינו, כי מה תזיק לנו בעניני האמונה, אם הנפש היא כח
והכנה לבד מהתמזג היסודות ואח"כ כשתתגדל תעלה מעלה מעלה
עד שיש בה כח לחיות גם אחרי הפרדה מהגוף. או בשעת בריאת
הגוף תרד הנפש משמי מרומים, והיא בעצמותה דבר מחוץ לגוף?
אשר באמת לפי דעה הזאת יצדקו כל קושיות הבעל עקדה ע"ש.

ואם תשאלני: הלא אם תפריד הגוף אין בשום יסוד בפני
עצמו כח והכנה לנפש? אז גם אנכי אענך, הלא אין מזה ראיה, אולי
כלם ביחד בהשתלבות המרכבים יולידו נפש. ובפרט כאשר עינינו

ראות בכל הטבע, כל אחד בפני עצמו אין בו הדבר ההוא, ובהתמזגם
יולד דבר שלישי נכון וקיים. ואם תאמר, הן כל זאת מצד טבע
פשוטיי ואין שינוי בבחירתם, אכן נפש האדם יש בה מן השינוי
והתמורה ובחירה   רצונית מה שאין כן בכל הטבע ואיך אפשר
מהתמזג היסודות תוליד בנפש כח לבחירה רצונית? נגד הקושי׳
הזאת אשאלך לפי דעת שהנפש איננה מהתמזג היסודות, רק עצם
נפרד ממעל, איך יתכן שיהי׳ בה התקבלות השינוי, כי הוא חלק
ממרומים למעלה מגלגל הירח אשר אין בהם שום שינוי ובחירה
רצונית, אם לא שתאמר שהנפש נבראת מן השם בכח, שיש בה
בחירה חפשיית, ולכן מה איכפת לך עתה לפי דעת הרמב״ם ז״ל ג״כ,
שאע״פ שהנפש מהתמזג היסודות, בכל זאת יש בה כח בחיריי
לשנות כרצונה וכחפצה. והטעם נסתר מנגד עינינו, כמו באמת אין
לנו יד בכל חקי הטבע הראשיים, ונסתרים מעין גבר.

ואף אם אסכים לדעת זו שהנפש הוא דבר מחוץ לגוף ואיננה
כח והכנה לבד, והרמב״ם ז״ל טעה בדבר זה, אשר לא נודע עוד
בדורו, העל כן נבזנו אנחנו, ונשימה תורותיו לשמצה? קרא בגרון
נגד נביאי אמת, אשר עמדו בסוד ד׳, מדוע הציבו לדמיון המון כי
קדרות שמש וירח או רעידת הארץ, אשר באמת כל אלה על פי חקי
הטבע יסובו, והתוכנים בזמנינו יחשבו עתם ורגעים, הם עונשי השם
להכות ולענוש את כל בני התבל כמו השמש יהפך לחשך והירח
לדם, וכן אמרו חז״ל בסוף סוכה [כט ע״א] לוקי [צ״ל ליקוי] לבנה
סימן רע לשונאיהם של ישראל ע״ש? או דבר בפה מלא סרה על חז״ל
אשר לא ידעו כי הארץ כדוריית היא, ודמו כי אך שטחיית, כחצי
עגול, והשמים שוכבים עליהם? אלא הנח לדברים כאלה, שכבר צוחו
בהם קמאי ובתראי ואל תהי כסיל שונה באולת!

ומה שעמדת לימין הדת, להראות כי הרמב״ם ז״ל כפר
בתחיית המתים, בדבר שלא ידעת ולא הבינות פרשת רשת הכפירה
על אדוננו הרמב״ם ז״ל, אולם הה! ותלכד רגלך. כתבת בלשון

מדברת גדולות, וז"ל "תחיית המתים שלך היא של אריסטו
ומפרשיו, לא של אבותינו; שלך היא לנפש,ושלנו לגוף ולנפש, שלך
לחכמים וטובים, ושלנו לטובים ולרעים, לחכמים ולטפשים." ובסוף
המאמר הבאת דברי הרמב"ם ז"ל: "כי השלמות האחרון אין בו
מעשים ולא מדות, אבל הוא דעות לבד, ואמרת כי השלמות האחרון
הוא הנכבד בלי ספק, והוא סבת החיים המתמידים, לא זולתו (בח"ג
פ' כז). הרי מבואר כי גם גנוב רצוח ונאוף יוכל הפילוסוף המשכיל
לקנות לו חיי העוה"ב ולאו בזכותא תלי' מלתא, אלא בידיעת
האמתיות תלי' מלתא, ראה מה בין העה"ב שלך לעוה"ב שלנו!"

דבריך אלה באמת אינם ראויים להשיב עליהם, אך להשכילך
בינה אצא הפעם, ולפרש לך כל דברי הרמב"ם ז"ל באלה הענינים,
ובכונת המאמרים האלה, ואז תדע כי כל השגתך היה רק בעבור שלא
הבינות הטיב [!] דבריו, ולא שמת לבך עליהם, ורק אהבת הנצוח
והקלקול גרמה להביאך על הלום, לדבר סרה עליו, ולדמותו
להפילוסוף המובא בכוזרי מאמר ראשון כי אין הקב"ה מבט במעשה
בני אדם רק במחשבות וידיעות לבד. אך אם אתה לו שמעני, אבאר
לך באר הטיב [!] דברי הרמב"ם ז"ל במה שאמר כי השלמות האחרון
אין בו מעשים ולא מדות רק הוא דעות לבד. אך בתחלה נתקור איזה
דבריו יקראו דעות אשר אליהם כיון הרמב"ם ז"ל? לדעתי, גם לדעת
כל משכיל בר לבב, יקראו אלו דעות לדעת כי יש מצוי ראשון, והוא
יודע, ומשגיח, ומעניש, ונותן שכר טוב לעושי רצונו, קנצי למילין,
שנאמנין בכל התורה, או לפחות בעיקרי הדת שהעמיד הרמב"ם ז"ל
בעצמו, והדעות הללו באמת הן הנכבדות בלי ספק.

אכן באיזה צד ואופן נגיע אל הדעות הנכבדות הללו? אין
להם דרך אחר רק ע"י מעשים ומדות טובות. ואין לך מעשים ומדות
טובות יותר מאשר צוה השם בעצמו ע"י נביאו נאמן ביתו, כאשר
באר הטיב [!] הרמב"ם ז"ל בעצמו בשמונה פרקיו ע"ש. ואל תטעה
לומר כי כאשר באנו אל הדעות אמיתיות נעזוב המעשים ולא נצטרך

עוד אליהם. כי בעת אשר כבר עזבנו מצות השם, אשר צונו ע"י
משה נביאו, לא יוכל לעזוב אותם, רק על שני אופנים, או שנכפור
בהם ולא נודו שהשם צום, או נודה ולא נרצה לעשותם, ובשניהם
עזבנו ברגע זו השלמות האחרון, ולא נשאר בידנו כלום. כי כאשר
לא נעשה מעשה התורה היאך נודה בדברי השם ובנביאיו
והתחברותו והשגחתו למין האנושי? אך מפני מה קורא הרמב"ם ז"ל
[את הדעות] <u>השלמות האחרון</u>? הוא, כי הוא ז"ל יכונן כל מעשי בני
הטבע תכלית אל תכלית, כשלהבת הקשורה בגחלת, ולדוגמא, כל
מעשי בני האדם בעוה"ז, עשרו גבורתו חכמתו ויכלתו, יכון האדם
בהם לתכלית כדי שיוכל לעשות מעשי השם בשלמות כמ"ש
הרמב"ם ז"ל בח' פרקיו, ע"ש, ותכלית המעשה שיוכל ע"י
להשגת השם לדעת אמיתו ואחדותו, והוא באמת השלמות האמיתי
כי בלי דעת השגת השם ואחדותו המעשה אינה כלום כמו שאמרו
חז"ל רחמנא לבא בעי.[8] וכן תפלה בלא כונה כגוף בלא נשמה, וכן
גבי קרבן שפוסל במחשבת חוץ לזמנו או חוץ למקומו,[9] וכן מלאכת
שבת צריכה להיות העקירה משעה ראשונה לכך ונתכוין לעשות
עקירה ברה"י והנחה בר"ה, ע' שבת דף ה ע"ב, כי איך אפשר
שתתקבל המעשה אם אין הכונה רצויה לצד השם. אמנם מחשבה
והשתכלות לבד בלי מעשה בודאי אינה רצויה, כי איך תתרצה
המחשבה אם לא נשמור לעשות אשר צונו במצותיו; אך אחר המות,
או בימי עוה"ב, אין בהם מעשה כלל כההיא דאמרו עוה"ז דומה
לערב שבת כל מי שמכין בערב שבת, אוכל בשבת,[10] רק מחשבה
לבדה איתא כההיא דאמרו צדיקים יושבים ועתרותיהם בראשיהם
ונהנים מזיו השכינה.[11]

וא"כ שמעית מכל זה כי דעת הרמב"ם ז"ל אינה כפי הבנתך,
שאף רצוח גנוב ונאוף יוכל הפילסוף ויזכה לחיי העוה"ב. חלילה

8. סנהדרין קו ע"ב (גירסת רש"י), ילקוט שמעוני, שמואל א, רמז קכד.
9. פסחים ס ע"א, זבחים סד ע"ב–סה ע"א.
10. שמחות ב, ג.
11. ברכות יז ע"א.

וחלילה אדרבה שהכופר במצוה אחת, ואומר אינה מן השמים, אין לו
חלק לעוה"ב ומצוה לשנאו ולאבדו בעוה"ז ויצא מכלל ישראל
ונקרא אפיקורוס, כי הוא כופר בתורה מן השמים. אולם כל הדברים
הללו לא נאמרו רק נגד האיש הישראליי לבד, אשר כבר נכנס
במסורת הברית וקבל עליו תורת אמת, ולא כמו שבאת אתה
בעקיפין, לדבר עליו סרה, כי הדברים הללו דבר אף נגד מי שאינו
ישראלי, חלילה, וכי עינינו תנקר, כי הרמב"ם ז"ל הזהירנו כמה
פעמים לאהבם ולכבדם ולשמור ממונם ולבקש שלומם וטובתם כל
הימים? ועוד איך אפשר דבר כזה להאמר אם הגוים לא יאמינו בי"ג
עקרי דתנו מצוה לשנאם ולאבדם? הלא בין עקרי הדת הוא כי תורת
משה לא תשתנה, ואיך אפשר להכביד עיקר כזה על שום אומה
ולשון, אם לא שנכריחם לקבל דתנו ולהיות לעם אחד. והוא סותר
ומנגד לדברי הגמר' והרמב"ם ז"ל בעצמם, שאמרו קשים גרים
לישראל כספחת בבשר החי,[12] וכן אמרו אין מקבלין גרים לימות
המשיח, כשם שלא קבלו בימי דוד ושלמה.[13] נשמע מזה, כי התורה
לא הקפידה להעמיס עֵלֵנו ודתנו על עם אחר, ובכל זאת אמרו חסידי
אומות העולם יש להם חלק לעוה"ב,[14] ואמרו הוי מתפלל בשלומה
של מלכות.[15] וכל הדברים הללו העתיקם הרמב"ם ז"ל בהלכותיו.[16]
ואתה באת לעורר מדנים בינינו לבין האומות אשר אנו מתגוררים
ביניהם בדברך סרה על כבוד אדונינו הרמב"ם ז"ל כי הוא מצוה
עלינו לשנאם ולאבדם. שקר אתה דובר, ועל דברים כאלה נאמרו
יכרת ד' כל שפתי חלקות![17]

אמנם בעיקר קושייתך אשר הקשית לשאול על הרמב"ם ז"ל,
מאין יצא לו להכביד עלינו עול י"ג עקרים לעיקרי הדת והכופר בהם

12. יבמות מז ע"ב, קט ע"ב, קידושין ע ע"ב, נדה יג ע"ב.
13. יבמות כד ע"ב, עבודה זרה ג ע"ב.
14. תוספתא סנהדרין יג, א.
15. אבות ג, ב.
16. הלכות דעות ב, ו, הלכות תשובה ג, ה, הלכות גזילה א, ב, הלכות שכירות יח, א.
17 תהילים יב, ד.

13

אין לו חלק לעוה"ב? קושיתך זאת צריכה יישוב נכון באמת,
ובתחלה נחקור על גוף הקושי' כי היא מסתעפת לב' קושיות. האחת
הקושי' הנודעת כבר, איך אפשר בדבר אמונה הכרח הקבלה? ממה
נפשך אם אאמין, הרי כבר האמנתי מבלי צווי, ואם לא אאמין איך
תכריחני הצווי להאמין בדבר שאי אפשר לפי שכלי להאמין. אף אם
אומר האמנתי, הלא לבי בל עמי? והשניה, מאין יצא לו להרמב"ם
הדברים האלה שאם אינו מאמין בי"ג עיקרים הללו אין לו חלק
לעוה"ב?

ואומר אני אך תן לבך לדעתי ליישב שתי הקושיות ובתחלה
הקושי' הב', כי ידוע כי הרמב"ם ז"ל בכל הלכותיו הולך תמיד רק
אחרי מסדרי הש"ס, וקובע כל פסקיו כמוהם, וכאשר מצא המשנה[18]
כל ישראל יש להם חלק לעוה"ב, ואלו שאין להם חלק לעוה"ב
האומר אין תחיית המתים מן התורה, ואין תורה מן השמים,
ואפיקורוס, חלק אותם לי"ג סעיפים אשר יסתעפו ויתפרדו מן
הראשיים הללו. וכאשר ראה מאמר חז"ל[19] כל הכופר בע"ז כאלו
מודה בכל התורה כלה וכל המודה בע"ז כאלו כופר בכל התורה
כלה. לכן הביא ראשית האמונה והוא יסוד הא', שיש אלוה מצוי
ראשון, שלם בכל דרכי המציאות, ואין האחדות והאדנות אלא לו
לבדו. היסוד הב', יחודת השם, שאינו כאחד העובר והמתפרד
ומתדבק מחלקים. היסוד הג', שלילת הגשמות. היסוד הרביעי, כי
הוא קדמון במוחלט, וכל נמצא זולתו בלתי קדמון, רק כלם נבראים
עפ"י דברו. היסוד החמישי, שראוי לעבדו ולגדלו ולא יעשו כן למי
שהוא תחתיו במציאות. אלה החמשה יסודות הראשיים בענין אלוקי,
מוצאם מדברי חז"ל כל הכופר בע"ז כאלו מודה בכל התורה, וכל
המודה בע"ז כאלו כופר בכל התורה כלה, והמודה בע"ז בודאי אין
לו חלק לעוה"ב.

והיסוד השישי, הנבואה. היסוד הז', נבואת משה היתה

18. סנהדרין י, א.
19. ספרי דברים, פיסקא נד.

אמיתית ושהוא ראש לנביאים. היסוד הח', היות התורה כלה מן השמים מפי הגבורה. היסוד הט', כי לא תשתנה ועליה אין להוסיף ואין לגרוע. הד' יסודות הללו כלולים תחת השם "אין תורה מן השמים." היסוד העשירי, כי הוא היודע כל, והמשגיח. היסוד הי"א. כי הוא הנותן שכר טוב, ויעניש, למי שיעבור על מצותיו. היסוד הי"ב, ימות המשיח. היסוד הי"ג, תחיית המתים והוא ימי עוה"ב. הד' יסודות הללו כלולים במאמר אין תחיית המתים מן התורה, כי תחיית המתים הוא ע"צ השכר והעונש, כאשר אבאר. ולולא שהקב"ה יודע ומשגיח על פרטי מין האדם, מאין לו להעניש או לתת שכר לעושי מצותיו אם אינו משגיח כלל. וגם ימות המשיח ג"כ כלולים בתוך שכר ועונש, כאשר ירצה השם להרים קרן אומה השפלה ע"פ ההשגחה פרטית וישלם שכרה בעוה"ז לעיני כל. והדברים הללו נאמרים בספר העיקרים פרק יב [צ"ל פרק יג] מאמר א' באר הטיב [!], וז"ל ג' עיקרים הללו, ר"ל מציאות השם, שכר ועונש ותורה מן השמים, הג' עיקרים כוללים לדת אלהית, שכל הכופר באחד מהם יצא מכלל בעלי הדת האלהית ואין לו חלק לעוה"ב . . . עד שיודה בהם ובשרשים הנתלים בהם וכו', והמאמין בעיקר הג' שהוא השכר והעונש צריך שיאמין בידיעת ה' והשגחתו, ושיש שם שכר אם נפשיי ואם גופני, וכל מי שיכפור שורש מאלו השרשים המסתעפים מן העיקרים או נתלים בהם, כאלו כופר בעיקר עצמו וכו' עכ"ל ע"ש.

ואמנם תחיית המתים הם ימי עוה"ב שמפרש הרמב"ם באר הטיב [!] מאוד. אך מאין יצא לו להרמב"ם ז"ל שתחיית המתים כלולים בימי העוה"ב ולא בימי ימות המשיח? לדעתי לקוחים דבריו מסתם גמר' מפורשת, וז"ל המשנה: ואלו שאין להן חלק לעוה"ב, גמר', וכל כך למה? תנא הוא כפר בתחיית המתים לפיכך לא יהי' לו חלק בתחיית המתים, שכל מדותיו של הקב"ה מדה כנגד מדה. א"כ ששאלת הגמר' היתה וכל כך למה? שפי' למה לא יהי' לו חלק לעוה"ב, ומשני הוא כפר בתחיית המתים לפיכך לא יהי' לו חלק

בתחיית המתים, מכלל דתחיית המתים היינו העוה"ב, דאל"כ אינה מדה כנגד מדה, הוא כפר בעוה"ב לפיכך לא יהי' לו חלק בתחיית המתים, אלא דתחיית המתים היינו העוה"ב והבן.

ומעתה נכונים המה דברי הרמב"ם ז"ל מאוד בטעמם, שכותב פרק ח מהלכות תשובה [ה"א] וז"ל: הטובה הצפונה לצדיקים הוא חיי העוה"ב, והוא החיים שאין עמם מות והטובה שאין עמה רעה כו' כו' ע"כ, כי לקוחים כל דבריו מדברי הגמ' הנ"ל. ואף שיש אגדות רבות החולקות על משמעות הגמ' הזו, אין אחריותם על הרמב"ם ז"ל, כדרכו תמיד אף לענין הלכה היכא שיש מחלוקת. אמנם השכר והעונש שמביא הרמב"ם ז"ל כמה פעמים, ומביאו ליסוד האחד אשר, שהקב"ה מעניש ונותן שכר טוב לאוהביו ולשומרי מצוותיו, השכר ועונש הזה הוא מיד אחר המות, שמקבלת הנפש שכרה או ענשה, ואין זה העוה"ב שחשבת והוכחת בדבריך כי לדברי הרמב"ם ז"ל אין דין ואין חשבון לאחר המות אלא הרשע נכרת ונאבד כבהמה, חלילה להרמב"ם ז"ל מדבר זה אשר צועק מתיד כברוכיא בכל מקום כי יש שכר ועונש אחר המות ואתה תחפא עליו דברים אשר לא כן.

ומה שאמרת תחיית המתים שלך היא לנפש, שלנו לגוף ולנפש, הלא אם היה לך שכל בקדקדך היה לך לשאול לפי דעתך קושיא יותר עצומה, והיה לך לומר כך: הן הרמב"ם מודה בהשארת הנפש לאחר המות, א"כ הנפש איננה מתה בשום פעם, ומהו יקרא תחי' מאחר שעדיין לא מתה והיא בקיומה קודם מות ולאחר המות, ומהו התחי' שתהי' אז יותר משעת מתה? אכן באמת לא ירדת לסוף כונתו בזה, כי גם הרמב"ם מודה שהתחי' שתהי', תהי' ביחד לנפש ולגוף, ויזדכך הגוף ויהיה בכנפש, ויעלה מעלה מעלה, ולא יהי' אז לא אכילה ולא שתי' ולא תשמיש כו' כי אם השגת השם לבד כמו שמצינו מעלת החסידים והנביאים בזה העולם מה שתשיג הנפש לבדה בהפרדה מן הגויה כמו ולא אכל משה לחם ארבעים יום, וכן

אליהו, ויונה חי במעי הדג ושאר דברים רבים שאי אפשר לפורטם פה, וכמו כן יהיו אז כל ישראל נקיים וברורים אחרי אשר כבר נענשו וקבלו עליהם דינם ועונשם על חטאם ומרים ויהיו אחרי כן זכים ותמימים לקבל כח שפע אלוה. וכמו כן לשון הרמב"ם ז"ל וז"ל: וכאשר יאמין האדם אלה היסודות כלם ונתברר בה אמונתו בד' הוא נכנס בכלל ישראל, ומצוה לאוהבו ולרחם עליו ולנהוג עמו בכל מה שצוה הש"י איש לחברו מן האהבה והאחוה, ואפילו עשה מה שיכול מן העבירות מחמת התאוה והתגברות הטבע הגרוע הוא נענש כפי חטאיו אבל יש לו חלק לעוה"ב והוא מפושעי ישראל וכו' עכ"ל. וראה גם דברי הראב"ד ז"ל החולק תמיד על הרמב"ם ז"ל אומר בפ"ח מלכות תשובה [ה"ב] וז"ל: דברי האיש הזה בעיני קרובים למי שאומר אין תחיית המתים לגופות אלא לנשמות בלבד כו' אבל אפשר שהבורא ית' ישים גויתם חזקות ובריאות כגוית המלאכים וכגוית אליהו ז"ל עכ"ל. ואומר רק קרובים ולא החליט בודאי שיאמר כי הרמב"ם ז"ל סובר שאינו תח"ה רק לנשמות בלבד אלא אומר קרובים דבריו ואתה מהרת והחלטת דברים שלא היו ולא נשמעו מהרמב"ם ז"ל.

ומה שאמרת "אפילו היה החלום הזה אפשר להתקיים, עדיין אין זה השכר אשר אנחנו מקוים, כי הנפש בהתחברה באל לא תהיה עוד בריה בפני עצמה, ולא יהיה עוד הצדיק נמצא באישיותו, ולא זוכר מעשיו, ולא נהנה כלל בקבלת שכרו, אבל הוא נהפך להיות חלק מאלוה, ואישיותו וזכרון מעשיו אובדים לגמרי" ע"כ. דבריך אלה יאותו יותר לנשים הזקנות, ולא לך לוצאטו! כי איך תדמה בנפשך שקר לחשוב על הרמב"ם ז"ל כי הוא סובר שיתוספו נשמת הצדיקים על ענין אלוה ויהיו חלק מאלהי? דבר עוד הפעם אלה הדברים, "כי יתוסף נשמתם על אלוה". וכי חסר הוא שיתוסף? ואיך אפשר על בלי תכלית בכל צד שיתוסף עליו? איש בער לא ידע וכסיל לא יבין דברי הרמב"ם ז"ל וחושב על רבינו משה דברים שלא אמרם

פתי שבפתאים.

ואף לו יהי כדבריך שהרמב"ם ז"ל סובר שיתוספו נשמת צדיקים על כח אלוה, איך תאמר: ולא יהי' הצדיק נמצא באישיותו ולא זוכר מעשיו. אם יהי' לאלוה, איך אפשר שלא יהא זוכר מעשיו? ועוד שזה לא יקרא בעיניך שכר טוב? ואיה שכר גדול יותר מזה? אמנם דברי הרמב"ם ז"ל סותרים דבריך לגמרי, וחלילה לו לאדם גדול הזה לומר או לחשוב דברים כמו אלה, שתהי' נשמת הצדיק חלק מאלוה, וז"ל הרמב"ם ז"ל: "ונהנים מזיו השכינה, ר"ל שאותן הנשמות מתענגות במה שמשיגות ויודעות מאמיתת הבורא יתב' כמו שמתענגנות חיות הקודש ושאר מדרגות המלאכים במה שהם משיגים ויודעים ממציאותו." ועפ"י הדברים האלה איך אפשר לחשוב על הרמב"ם שסובר שיהי' חלק מאלוה אחרי שאומר בפירוש משיגות ויודעות, שאם יהי' לחלקו איך שייך לומר משיגות ויודעות כשם שהמלאכים וחיות הקודש, וכי המלאכים וחיות הקודש הם חלק אלוה? אוי לפה חנף שאומר על הרמב"ם דבר כזה! וכן אומר על "ועטרותיהם בראשיהם – השארות הנפש בקיום המושכל להם והוא הבורא,"[20] כונתו שישיגו את עצם השם הנכבד, וזה כונתו במה שאמר להם בלשון רבים, כי לפי דעתך שיתוספו לחלק אלוה הלא כלם יהיו אחד, ואיך שייך לומר "להם"? אך במה שאמר וחיות הוא רוצה לומר המושכל והוא דבר אחד אולם לא המשכיל והוא דבר אחד רק המושכל והוא, וזה אמת וברור ורצונו שלא ישכילו בני אדם אז בדבר אחר, רק באלהים לבדו ועיין במורה ח' א' פרק שמונה ושישים, ודבר זה אסור לגלות לפני עם הארץ.

ואשר דברת בפיך והקשית לשאול נגדו וז"ל:

ואחרי אשר פקח ד' את עינינו להבין סתריך ראינו כי גם במאמרך על תחיית המתים אמרת ברמז מה שיבטל אותה, כי אמרת שתחיית המתים היא מופת ומעשה נסים, ובסוף אמרת

_____

20. לשון הרמב"ם בהקדמתו לפרק חלק.

כי המופת לא יתכן שימשך ויאריך ענינו ושהמטה אשר נהפך לנחש הוצרך שישוב למטה, א"כ לפי דבריך אפילו יהיו המתים לא יתכן שישארו בחיים, אבל ימיתו מיד, אחרי שתחיית המתים מופת והמופת לא ימשך ע"כ.

עתה הראית לדעת כי איש נבוב אתה, כי לו יהי כדבריך כאשר הבינות, שכל מופת לא ימשך, א"כ הרם כשופר קולך והגד להרמב"ם ז"ל פשעו כי כפר גם במן שירד ארבעים שנה, ורצננצת המן שצוה השם להניח לדורות ולא נתבאש, ושלא בלו השמלות והמנעלים כל ימי לכת ישראל במדבר, ומטה אהרון שפרחו בו שקדים והיו המטה והשקדים לאות לבני ישראל עד גדול הארץ, ועוד רבים כדומה. אכן דברי הרמב"ם ז"ל מפורשים באר היטב [!] בכ"ט משני ע"ש, כי כל הדברים הללו הם רק נגד שינוי הטבע נאמרו, אכן באמת יש שני מיני מופתים, מופתים עוברים, ומופתים עומדים. מופתים עוברים ישלטו בממשלתם כל ימי הצורך בהם, וכאשר יעבור הזמן ואין נצרכים עוד, מיד ישיבו לטבעם הראשון. ויש מופתים שנצרכים להם ימים רבים ויעמדו ימים רבים כמו המן והשליו ובליאת הבגדים ושקדים של מטה אהרן, יעמדו כל ימים הנצרכים להם, ואח"כ כשאין נצרכים ישיבו לטבעם הראשון, וכן וישבות המן ממחרת באכלם מעבור הארץ,[21] כיון שהיה להם תבואת ארץ כנען מיד וישבות המן וכן בכל נסי השם.

אכן תחיית המתים בעצמותה אינה על צד המופת כלל רק ע"צ השכר, כי איך יתכן אז מופת בדבר שלא ימשך אחריו שום דבר אחר, כי הוא התכלית האחרון והשלמות הגדול, לכן יהיו החיים הללו חיים נצחיים לבלי תכלית, ודוק. ועוד ראה גם ראה כי בעלילת דברים אלה יצאת להלחם נגד הרמב"ם ז"ל, ועתה אוחז החבל נגדו בשני ראשין. בתחלה אמרת כי הרמב"ם סובר שיהיו הצדיקים חלק אלוה ויתוספו עליו ועתה אמרת כי אמר ברמז דבר שיבטל אותה כי

---
21. יהושע ה, יב.

19

ימיתו מיד, שת"ה מופת והמופת לא ימשך. ואיך אפשר מי שהוא חלק אלוה שישוב וימות, ולא יהי' לו חיים נצחיים. בלכול דברים אני רואה כאן, שמבלבלים מוח הקורא, וראש לכל רואה האגרת.

והקושי' הא' שהבאתי לעיל שמסתעפת מדבריך וז"ל: והשנוי והקלקול השני הוא ענין העיקרים אשר הציב להיות כמו יסודות לאמונתינו, המצאה אשר לא צוו ולא דברו קדמונינו ז"ל ולא עלתה על לבם מעולם וכו'. והרמב"ם קבע הלכה מה אנו חייבים להאמין ומה אנו חייבים שלא להאמין, וזה בלא ספק שנוי וקלקול גדול באמונת ישראל ע"כ. באמת על הקושי' הזאת עמדו ראשונים ואחרונים ולא הועילו כלום, אמנם מקום הניחו לי להתגדר בתרוץ זה בהקדמתי לספרי הגדול מוסדות אמונה לתרץ הקושי' הזאת באריכות ולברר וללבן כל הספיקות אשר יסתעפו ממנה. אכן עתה קצרו העת והגליון להעתיק כל הדברים הללו, ואעתיק לך פה רק הצריך לעניננו, והיותר כמוס אתי, רשום בכתובים.

ידוע, כי כל רעיון נופל תחת סוגים ראשיים: המחוייב, והאפשר, והנמנע. ואמנם המחוייב והנמנע אחדים המה אלא ההפך המחוייב הוא הנמנע והפך הנמנע הוא המחוייב. ד"מ כשנקח קו ב' אמות ונעבור בקולמוס כנגדו בכל פעם חצי הראשון, דהיינו אמה, ואח"כ חצי אמה, ואח"כ שליש אמה, ואח"כ חצי שליש, לעולם לא נגיע בשבר הזה להשלים הקו של ב' אמות לא פחות ולא יותר, דהיינו נמנע, ובאמת מחוייב הוא שלא יוכל להשלימו כי בכל פעם אשר יוסיף לא יוסיף יותר מחצי הראשון אשר עמד אצלו בראשונה, וכן לעולם כי כל שבר קטן באחרונה כחצי הראשונה, ומעתה על המחוייב והנמנע לא יפול בשום אופן תאר אמונה, כי איך יפול על ידיעה ברורה אמונה, אחרי אשר כבר הוחלטה לידיעה ומחוייבת להיות ומפני זה לא נכתב בכל התורה כלה והאמנת היום, רק וידעת היום,[22] שתהי' בידך ידיעה ברורה ואמתית, אחרי הבאת המופת, וכן

_____

22. דברים ד, לט; ט, ג.

דוד אומר לבנו דע את אלהי אביך,[23] ולא אמר האמן באלוהי אביך, כי אמונה לא תצדק כי אם על דבר אפשריי, אפשר להיות ואפשר שלא להיות, ואין ראיה והכרעת המופת על שום צד מהצדדים, אז יצדק שם אמונה, כי אאמין שיהי' ויתמלא הדבר ההוא, אף שיש באפשרותו שלא להיות.[24]

---

23. דברי הימים א, כח, ט.

24. ולא אכחד ממך דבר יקר אשר אמרתי בפרוש פרשה סתומה מאוד בתורתנו הקדושה. בראשית טו: אחר הדברים האלה היה דבר ד' אל אברם במחזה לאמור אל תירא אברם אנכי מגן לך שכרך הרבה מאוד. ויאמר אברם אדני אלהים מה תתן לי? ואנכי הולך ערירי! ובן משק ביתי הוא דמשק אליעזר. ויאמר אברם הן לי לא נתת זרע והנה בן ביתי יורש אותי! והנה דבר ד' אליו לאמר לא יירשך זה! כי אם אשר יצא ממעיך הוא יירשך, ויוצא אותו החוצה, ויאמר הבט נא השמימה וספור הכוכבים אם תוכל לספור אותם, ויאמר לו כה יהיה זרעך. והאמן בד' ויחשבה לו צדקה!! הפרשה הזאת סתומה לדעתי מאוד מאוד, כי בכל מפרשי הפשט אשר ראיתי לא מצאתי נחת רוח בדבריהם, כי שני הכתובים הללו יסובו על מרכז אחד, ד' מה תתן לי? ואנכי הולך ערירי ובן משק ביתי הוא דמשק אליעזר, והיינו ממש כתוב השני, הן לי לא נתת זרע. והנה בן ביתי יורש אותי, והוא מאמר הראשון בשנוי לשון קצת? ועל כל זאת תמיה אני, אחרי אשר הוציא אותו אלקים החוצה ויצוהו לספור הכוכבים ויאמר לו כה יהי' זרעך, אמר הכתוב והאמין בד' ויחשבה לו צדקה. מהו ההאמנה שייך כאן אחרי אשר כבר דבר אתו אלהים, ויאמר לו כה יהי' זרעך הוא כבר מחוייב להיות, ועל המחוייב לא תפול אמונה? וכי אפשר לאדם שלא להאמין בדברי השם בדברו אתו אל פנים ואמר לו כה יהי' זרעך? הקושיות הללו אלצונו לפרש הפרשה הזאת בענין אחר והוא בהקדימי הקדמה אחת. ידוע כי יש בני אדם שיולידו בנים ובנות בשחרות ימיהם או עכ"פ בחצי ימיהם, והנה משך ימי חייהם יתענגו בהם ויהיו להם נחת רוח במה שיגדלום וילמדום וישאו להם נשים וכדומה. ויש אשר יולידו בנים ובנות רק לעת זקנתם לבד או אף גם ילדו לאחר מותם, בהניחם אשה מעוברת. ומעתה נבוא להבין דברי הפרשה, כי בעת אמר לו אלהים שכרך הרבה מאוד השיבו אברם ראשון ראשון ד' אלקים מה תתן לי? כלומר למה תתן לי שכר הרבה, ורצונו עושר ונכסים בעוה"ז? ואנכי! כל זמן שאני הוא כלומר באשיות, הולך ערירי, ר"ל כל ימי חיי אני הוא לבדי בלא בנים, ולא אדע שום עונג ונחת רק ובן משק ביתי הוא דמשק אליעזר כלומר שכל עסקי ביתי ישקו רק על פיו, ואח"כ מוסיף הכתוב ואומר הן לי לא נתת זרע כלל ורצונו שכבר זקן אנכי ואולי לא אוליד כלל והנה בן ביתי יורש אותי, כלומר אולי גם בן ביתי יורש אותי אף לאחר מיתתי, ולא יותר לי שום בן. אז ענהו השם על שאלתו האחרונה לבדה, לא יירשך זה כי אם בנך אשר יצא ממעיך. ועל שאלתו הראשונה כי כבר הוא זקן וכל ימי חייו אין לו עונג ונחת מבניו, לא ענהו. וגם אברהם אבינו עוד לא שאל פעם שנית שאלתו הראשונה אך היה בטוח בדברי השם כיון שאמר לו שיהי' לו בן בודאי יגדלהו וינשאהו, כי יאריך לו השם ימים לראות בשמחת בנו, ויתענג עוד ממנו. לכן כתוב והאמין בד', ר"ל, על שאלתו הראשונה, לכן ויחשבה לו צדקה, כי חשב לו לצדקה יען לא שאל פעם שנית שאלתו הראשונה כמו שמצינו אצל דוד היסגרוני בעלי קעילה [בידו]? הירד שאול? [שמואל א, כג, יא] והבן [הערת הכותב].

ולפ״ז נאמנו מאוד דברי הרמב״ם ז״ל במאוד מאוד, כי אין כונת הרמב״ם ז״ל להעמיד עקרי הדת לחכם גדול ומבין מדעתו ויש לו ראיות ברורות על מציאות השם ואחדותו והתיחדו עם נביאיו, כי באיש הזה לא שייך אמונה כי כבר הוא יודע, ואצלו מחוייב כבר להיות והאמונה קטנה מהכיל הידיעה הברורה, ואז כבר נקרא דעות. ומה ימתק לנו עתה דברי המורה בח״ג פרק כז באמרו כי השלמות האחרון אין בו לא מעשים ולא מדות אלא דעות בלבד, כי אחרי אשר כבר עלה מכל אמונה למעלה להשכיל להטיב לדעת את ד׳ ואת טובו בידיעה גמורה והשגה שלימה. אולם הרמב״ם בצותו לנו הי״ג עיקרים הוא דיבר אל כל קהל ישראל המון רב מסוף העולם ועד סופו, אשר יש ביניהם כמה וכמה אנשים שאין בכחם להשיג בידיעה ברורה השגת השם ועיקרים אשר בית ישראל נשען עליהם, צוונו והעמיד הי״ג עיקרים הללו שיאמינו עכ״פ בהם שהם אפשרים, ולא יהי׳ בעיניהם מן הנמנעות כי כל האומר על העיקרים הללו שהם מן הנמנעות הוא כופר בד׳ ובמשה עבדו, והוא אפיקורוס גמור ומצוה לשונאו ולאבדו, והוא בכלל המורידין ולא מעלין שאמרו בגמר׳.

ובזה דברי הרמב״ם ז״ל מובנים וברורים מאוד למי שהבין בהם ולא העמיס עלינו עול כבד יותר מחז״ל חלילה, כי הוא צועד תמיד בעקבותם, ואינו זז מהם, ובוחר במשנתם, וכל בעל מודה בזה, שאם ימצא איש שיאמר על הדברים האלה שהם מן הנמנעות הוא כופר בתורה כלה ואין לו חלק לעוה״ב, ומשנה מפורשת היא כאשר הבאתי לעיל. ואיך תאמר המצאה שלא צוו ולא דברו קדמוננו ולא עלתה על לבם? ודברי הרמב״ם ז״ל ברורים ואמיתיים ולא יחלקו עליהם אלא מי שנשתגע ונהפך לו מוחו ואמונתיו אמונות נכוחות אשר יאמין האדם בהם וחי לעולם, ועיקריו עקרי הדת אשר לא יליזו מנגד עינינו. ואם אין בנו כח להשיגם על צד המופת, ותהי׳ הכרתינו וידיעתינו ידיעה ברורה, בכל זאת בני מאמינים אנחנו להאמין שבאפשרות הש״י לענוש ולגמול ולהצמיח קרן ישועה ולהחיות מתים לנו [ו]לבנינו, ואלהינו עושה טוב ומטיב לכל, ומה שכעת

באפשריותו, יקיים האל במהרה בימינו אמן.

עוד אחת ואני מרעיש עליך כל דברי הש״ס לולא יראתי מפני האריכות אכן מעט אביא נגד עיניך, ואעירך על דבר אחד אשר לא למדת ולא הגית בם והוצאת מפיך מלין לדבר על מאור עינינו הרמב״ם ז״ל, וז״ל:

כבר פירש הרמב״ם בהלכות ממרים פרק ב׳ כי זה שאין ב״ד יכול לבטל דברי ב״ד חבירו אינו אלא בגזירות ותקנות ומנהגים שגזרו ותקנו והנהיגו ב״ד ראשון ופשט הדבר ישראל, אז אין ב״ד יכול לבטל דבריהם. אבל ב״ד שדרשו באחת מן המידות וכו׳ הרי זה סותר וב״ד אחר יכול לבטל דבריהם כמו שנאמר אל השופט אשר יהיה בימים ההם. ולזאת אשיב כי החילוק הזה שהרמב״ם מחלק בין תקנות ופסקי הלכות אין לו כלל על מה שיסמוך והוא הפך ממש מכוונת המשנה, כי המשנה עוסקת כאן לתת טעם למה הוזכרו דברי היחיד בין המרובין, ואמרה שזה כדי שיוכל לסמוך עליהם הדורות הבאים, לפי שבלעדי סמך היחיד אין ב״ד יכול לבטל וכו׳. וזה יצדק בפסקי הלכות שבהם מזכירין תמיד דברי היחיד, אך זה אין לו מקום כלל בגזירות ותקנות, כי באלה אין דרך המשנה להזכיר דברי החולקים, קראת מימיך: גזר פלוני כך וכך, התקין פלוני כך וכך, ופלוני חולק עליו? עכ״ל.

בתחלה אעיר לפניך קושי׳ אחת על מסדר המשניות הללו אשר לא עמדו עליה לא גייגער, ולא אתה, כי מה לו למסדר המשנה להביא המשניות הללו למה מזכירין דברי שמאי והלל וכו׳, ושניה למה מזכירין דברי היחיד בין המרובים וכו׳,[25] כאן אחר שלש משניות הראשונות ולמה לא הביאם אחר סוף כל המסכתא אחר שכלו כל המחלוקת דאז הוי שייך טפי לאתויי ולהקשות למה מזכירין דברי היחיד בין המרובין? ואם נאמר יען שפסקו מחלוקת

---

25. עדיות א, ד–ה.

הלל ושמאי וחכמים, הלא עוד בתר הכא יש מחלוקת אצל הפורט סלע ממעות מעשר שני?[26] ליישב הקושי' הזאת באמת הן הם דברי הרמב"ם ז"ל בהלכות ממרים שהבאת, כי המסדר כיון בכונה מיוחדת להביא עתה דברי המשנה למה מזכירין, כאשר הביא המשנה[27] הלל אומר מלא הין מים שאובין פוסל את המקוה וכו' שמאי אומר תשעה קבין וכו' ובאמת פסול מקוה הוא גזירה מדרבנן במים שאובין כמו שאומר רש"י ז"ל בפירוש מכות דף ג ע"ב בד"ה לא פסלוהו, פסול מקוה במים שאובין מדרבנן הוא ע"כ. ועיין נדרים דף מב בדברי הר"ן שם, וכאשר הביא המסדר המשנה את משנת פסול מקוה הביא מיד למה מזכירין להורות כי דין זה לא שייך רק בגזירות ותקנות כדברי הרמב"ם ז"ל בהלכות ממרים פרק ב שהבאת. ומעתה קושיתך תעלה בתהו ואינה צריכה יושב [צ"ל ישוב] עוד כי רוב מחלוקת הש"ס הם בגזירות ותקנות ומנהגים כמו כל הנשים דיין שעתן, פסול מקוה, מחלוקת בנטילת ידים, בי"ח דבר, ועוד רבים לא אוכל לפורטם עתה. ובאמת מעולם לא מצינו בכל הש"ס שמביא אין ב"ד יכול לבטל, רק על תקנות וגזירות כמו בריש ביצה [ה ע"א] לענין עטור שוקי ירושלים בפירות בהשולח[28] לענין תקנת הגט, וכדומה, ובקרב אי"ה אוציא לאור ספרי הגדול מאמר המחלוקת בו נחלקו כל מחלוקת המצויה בש"ס איש איש על דגלו, ותראה נפלאות.

טרם אחתום אגרתי, אביע לך כל רוחי, כי לא להרבות כבודי או חלילה להשפיל כבודך יצאתי נגדך בדברי חרפות כמו אלה, כי יודע כל באי עירי כי אין דרכי בכך, לבלות ימי בביקור דברי זולתי, כי מה יתן לי ומה יוסף, אם צדקו דברי זולתי, אם יצאה שגגה מה מתחת ידו? אך כבוד הדת וכבוד הרמב"ם ז"ל אשר אני מתאבק בעפר רגליו המה הרהיבוני ונתני בנפשי יתר שאת ועוז להכותך בשוט לשוני ולשפוך חמתי עליך. אכן השענתי על המקרא ונקלה

26. שפ, א, ט.
27. שם, א, ג.
28. גיטין לו ע"ב.

אחיך לעיניך,[29] ולא הודעתי האגרת ברבים טרם שלחתיה לך, אולי תועיל לך תוכחתי ותשיב תראה שנית בעין פקוחה אגרתך ותסיר ממנה כל הצנינים המכאיבים הדת וגדולי עמנו ותתקיים בך בעצמך דברי הגמ' כיון שנקלה הרי הוא אחיך,[30] ותודה בקהל עם כי חטאת, אז תהי' לאיש מצליח, גם לי תהי' צדקה.

דברי אוהב האמת יותר מנפשו

נחמן יצחק הכהן פישמאן איש לבוב

פה לבוב יום ג' פ' בהעלותך, אך לבל תהי הלהב עולה מאליה[31]

התשובה אשר תשיבני על זאת היא תצוה עלי לבל אודיע האגרת הזאת ברבים, ואם תתמהמה להשיבני אחקקנה בדפוס, ותהי' למזכרת נצח.

---

29. דברים כה, ג.
30. מגילה ז ע"ב.
31. ראה רש"י, במדבר ח, ב.

25

שלשה מכתבים מאת הרב יוסף קאפח

ב"ה יג כסלו תשמ"א

כבוד הד"ר מנחם קלנר

שלום

לשאלתך, נכון כל חכמי ימי הביניים לא היה לפניהם הנוסח
האחרון והסופי של פירוש המשנה. יעיין מר במבואי לסדר זרעים
שם בארתי כי הרמב"ם המשיך כל ימי חייו לתקן ולהגיה, להוסיף
ולגרוע בפירושו למשנה. נכון שהרמב"ם כתב את המורה שנים
רבות לאחר פירוש המשנה וכפי שבארתי במבואי למורה הנבוכים
מהדורתי. ותוספת זו ביסוד הרביעי[1] הוסיפה במשנה בסוף ימיו
בכתב ידו הרהוט שהיה רגיל בו בסוף ימיו ואשר אנו מכירים אותו
מהרבה תקונים מאוחרים בפירוש המשנה ומכמה אגרות, וכפי
שציינתי בהע' 34 בפירוש המשנה מהדורתי, ויש בפירוש המשנה
מהדורתי מאות תקונים שלא ראו אותם חכמי ימי הביניים, וכפי
שהסברתי את הענין במבואי לסדר זרעים.

בהוקרה

יוסף קאפח

---

1. "ודע כי היסוד הגדול של תורת משה רבינו הוא היות העולם מחודש, יצרו ה' ובראו
אחר ההעדר המוחלט. וזה שתראה שאני סובב סביב ענין קדמות העולם לפי דעת
הפילוסופים הוא כדי שיהא המופת מוחלט על מציאותו יתעלה כמו שביארתי ובירדרתי
במורה."

לכבוד הג"ר יוסף קאפח שליט"א

אחדשה"ט

בהרבה מקומות כותב כת"ר שאינו נכון לתרגם את המלה
"אעקתאד" כ"אמונה", ואין ספק שהצדק אתו. לכן, תמה אני למה
תרגם כך בהקדמת הרמב"ם לפרק חלק יסודות ז' וח' ובסיום
היסודות?

המכבדו כערכו הרם

מלך שפירא

כבודו צודק והנני מעתיק לך איך מתוקן אצלי.

"היסוד השביעי נבואת משה רבנו והוא <u>שנדע</u> שהוא"

"היסוד השמיני והוא <u>שנדע</u> שכל התורה וכו'"

בסיום

"לפי שראיתי שיש תועלת <u>בדעה</u> לפי שאני . . . אלא אחר
התבוננות וישוב הדעת ועיון <u>בסברות</u> נכונות ובלתי נכונות,
וסכום מה שצריך <u>להיות בדעה</u> מהם ובירורו <u>בהוכחות</u>
<u>וראיות</u> וכו'.[1]

בכ"ר

יוסף קאפח

---

1. ראה עמית קאפח, 'הערות מהר"י קאפח לפירוש המשנה מהדורתו', מסורה ליוסף ד
(תשס"ה), עמ' 308–309.

לק"י יום ג' לסדר "תהיין לראש יוסף" י' טבת התשנ"ט

לכבוד הרה"ג יוסף קאפח שליט"א

בעת לימודי פירוש המשנה של רבינו הגדול במהדורת
כת"ר, ראיתי שבמסכת תרומות פי"א ה"ג בענין "ואין מביאין
בכורים משקין אלא היוצא מן הזיתים ומן הענבים", העיר כת"ר
בהערה 18 שבמה"ק היה כתוב "ואין הלכה כר' יהודה" ותוקן
במה"ב ל"והלכה כר' יהודה", וכ"פ רבינו בהל' בכורים פ"ב הל'
(ד) [ה], והעיר כת"ר על חזרה זו של הרמב"ם גם במהדורתו למשנה
תורה עמ' רסא.

אולם בהגיעי למסכת חלה פ"ד הי"א ראיתי שבענין יוסף
הכהן שהביא בכוריו יין ושמן ולא קבלו ממנו, כתב רבינו בפירושו:
"זוהי הסברא הנכונה, ויתבאר כל זה במסכת בכורים שאין מביאים
בכורים משקין. ומה שנתבאר במסכת תרומות באמרם אין מביאים
בכורים משקין אלא היוצא מן הזיתים ומן הענבים בלבד, היא סברת
ר' יהודה לבדו שלומד לבכורים מן התרומה כמו שביארנו בתלמוד,
וכבר ביארנו את זה במסכת תרומות."

ולכאורה, דברים אלו מתאימים לנוסח מה"ק בתרומות,
וחשבתי שאולי שכח רבינו הגדול למחקם במה"ב כפי שהעיר כת"ר
במקומות אחרים: ברכות ז, א הערה 5; שביעית ב, ב הערה 7;
שביעית ה, ט הערה 18; ערלה א, ב הערה 5. אולם בנד"ד לא העיר
כת"ר דבר.

עוד אשאל מכת"ר אודות מ"ש בקטע הנ"ל בסוף מס' חלה
"ויתבאר כל זה במסכת בכורים", ולא מצאתי ענין זה במס' בכורים,
וכת"ר במהדורתו לא העיר דבר.

בהזדמנות זו אודה לכת"ר על העונג והשמחה שנגרמו לי
לאורך שנים ואי"ה לאי"ט מלימוד כתבי הרמב"ם וחיבורים נוספים
במהדורותיו של כת"ר. וכמצוותם של כהנים אברך את כת"ר בברכה

המשולשת: "יברכך ה' וישמרך. יאר ה' פניו אליך ויחנך. ישא ה' פניו
אליך וישם לך שלום."[1]

ויה"ר שיקויימו בנו דברי הנביא: "כה אמר ה' צבאות צום
הרביעי וצום החמישי וצום השביעי וצום העשירי יהיה לבית יהודה
לששון ולשמחה ולמעדים טובים ואמרת והשלום אהבו."[2]

בברכה ובכבוד

כרמיאל כהן

לק"י

כבוד הכהן המברך נ"י

לכאורה כב' צודק ונראה שהרמב"ם שכח להעיר מיד על
ההלכה, ומשכחתו של הרמב"ם נדבקתי גם אני, וד' הטוב יכפר בעד.

כ"ד יוסף קאפח

---

1. במדבר ו, כד–כו.
2. זכריה ח, יט.

קטעים מכתבי הרב יחיאל יעקב וויינברג על דבר הגישה
הנכונה להבנת דברי הרמב"ם

1. אמנם ידעתי שהגר"ח[1] בחידושיו מפרש דברי הרמב"ם, שכוונתו
לומר שמה שאינו מועל לאחר שנעשתה אפר, והרי בקדושת בה"ב
מועל גם באפר, הוא משום דכתיב "חטאת היא" ובא הכתוב להוציא
אפר אף מקדושת בדה"ב. ואף שהיא חריפות גדולה וראויה לגאון
שכמותו, מ"מ פשטות לשון הרמב"ם אינה כן, כמבואר למעיין אוהב
אמת לאמתו (וכבר אמרתי, שחידושי רבינו הגר"ח הם אמיתיים
מבחינת העיון העמוק, אבל לא תמיד במובן היסטורי, כלומר,
בכוונת הרמב"ם עצמו, שדרך לימודו היתה אחרת מזו של הגר"ח.
ואין זה מקפח ערכו של גאון שכלי זה, שראוי הוא להקרא "רמב"ם
חדש", אבל לא תמיד כמפרש הרמב"ם, אלא שמרן הגר"ח הגיע
בחריפותו לאותן מסקנות שהרמב"ם ז"ל הגיע להן בדרך לימודו
הוא).[2]

2. והנה כבר השריש לנו הרשב"א באחת מתשובותיו,[3] דמוטב לנו
לומר שהרמב"ם שכח סוגיא מפורשת מלומר שהרמב"ם פירש סוגיא
נגד משמעותה. . . . ולפי דעתי מה שעמלו כמה מחברים להציל את
הרמב"ם מהשגגות ע"י שהם עוקרים סוגיות ערוכות ע"י פלפול חריף,
הוא נגד האמת הפשוטה. ומוטב לנו להניח את הרמב"ם כמו שהוא
מלעקם את המפורש בגמ' נגדו.[4]

3. ולא באתי ח"ו לקפח את דבריו החריפים בישוב פסקי הרמב"ם,
ואדרבא אני מתפעל מיושר הגיונו ומנועם דבריו הנחמדים, אלא

1. רבי חיים סולוביייצ׳יק.
2. שרידי אש, חלק ב סימן קמד.
3. לא מצאתי.
4. שם, חלק ב סימן קסב.

לפענ"ד דברי כת"ר מכילים חידושים גדולים שאינם מדרכו של
הרמב"ם ז"ל, ואינם מתישבים בלשונו. לכן ארשה לעצמי להציע
לפני כת"ר דרך אחרת בביאור הסוגיות שלפנינו, אולי יתישבו דברי
הרמב"ם בפשטות.[5]

4. אמנם, לא אחד אשר בלבבי, כי אין דעתי כדעת החוקרים החדשים,
שכל ספרי הפלפול הם יגיע לריק. לא כן הדבר! ההשתדלות של טובי
הגאונים, ז"ל, הועילו להתפתחות המחשבה התורנית התלמודית
ולבירור ולביהור המושגים התלמודיים. זכה הרמב"ם, ז"ל, אשר
לכתחילה נתכוין לחתום תורה בלימודה, כי ספרו הגדול נעשה
למבוע גדול וליצירה גאונית של הרוח העברי. לולי רבותינו
הגדולים גאוני הדורות האחרונים, הי' נעשה לימוד הגמרא לימוד
יבש ומשעמם. הם עשו אותו לים החכמה והתבונה, אשר כל כשרון
מוצא בו מקום להתגדר בו. אבל כל זה אינו פוטר אותנו מן החובה
לעמול ולרדת לכוונת הרמב"ם עפ"י דרכו הוא וסגנון לימודו הוא.[6]

5. כבר נועזתי ואמרתי להג"ר משה סולובייציג ז"ל (אביו של הגרי"ד[7]
נ"י) שחידו"ת של אבי' הגאון ר"ח הם אמת מבחינת ההגיון אבל לא
מבחינת אמת ההיסטורית. לר' חיים הי' דרך לימוד אחרת משל
הרמב"ם.[8]

6. קראתי את מאמרו של הגרי"ד סולובייציג על דודו הגרי"ז[9] זצ"ל.[10]
השפה היא נהדרה ונאדרה והסגנון הוא מקסים. אבל התוכן הוא

5. שם, חלק ג סימן קלב.
6. שם, חלק ג סימן קלג.
7. רבי יוסף דב סולובייצי'יק.
8. ממכתבו לד"ר גבריאל חיים כהן (כז טבת תשכ"ה).
9. רבי יצחק זאב סולובייצי'יק.
10. "מה דודך מדוד", הדואר (תשכ"ד), עמ' 752–759 (= דברי הגות והערכה, ירושלים
תשמ"ב, עמ' 57–97.

מוגזם ומופרז מאד. כך כותבים אנשים בעלי כת, כמו אנשי חב"ד
ובעלי המוסר. מתוך מאמרו מתקבל הרושם כאלו התורה לא נתנה
ע"י מרע"ה חלילה כי אם ע"י ר' חיים מבריסק זצ"ל. אמת הדברים כי
ר' חיים הזרים זרם חדש של פלפול ע"ד ההגיון לישיבות. בהגיון יש
לכל אדם חלק, ולפיכך יכולים כל בני הישיבה לחדש חידושים
בסגנון זה, משא"כ בדרך הש"ך ורעק"א צריך להיות בקי גדול
בשביל להיות קצת חריף. ולכן משכל אנשי הישיבות מתאוים להיות
"מחדשים" הם מעדיפים את ר' חיים על כל הגאונים שקדמו לו.
שאלתי פעם אחת את הגרי"ד בהיותו בברלין: מי גדול ממי: הגר"א
מווילנא או ר' חיים מבריסק? והוא ענני: כי בנוגע להבנה ר' חיים
גדול אף מהגר"א. אבל לא כן הדבר. הגר"א מבקש את האמת
הפשוטה לאמתה, ולא כן ר' חיים. הגיונו וסברותי' אינם משתלבים
לא בלשון הגמ' ולא בלשון הרמב"ם. ר' חיים הי' לכשלעצמו רמב"ם
חדש אבל לא מפרש הרמב"ם. כך אמרתי להגאון ר' משה ז"ל אבי'
של הגרי"ד שליט"א.[11]

7. מאמרו היקר "משמעון הצדיק וכו'"[12] (השם הוא סנציוני קצת ועלול
לעורר קצת תמהון וקצת גיחוך) קראתי, ונהנתי הרבה הן מתכנו והן
מסגנונו המזהיר. כפה"נ נכתב מתוך מגמה להגן על האנציקלופדיא
מפני מבקרי', ובבחינה ידועה צודק כת"ר, כי המחשבה התלמודית
לא נפסקה מעולם. מ"מ אין לומר כי התלמוד לא נחתם. האיסור
להוסיף או לחלוק עלי' הוא כבר בגדר חתימה, אלא שאין זו חתימה
רשמית של עורכים או של ועד גדול כי אם חתימה אנונומית ע"י קול
העם כולו. בהקדמתי לספר "מחקרים בתלמוד"[13] נגעתי בשאלה זו
מנקודת-ראות אחרת. יעי' נא שם.

ע"ד הקובלנא של המבקרים על שמכניסים באנצ'יק' פלפולי

11. ממכתבו לד"ר גבריאל חיים כהן (יט כסלו תשכ"ו).
12. הצופה, כח תשרי תשי"ג (נדפס שנית בהמעין, ניסן תשס"ז, עמ' 5–8).
13. = כתבי הגאון רבי יחיאל יעקב וויינברג, חלק א סימן צד.

האחרונים וכו', יש לדון בה בכובד ראש. בין אנשי המדע נפוצה
הדעה כי דברי האחרונים אינם "המשך" התלמוד, כי אם הסעה
למהלכי-מחשבה אחרים. ובעיקר קובלים עליהם על שאינם עוסקים
בבדיקת המקורות ובתיקון הגרסות ואינם עמלים להבין את הדברים
כפשוטם ולבאר דברי חז"ל על דעת אומריהם (ולא על דעת הדורות
האחרונים שנתרחקו הרבה מעולם המחשבה של התלמוד וראשוני
מפרשיו). בעיני המבקרים פלפולי האחרונים הם "סילופים" בדרך
חריפות מלאכותית. אבל כת"ר צודק בעצם רעיונו כי לאמתם של
דברים פלפולי האחרונים הם חידושי מחשבה מקורית בצורה של
פרשנות לקודמים.[14] ספרותנו היא בעצם ספרות של פרשנות. נקח נא
פירושי האגדה, הקבלה, הפילוסופיא לתורת משה שמכילים רעיונות
מקוריים בצורה של פרשנות. וכן הדבר בפירושי התלמוד, מפרשים
ומבארים ובאותה שעה – מחדשים וממשיכים! וכך נאה לנו. שמירת
החבית וגם את יינה אבל גם חידוש ויצירה. וזה הפירוש העמוק של
כל מה שתלמיד ותיק עתיד לחדש וכו'.[15] העיקר: להשאר בתחום
הרוח העברי המקורי ולא לפרוץ הגדר ח"ו. פריצת הגדר בכוונת
מכווין פירושה לתעות ולתהות במדבר הרוח.

לפענ"ד צריך ידידנו הגרי"ש [!] זווין לדקדק יותר בהבאת
מקורות ראשונים ודעות גאוני קדמאי ובתראי של בבל, שהם הי'
באמת ממשיכי התלמוד במובן העמוק של מלה זה [!]. משא"כ
האחרונים. הם ממשיכים את חוט המחשבה של התלמוד, אבל אין
לכנותם ממשיכי התלמוד. בשעתו אמרתי להגר"מ סולובייציג ז"ל
בנו של מרן הגרח"ה ז"ל כי חידושי אבי' הגז"ל הם אמתיים מבחינת
המחשבה ההגיונית, אבל אין הם אמתיים מבחינה היסטורית.
להרמב"ם ז"ל היתה דרך למוד ומחשבה אחרת לגמרי. הבאתי ראיות
חותכות, שבתשובות הרמב"ם לא נמצא אף דבר אחד הדומה

14. ראה שם, חלק ב עמ' קז–קטו, וספרי *Between the Yeshiva World and Modern*
Orthodoxy (London, 1999), pp. 143, 193 n. 92.
15. ויקרא רבה כב, א.

במהותו לחידושי הגר"ח ז"ל. הרמב"ם מתרץ א"ע באופן אחר
לגמרי. הוא אומר: לי גירסא אחרת, פירוש אחר, או: טעות המעתיק
או הכורך וכו'. וגם טעיתי ושכחתי! . . .[16] אבל אין לקפח שכרו של
הגר"ח חלילה, בו קם לנו רמב"ם חדש שהנהו פאר למחשבה
התורנית.[17]

8. זכורני שפעם נתן [הרב וויינברג] שיעור פתיחה בישיבת עץ חיים
במונטרה על מס' בבא קמא והביא רמב"ם בעניין גזלן, וקושיית
הראב"ד עליו, ותירוץ של ר' חיים מבריסק. לפתע דפק על הסטנדר
ואמר: "ביי מי איז ברור אז ר' חיים איז ניט אמת. פאר וואס"? ער
זאגט אזוי גוט אז ער מאכט דעם ראב"ד פאר א עם הארץ" [ברור לי
שתירוצו של ר' חיים איננו אמת, למה? כי הוא אומר כ"כ טוב
שהופך את הראב"ד לעם הארץ].[18]

16. הנקודות במקור.
17. ממכתבו לרב יהושע הוטנר (יז אדר תשי"ג).
18. הרב אברהם אבא וינגורט, "עיון במשנתו של הרב וויינברג זצ"ל", המעין, לז (ניסן
תשנ"ז), עמ' 29.